Bringers of War

Bringers of War

The Portuguese in Africa during the Age of Gunpowder
and Sail from the Fifteenth to Eighteenth Century

John Laband

Frontline Books, London

Bringers of War

This edition published in 2013 by Frontline Books,
an imprint of Pen & Sword Books Ltd,
47 Church Street, Barnsley, S. Yorkshire, S70 2AS
www.frontline-books.com

ISBN: 978-1-84832-658-3

For more information on our books, please visit
www.frontline-books.com, email info@frontline-books.com
or write to us at the above address.

Printed and bound in India by Replika Press Pvt. Ltd.
Designed and typeset in Baskerville by Wordsense Ltd, Edinburgh

Contents

Illustrations

Colour Plates

Black-and-White Plates

Maps and Diagrams

Glossary

abuna	head of the Coptic church in Ethiopia
al-Maghrib al-Aqsa	The far west; Arab coastal region of North Africa
al-makhzaniya	standing army of the ruler of Morocco
almadia	light, long vessel that plied the Zambezi river
amba	flat-topped mountain with precipitous sides in Ethiopia
aventureiro	Portuguese noble without enough money for cavalry service, who fought on foot
awenekongo	see *mwenekongo*
bahrnagash	governor of the coastal province in Ethiopia
beylerbey	Ottoman regent in *al-Maghrib*
canarin	Christian Indian from Goa
changamire	Rozvi ruler
chavas	Ethiopian mounted warrior
chikunda	military retainer on a *prazo* in the Zambezi valley
Dar al-Harb	lands of war; regions not ruled by Muslims where war against non-believers was sanctioned
Dar al-Islam	lands of Islam; regions governed by Muslims
degredado	Portuguese criminal serving out his sentence in exile
dikota (pl. *makota*)	great nobleman in Ndongo
donataria	concession of feudal lordship granted by the Portuguese crown to develop a colonial territory
donatário	proprietor of a *donataria*

Estado da Índia	Portuguese empire east of the Cape of Good Hope
feira	fair or market
feitoria	Portuguese trading station or 'factory' overseas, usually guarded by a fort
fidalgo	Portuguese nobleman of middling or lesser rank; gentleman
fidalguia	Portuguese traditional nobility
fronteiro	minor nobleman serving in a Portuguese fortress in Morocco; trained arquebusier
gult	land granted by the Ethiopian ruler in return for the *gult*-holder's military and other services
hajj	pilgrimage to Mecca; one of the five pillars of Islam
ijiko	see *kijiko*
imam	leader of prayers at the mosque; Muslim religious leader
imbari	see *kimbari*
jihad	holy war to create a setting in which Islam can be properly practised
karonga	paramount ruler of the Maravi chiefdoms
katama	peripatetic royal encampment of Ethiopian rulers
kijiko (pl. *ijiko*)	enslaved royal officials and army officers in Ndongo
kikumba	army baggage train of carriers in Kongo
kimbari (pl. *imbari*)	professional military elite in Ndongo recruited from free men and warrior slaves
kitomi	priests of the ancient spirits of place in Kongo
lemd	lion skin worn by the elite in Ethiopia
lupanga	short sword carried by Kalanga warriors in Mutapa
makhazan	storeroom; cultivated coastal lowlands of Morocco; government
makota	see *dikota*
maliki	ruler of a city-state on the southern Swahili coast

mambo	ruler of the Lundu kingdom
mfalane	ruler of a city-state on the northern Swahili coast
mhondoro	Kalanga spirit mediums
Mouros	Moors, or Muslims generally
muhongo	queen of Matamba
mwenekongo (pl. *awenekongo*)	ruler of Kongo
mwenemutapa	ruler of Mutapa
mwisikongo	nobles or clan chiefs in Kongo
mzungu (pl. *wazungu*)	Swahili term for a foreigner; an Afro-Portuguese
negus	ruler of Ethiopia
ngola	ruler of Ndongo; iron regalia that represented the ruler
nyika	wilderness inland from the Swahili coast
nzimbu	cowrie shells used as currency
pombeiro	itinerant African slave agent and trader in the Angolan interior
pombo	lightly armed foot scout in Angola
prazeiro	holder of a *prazo*
prazo de coroa	leased crown estate in the Zambezi valley
Reconquista	the reconquest of Christian lands (especially in Iberia) from the Muslims
renegado	Christian renegade serving in the Moroccan army
sertanejo	private Portuguese adventurer and trader; backwoodsmen
sesmaria	land grant in the Portuguese empire
sharif	courtesy title of Muslim ruler claiming descent from Fatima, the daughter of the Prophet Mohammad
siba	rebellion; the lawless borderlands of Morocco
soba	Mbundu chief
soldado	young, unmarried Portuguese soldier serving in the Indies
sono	war leader in Mutapa

tellek saw	Ethiopian warrior living a life of chivalry and honour
terço	Portuguese infantry formation of pikemen with a sleeve of arquebusiers (*tercio* in Spanish)
trace italienne	fortress designed with angular bastions connected by curtain walls of the same height
waungwana	patricians of the Swahili coast
wazungu	see *mzungu*

Chronology

Date	Atlantic Africa (Morocco, Angola and Brazil)	Date	*Estado da Índia* (Swahili coast, Ethiopia, Mutapa and Zambezi valley)
1385	**Accession of João I**		
1415	Portuguese capture Ceuta		
1481	**Accession of João II**	**1481**	**Accession of João II**
1482	Portuguese found São Jorge da Mina		
1483	Cão enters Congo river		
		1488	Dias rounds Cape of Good Hope
1491	Portuguese embassy to Kongo		
	Mwenekongo baptised		
1494	Treaty of Tordesillas		
1495	**Accession of Manuel I**	**1495**	**Accession of Manuel I**
		1498	V. da Gama reaches Swahili coast on way to India
1500	Portuguese discovery of Brazil		
		1502	Da Gama's second voyage to Indies
		1505	De Almeida sacks Kilwa and Mombasa and seizes Sofala
		1508	*Jihad* by Adal against Ethiopia
1509	Kongo pays in slaves for Portuguese military assistance	1509	Portuguese naval victory off Diu in Gujarat
		1510	Portuguese capture Goa
		1511	Portuguese capture Melaka

Date	Atlantic Africa (Morocco, Angola and Brazil)	Date	*Estado da Índia* (Swahili coast, Ethiopia, Mutapa and Zambezi valley)
		1512	Portuguese select Moçambique Island as main base on Swahili coast
			First Portuguese expedition up Zambezi river
		1513	Portuguese fail to capture Aden
		1515	Portuguese capture Hormuz
		1517	Ottomans conquer Egypt
			Ethiopia defeats Adal
1518	Dom Henrique first black bishop in Africa		
1519	Portuguese embassy to Ndongo		
1521	**Accession of João III**	**1521**	**Accession of João III**
		1525	Ottomans conquer Yemen
		1527	Start of Grañ's *jihad* against Ethiopia
		1528	Portuguese sack Mombasa again
		1529	Grañ's victory at Shimbra-Kure over Ethiopia
		1531	Portuguese establish Zambezi bases at Sena and Tete
1534	Portuguese colonisation of Brazil begins		
		1535	Grañ captures Aksum
			Ottomans capture Basra
		1538	Ottomans capture Aden
		1540	Mutapa permits Portuguese trade on plateau
		1541	Portuguese naval expedition to Red Sea
			C. da Gama's expedition to Ethiopia
		1542	Da Gama's victories at Amba Senait and Antalo plain

Date	Atlantic Africa (Morocco, Angola and Brazil)	Date	*Estado da Índia* (Swahili coast, Ethiopia, Mutapa and Zambezi valley)
		1542	Grañ defeats Portuguese at Wofla; execution of da Gama
		1543	Portuguese and Ethiopian victory at Weyna Dega; death of Grañ
		1546	Fort São Sebastião begun on Moçambique Island
		1555	Jesuit missionaries enter Ethiopia
1556	Ndongo breaks free from Kongo overlordship		
1557	**Accession of Sebastião**	1557	**Accession of Sebastião**
		1558	Fort São Sebastião completed
			Portuguese forts completed at Muscat
1559	Portuguese embassy to Ndongo		
		1561	Martyrdom of Jesuits in Mutapa
1568	Jaga incursion into Kongo		
1571	Portuguese expedition to expel Jaga	1571	Barreto's expedition up Zambezi
	De Novais appointed Governor of Angola		
		1572	Barreto eliminates Swahili traders at Sena
			Barreto defeats Tonga
		1573	Barreto dies at Sena
		1574	Homem's expedition to Manyika
		1575	Homem defeats Uteve but retires from Manyika
			Homem's expedition from Tete to secure silver mines
1576	Moroccan war of succession	1576	Portuguese garrison in Chicova overrun
	De Novais founds Luanda		
1578	Portuguese invasion of Morocco		
	Sa'adians defeat Portuguese at Battle of the Three Kings		

Date	Atlantic Africa (Morocco, Angola and Brazil)	Date	*Estado da Índia* (Swahili coast, Ethiopia, Mutapa and Zambezi valley)
1578	Accession of Henrique	1578	Accession of Henrique
1579	Start of Ndongo–Portuguese wars		
1580	Portuguese crown falls to Spain		
1581	Accession of Filipe I (Felipe II of Spain)	1581	Accession of Filipe I (Felipe II of Spain)
1583	Portuguese defeat Ndongo at Cambande		
		1585	Ali Bey raids Swahili coast
		1586	Zimba defeat Portuguese at Sena
		1587	Portuguese sack Faza
		1588	Ali Bey captures Mombasa
1589	Ndongo defeat Portuguese at Ngwalema	1589	Zimba attack Swahili coast
			Zimba sack Kilwa
			Zimba and Portuguese capture Mombasa; they expel Ali Bey
			Zimba repulsed at Malindi
		1592	Portuguese expedition against Zimba in Zambezi valley fails
		1593	Construction begins on Fort Jesus in Mombasa
		1595	Dutch enter Indian Ocean
		1597	Prazeiros aid Mutapa against invading Maravi
1598	Accession of Filipe II (Felipe III of Spain)	1598	Accession of Filipe II (Felipe III of Spain)
1598	Dutch raid São Tomé and Príncipe		
		1600	English East India Company receives charter
			Prazeiros aid Mutapa in expelling Maravi
		1602	Formation of Dutch East India Company (VOC)

Date	Atlantic Africa (Morocco, Angola and Brazil)	Date	*Estado da Índia* (Swahili coast, Ethiopia, Mutapa and Zambezi valley)
1604	Portuguese capture Cambande		
1606	Dutch open trade with Loango		
		1607	First VOC siege of Fort São Sebastião
			Madeira begins involvement in Mutapa civil wars
		1608	Second VOC siege of Fort São Sebastião
		1613	Madeira suppresses revolt in Zambezi valley
1617	Portuguese found Benguela		
1621	**Accession of Filipe III (Felipe IV of Spain)**	**1621**	**Accession of Filipe III (Felipe IV of Spain)**
1621	Dutch West India Company founded		
		1622	Portuguese lose Hormuz to Persia
		1623	Maravi raid Mutapa
1624	Portuguese install puppet ruler of Ndongo, Filipe Hari		
1625	Dutch fail to capture São Jorge da Mina		
1626	Queen Nzinga of Ndongo strikes alliance with Imbangala		
1628	Imbangala betray Nzinga in war with Portuguese		
		1629	Prazeiros begin involvement in Mutapa wars of succession
1631	Nzinga conquers Matamba	1631	Yusuf's successful revolt and capture of Mombasa
	Dutch capture Recife in Pernambuco		Rising in Mutapa drives Portuguese from plateau
		1632	Portuguese naval expedition fails to recapture Mombasa
		1632	Expedition restores Portuguese presence in Mutapa

Date	Atlantic Africa (Morocco, Angola and Brazil)	Date	*Estado da Índia* (Swahili coast, Ethiopia, Mutapa and Zambezi valley)
		1633	Yusuf evacuates Fort Jesus; Portuguese reoccupy Mombasa
		1634	Jesuits expelled from Ethiopia
		1635	Portuguese–English truce
		1636	Portuguese sack Pate
1637	Dutch capture São Jorge da Mina		
		1638	Death of Yusuf
1640	Portuguese throw off Spanish rule		
1640	**Accession of João IV**	**1640**	**Accession of João IV**
1641	Dutch capture Luanda	1641	VOC captures Melaka from Portuguese
	Kongo and Ndongo-Matamba ally with Dutch		
1645	Ndongo-Matamba defeats Portuguese at Massanagano		
	Portuguese revolt against Dutch in Pernambuco		
1646	Portuguese defeat Ndongo-Matamba and Dutch allies at Cavanga		
1648	Brazilian expedition recaptures Angola from Dutch		
		1650	Portuguese forts at Muscat fall to Omanis
		1652	Omanis raid Pate and Zanzibar
1654	Dutch driven from Brazil	1654	Prazeiros involved in new Mutapa succession wars
1655	Start of Portuguese–Kongo wars		
1656	**Accession of Afonso VI**	**1656**	**Accession of Afonso VI**
1656	Kongo cedes territory to Portuguese and accepts tributary status		
1657	Portuguese recognise Nzinga as Queen of Matamba and Ndongo		

Date	Atlantic Africa (Morocco, Angola and Brazil)	Date	*Estado da Índia* (Swahili coast, Ethiopia, Mutapa and Zambezi valley)
		1658	Portuguese lose Ceylon to the VOC
		1661	Omanis sack Mombasa but fail to take Fort Jesus
1662	Peace concluded between Portuguese and Dutch		
1663	Nzinga dies	1663	Portuguese conclude peace with Dutch
1665	Portuguese victory over Kongo at Mbwila		
		1668	Omanis sack Diu
1670	Portuguese defeat at Kitombo in Nsoyo	1670	Omanis sack Moçambique but fail to take Fort São Sebastião
1670	Revolt of Filipe Hari in Ndongo		
1671	Defeat and death of Filipe Hari		
		1676	Omanis sack Diu again
1681	Portuguese involved in succession disputes in Matamba and Kisanje		
	Matamba defeats Portuguese at Katole		
1683	**Accession of Pedro II**	**1683**	**Accession of Pedro II**
1683	Peace concluded between Portuguese and Matamba		
		1684	Rozvi defeat prazeiros and Mutapa at Mahungwe
1689	Portuguese–Matamba war		
1690	Peace concluded between Portuguese and Nsoyo		
1692	Portuguese–Matamba war	1692	Rozvi drive Portuguese from Mutapa plateau
		1696	Omanis besiege Fort Jesus
		1697	Three Portuguese naval expeditions fail to lift siege
		1698	Fort Jesus falls to Omanis; fourth Portuguese naval expedition ineffective

Date	Atlantic Africa (Morocco, Angola and Brazil)	Date	*Estado da Índia* (Swahili coast, Ethiopia, Mutapa and Zambezi valley)
1706	**Accession of João V**	**1706**	**Accession of João V**
		1727	Portuguese found Inhambane
		1728	Portuguese retake Fort Jesus from Omanis
		1729	Omanis recapture Fort Jesus
		1730	Portuguese naval expedition fails to take Fort Jesus
1744	Portuguese–Matamba war		
1750	**Accession of José I**	**1750**	**Accession of José I**
1773	Start of war with Viye and Mbailundu in Benguela highlands		
1776	War with Viye and Mbailundu concluded		
1777	**Accession of Maria I and Pedro III**	**1777**	**Accession of Maria I and Pedro III**
		1781	Portuguese found settlement at Delagoa Bay
1834	**Accession of Maria II**	**1834**	**Accession of Maria II**
		1835	Ngoni overrun Zambezi valley
1853	**Accession of Pedro V**	**1853**	**Accession of Pedro V**
		1854	Emancipation of slaves in the Portuguese empire on royal lands
		1856	Portuguese free all slaves belonging to town councils and the church

Introduction

It is now nearly forty years since Portugal finally abandoned the debilitating, decades-long military struggle to hang on to its empire in Africa. When it withdrew from its African territories in 1974–1975 it was the last of the erstwhile colonial powers to do so. In common with all the other empire-building European states that had brutally apportioned Africa out between themselves in that cynical power-play familiar to us as the 'Scramble for Africa', Portugal had consolidated or acquired the greater geographical bulk of its African colonies only in the late nineteenth and early twentieth centuries. Yet Portugal's presence in Africa went back as far as the mid-fifteenth century, further than any other European power besides Spain.

During the fifteenth century the aggressive Portuguese ventured across the Mediterranean to North Africa and seized a string of strategic ports from the Muslim kingdom of Morocco. At much the same time their superbly designed, little ships gingerly felt their way down the west coast of Africa until they finally burst into the Indian Ocean with all its fabulous riches. All the way around Africa from the Mediterranean coast to the shores of the Red Sea the Portuguese made their belligerent presence felt, challenging Muslims wherever they found them with crusading zeal and fighting off their European and Indian Ocean competitors. Sometimes they gained no permanent foothold, and after enduring desperate battles and gruelling sieges abandoned Morocco, Ethiopia and much of the East African Swahili coast to their enemies. They had greater success in forcing their way up the Zambezi valley of southeastern Africa and settling there on enormous estates. In what is now Angola they fought sophisticated African kingdoms in interminable, vicious campaigns that yielded literally millions of slaves for the Portuguese plantations across the Atlantic Ocean in Brazil.

Today, few if any of these ferocious African wars fought from the fifteenth to the eighteenth century between the Portuguese and their diverse foes are familiar to anybody outside the ranks of professional historians. Yet in their drama and human interest, in their breathtaking variety of settings and in the array of military cultures pitted against each other, these conflicts deserve to be more widely known. All were waged on an unprecedentedly global scale that brought Africans directly into conflict with adversaries who had sailed from across the Mediterranean, the Red Sea, the Atlantic and the Indian Ocean. They were fought by warriors wearing heavy armour, or none at all, who wielded pike, spear or sword, cudgel or war hatchet, bow and arrow, crossbow, cannon, arquebus or musket. Soldiers went into combat on foot, on horseback or on board ship, and confronted their enemies in narrow city street or on open plain, in bastioned stone fortress or wooden stockade, in river inlet or rocky mountainside, in thick bush or rolling grassland. Wherever they campaigned it was in extremes of weather, in baking desert heat or in sweltering humidity, in tropical downpour, sleet or snow, or under the relentless, cloudless sky.

None of these far-flung and difficult military campaigns was a pushover for the Portuguese. Only in the last few decades of the nineteenth century did the gap in military technology and organisational efficiency between Europeans and Africans become so pronounced that colonial wars of conquest could logically have only one outcome. In the campaigns described in this book there was no automatic Portuguese superiority, and they fought (and often lost) against their assorted array of enemies on remarkably equal terms.

In *Bringers of War* considerable emphasis is placed on the nature of the widely differing societies confronting each other in war and, more particularly, on their diverging military cultures. Because the wars described in this book took place over the lengthy time span of several centuries and in such widely dispersed locations, it has not proved effective to cover them strictly chronologically, particularly since they so often occurred simultaneously. Instead, a regional approach has been adopted. Thus Morocco is treated first, followed by the Swahili coast in two sections, then Ethiopia, the Zambezi valley and Mutapa, and finally Angola. The focus also steadily widens from a single battle in the first chapter to multiple campaigns in the last, aimed primarily at capturing slaves. But no matter how the material is arranged, the purpose is constant: to awaken English-speaking awareness of a series of wars of colonial aggression and exploitation that deserve to be every bit as familiar as the contemporary Spanish conquest of the Americas.

The bibliography, which reflects the considerable published literature in English that relates to the many campaigns the Portuguese waged in Africa between the fifteenth and eighteenth centuries, is organised into sections that follow the sequence of the narrative. This enables readers to see which works I most relied upon when writing each chapter without having to wade through a mass of footnotes. Direct quotations are nevertheless fully cited in the end notes.

Deciding on the spelling of names and words not in English is challenging in a work that ranges across so many different societies. Orthography in African languages is constantly being adjusted, and the correct transliteration of words in Arabic into the letters of the Roman alphabet is problematic. I have therefore kept to the more established spellings in English where they exist, and have been guided by my sources where they do not. Terms not in English are explained when they first appear in the text, and those employed repeatedly are also listed in the glossary.

I wish to thank the Internal Grants Committee of Wilfrid Laurier University for awarding me a Book Preparation Grant to have the maps prepared and to help defray the cost of securing the rights to reproduce a number of the illustrations. Pam Schaus, the cartographer in the Department of Geography and Environmental Studies at Wilfrid Laurier, displayed admirable patience in transforming my clumsy sketches and instructions into elegant maps. I am very grateful to Michael Leventhal, the publisher of Frontline Books, for enthusiastically taking on this ambitious project, and to Kate Baker, the senior editor at Frontline, for her unfailingly cheerful encouragement, advice and assistance in shepherding the book to press. My thanks are also due to Joanna Chisholm for her eagle-eyed copy-editing. Fenella, my dear wife, also copyedited, staunchly took on the preparation of the index, and encouraged me along every step of the way. This book is dedicated to her.

CHAPTER ONE

The Battle of the Three Kings

Cockpit of War: The Struggle for Sixteenth-Century Morocco

The heavily forested, jagged Atlas mountains that massively thrust northeast across Morocco in a diagonal from the Atlantic to the Mediterranean are the kingdom's backbone. They hold back the rain clouds that sweep in from the ocean, so that in their eastern shadow the arid lands seep away into the Sahara desert. In the sixteenth century Moroccans regarded this region as the desolate realm of *siba* (rebellion), where the fierce mountain tribes and nomadic desert warriors lurked beyond the preserves of civilisation. To the west of the Atlas mountains, and defined to the north by their serrated geological offshoot, the Rif mountains, was the *makhazan* (storeroom), the cultivated coastal lowlands watered by the shallow rivers that find their way down from the highlands to the sea. There, the settled peasantry cultivated the kingdom's staple crops of wheat, barley and olives on terraced fields, and produced the superior sugar that was exported far and wide.*

The *makhazan* was also where the ports and cities lay, huddled tightly behind high, crenellated walls pierced by massive gates. The distinctively square-towered minarets of Morocco, each topped by its narrow lantern storey, thrust bravely above these daunting fortifications. Inside, and close by the mosques with their many cupolas, were the *madrasas* (colleges of religious learning), which were famed throughout the *Dar al-Islam* (Lands of Islam). Teeming city dwellers thronged the thriving bazaars and public baths; meanwhile, the rich and powerful took their private ease in luxurious mansions and palaces that presented blank walls to the noisy street, but inside afforded cool, lofty

---

* Queen Elizabeth I of England (d.1603) would have only Moroccan sugar in her household.

chambers, decoratively tiled, and shady, pillared courtyards where fountains played amid refreshing foliage.

In the *makhazan* of northern Morocco, where Fez was the ancient capital, the climate is a Mediterranean one. Wet, cool winters sheet the mountain tops with snow, while the scorching summers are without rain. Then the stubble of the harvested fields is baked to inflammable tinder, as are the shrubs and stunted cork oaks and other trees that mark their boundaries. The almond and citrus groves wilt and drop their leaves and only irrigation keeps them from dying.

When 4 August 1578 dawned, it was just such a late summer's day, with the sun remorselessly beating down out of a cloudless sky and the parched land a shimmering haze of breathless heat. In the open plain at the confluence of the Wadi Loukkos and its wide tributary, the Wadi al-Makhazin, twelve miles northwest of the town of al-Kasr al-Kabir,* two great armies confronted each other. Arrayed in a great crescent with the rising sun at its back, the host of the Sa'adian ruler of Morocco, a glinting cloud of horsemen swirling about the stationary masses of infantry on their mettlesome Barb steeds,† barred the road to the port of Larache. Determined to force its way through them to the supporting fleet they hoped to find at Larache, the heavily outnumbered Portuguese army and its few Moroccan allies, encumbered by its swollen baggage train and rabble of camp followers, were formed up in a tightly ordered, defensive hedgehog. The air quivered with the throbbing and rattle of drums, the shrilling and braying of trumpets and horns, staccato war cries and undulating prayers. Garish banners and standards of silk, velvet or brocade of every hue, embroidered with crosses or verses of the Qur'an, fluttered festively above the grim armies that bristled with pikes, spears and swords. Many soldiers carried crossbows, but there were dozens of menacing cannons too, and thousands of soldiers were armed with arquebuses – an early form of handgun. For this was already the gunpowder age, and both sides had embraced it with fierce relish.

Indeed, firepower would decide that terrible day of carnage, the Battle of Alcázarquivir as the Portuguese called it, after the nearby town of al-Kasr

---

* The town's name means 'The Great Fortress'.

† The Barb horse, a breed developed in North Africa with strong influence from the Arab breed, was the favourite war horse in the Muslim kingdoms of Egypt, the Maghrib and Spain.

al-Kabir, although the Moroccans named it after the Wadi al-Makhazin, the river whose banks and pools would run red with blood. More evocatively, it is remembered as the Battle of the Three Kings, called after the three monarchs who forfeited their lives during what was the greatest single military disaster the Portuguese would ever suffer during the course of their centuries of expansion overseas.

For the Moroccans fighting on both sides, the looming battle was the culmination of a hundred years of debilitating internal strife and foreign invasion that had sorely shaken their ancient kingdom. The Berbers were the original people of the land, and since ancient times had seen foreign overlords come and go: Carthaginians, Romans and even Vandals – crude barbarians migrating to Africa from their misty, northern European forests. Then in AD 642 the Arab warriors of Islam overran Egypt, precariously ruled by the Christian Byzantine empire, the faltering heir in the eastern Mediterranean of the Roman empire. The conquering Arabs swept on across Byzantine North Africa until, with exalting cries of *'Allahu Akbar!'** they finally spurred their steeds into the Atlantic surf.

To Arabs this region west of Egypt was *al-Maghrib al-Aqsa* (the far west), with Morocco at its furthest extremity. In the early centuries of Arab rule almost all the subjugated Berbers converted to Islam and joined the *Dar al-Islam*. Some of them were settled folk, agriculturalists or traders and town dwellers, but most lived in the *siba* (the tough mountain and desert lands) and held on to their language and customs long after they converted to Islam. They did not become more 'arabised' until the Bedouin – warlike desert nomads from Arabia drifting west in waves across *al-Maghrib* from the thirteenth century onwards – had forcibly settled among them.

At the turn of the sixteenth century, Morocco was beset by a time of troubles when rival dynasties contended bloodily for dominance, towns rose up in revolt against their exactions, and the Berber mountain tribes and Bedouin alike regularly raided the settled farmers of the plains. An ambitious Bedouin lineage, the Sa'adians, who hailed from the Saharan oases south of the High Atlas mountains (a region known as the Sus), saw how they could take advantage of the chaos to seize control of the Moroccan agricultural heartland,

---

* 'God is great!'

the *makhazan*. Their leading noble family claimed descent from Fatima, the daughter of the Prophet Mohammad, and so was recognised as *sharif* with all the attendant hereditary religious and political powers that implied.

In their bid to conquer the *makhazan*, the Sa'adian *sharifs* were spurred on by *marabouts*,* the holy men of the Islamic brotherhoods who were strongly established in the same desert borderlands where they had their power base. These brotherhoods followed the Sufi way of Islam that emphasised the internal dimension of the faith.†

As leaders of a potent Muslim spiritual revival in Morocco, the Sufi brotherhoods were deeply involved in practical politics, supporting and encouraging rulers who actively promoted their form of Islam. *Marabouts* were particularly concerned that the corrupt and ever-less-effective sultans of the reigning Wattasid dynasty in Fez were showing themselves powerless to prevent Portuguese Christians from seizing Morocco's strategic ports. That is why they turned to the Sa'adian *sharifs* with whom they were closely associated to overthrow the Wattasid sultans and lead a *jihad* (religiously sanctioned war) against the foreign infidels polluting Moroccan soil.

From the Portuguese point of view, their military occupation of Moroccan ports was only fair return for centuries of Muslim domination of their own country, and a guarantee that it could never recur. In 711 the Arab conquerors of *al-Maghrib* had triumphantly expanded their *jihad* across the narrow Strait of Gibraltar. They supplanted the Christian Visigoth rulers of the Iberian peninsula (*al-Andalus* as they called it) and established their own highly sophisticated, multicultural Moorish kingdoms with their abiding heritage of wondrous architecture.

Pushed up by the Moors to the very northern edges of Iberia, the rump Christian kingdoms embarked on a protracted struggle to evict the invaders.

---

* *Marabout* is derived from *murabit*, a warrior-monk who dwelt in a *ribat* (fortified residence of mystics) on the frontiers of Islam.

† Sufis strove for a mystical closeness to God and were not content with the routine observance of formal religious obligations and the conventional scholarly interpretation of religious law. Popular Sufism was associated with the cult of *awliya* (saints). These were revered *marabouts* (whether hermits or inspired warriors) who had attained union with God and taught the way to knowledge and salvation to the disciples who came to them in their desert retreats. On their death, the tombs of the *awliya* became sites of pilgrimage for the devout. In sixteenth-century Morocco two Sufi brotherhoods were particularly prominent: the moderately mystical Shadhiliyya and the more radical Qadiriyya with their belief in *jinns* (genies).

The *Reconquista* (reconquest) took nearly 800 years to accomplish, until in 1492 King Ferdinand of Aragon and Queen Isabella of Castile forced the surrender of Granada in southern Spain, the last of the Moorish kingdoms of *al-Andalus*. Tens of thousands of Muslim and Jewish refugees then sought refuge in Morocco, bringing with them their many skills, as well as their undying hatred for their Christian conquerors.

The Portuguese had freed their kingdom from Moorish rule in the mid-thirteenth century, more than 200 years before the Spanish* had done the same, but they could never quite convince themselves that they were secure from the threat of renewed North African invasions. As late as 1340 they had fought side by side with the Castilians (more usually their bitter rivals) at the Battle of Rio Salado near Seville to throw back a determined incursion led by the Sultan of Fez. Not surprisingly, therefore, the hallowed crusading tradition of the *Reconquista* remained vibrantly alive in the Christian culture of Portugal. This meant more than holding steadfast against the eternal enemy; it required carrying the crusade aggressively on to his own soil.

The opportunity arose during a time of internal turmoil in Morocco, and in 1415 King João I the Good of Portugal dramatically seized the port of Ceuta, strategically situated on its peninsula directly across the narrow strait from Gibraltar. Ceuta had long been the favoured embarkation point for Muslim armies invading Iberia, and for Moroccans, accustomed for centuries to being the aggressors, its loss was a devastating shock. Worse was to follow. Within the space of a few years the Portuguese had consolidated their initial success and captured a string of Moroccan port towns stretching from Ceuta, just within the Mediterranean, to Agadir, more than 500 miles south along Morocco's Atlantic coast.

Portuguese soldiers joining the colours to fight the infidel in Morocco regarded all Muslims – or *Mouros*† as they indiscriminately referred to them, no matter where in the world they encountered them – as the bitter hereditary enemies of the Cross. As such, *Mouros* could expect nothing from them other than suffering and death. In this merciless spirit the Portuguese seldom held Muslim prisoners for exchange or ransom as was the usual custom in wars

---

* 'Spain' was created by the fifteenth-century union of the crowns of Castile, Aragon and Granada.
† Moors.

between the Christian kingdoms of Europe. Instead, when they did not keep them as slaves they commonly slaughtered them out of hand – all too often, it seems, mutilating their corpses as well, as a sign of their contempt.

Not that the Portuguese were soft on themselves. Inspired by the martial, warrior ideals of the crusade and seduced by popular tales of chivalric, self-sacrificing romance, they welcomed hardship and adversity as challenges to be overcome. An ostentatious, even foolhardy disdain for the risk of death became central to their military culture and sense of self-worth. Consequently, wounds earned while performing reckless feats of suicidal valour under the admiring eyes of comrades-in-arms were prized as the indubitable marks of distinction and proven courage.

The fifteenth-century Moroccan wars spurred on the ambitious to ever more daring and ferocious deeds by providing the opportunity to be dubbed a *cavaliero fidalgo* (knight) for service to the crown. This brutal and reckless military culture contributed to decades of regular Portuguese victories against much larger numbers of enemies in Morocco. In later years all too many of these hardened veterans would mistreat the Muslims of East Africa with the same deliberate, heartless barbarism they had become accustomed to during their military apprenticeship in the bloodthirsty Moroccan wars.

Yet Portuguese military success in Morocco was not simply a consequence of crusading fanaticism and a pitiless military culture. Their initial victories were due to their mastery at sea* and to their gunpowder weapons deployed against Moroccans still mainly armed with traditional swords, spears and crossbows.

Black gunpowder, concocted from a mixture of charcoal, sulphur and saltpetre, as well as a very rudimentary form of gun, were both invented in China, probably as early as the ninth century AD. Between the eleventh and thirteenth centuries both were introduced into military use and spread very rapidly to the fearsome Mongol warriors of the Asian steppes. In the course of their rapid and terrifying conquests, the Mongols brought gunpowder technology to the Middle East and Europe by the middle of the fourteenth century. The military advantages of guns were enthusiastically embraced in late mediaeval Europe with its belligerent state system and incessant war-making. Europe took the lead over the Middle East in the development

---

* See Chapter 2.

of cannons and handguns primarily because its burgeoning mining and metallurgical industries provided the essential materials and expertise. By the end of the fifteenth century, European armies were fully equipped with gunpowder weapons.

Field artillery consisted of guns that were smaller and lighter than the enormously heavy siege cannons of the period. Even so, cast from bronze until better techniques in the mid-seventeenth century permitted them to be made of cast iron, they still weighed 4,500 pounds or more. Long, straining teams of oxen, horses or soldiers were required to tow them across country, and once they were lined up in front of an army for action there was little possibility of being able to move them again during a battle.* Moreover, after delivering an opening salvo the likelihood was that the enemy would overrun them before they could be reloaded. And not only were cannons dishearteningly immobile but they were also very inaccurate. A siege bombard at least had a castle's or town's high walls of masonry as a target, whereas a field gun could be expected to miss advancing ranks of soldiers altogether, firing over their heads or into the ground before them. But when a bounding, cast-iron cannon ball did make crushing, tearing contact with yielding human flesh, the effects were horrific, especially as a single ball could rip through several ranks of soldiers during its course.

At the beginning of the sixteenth century the most commonly used type of firearm on the battlefield was a four-foot-long handgun with a wooden stock and long metal barrel called an arquebus. It weighed between eleven and thirteen pounds and was light enough to hold up for firing with the butt against the shoulder or chest, depending on its design. During the course of the century the larger and more powerful musket was developed to supplement it. At six feet long and weighing twenty pounds it required a Y-shaped, metal support when firing it and a strong soldier to carry it.† Unlike modern machine-tooled rifles and artillery, arquebuses and muskets (as well as cannons) were all handmade, and there was none of the precise, machine-tooled uniformity we expect today. Gunsmiths worked to their own designs and assembled the

---

* Light, mobile field artillery that could move rapidly about the battlefield did not become available until the eighteenth century.

† By the seventeenth century the name 'musket' had become the generic term for all long-barrelled, hand-held firearms.

component parts with varying degrees of expertise. Depending on how much their owner was prepared to spend on them, these weapons could be very plain, or could be items of ornamental beauty with finely chased barrels and inlaid stocks.

But whatever the variation in design between them, until the late seventeenth century arquebuses and muskets shared two common characteristics: both were matchlocks and smoothbores. With a matchlock the trigger snaps back the 'serpentine' – a lever holding a two- to three-foot-long length of smouldering rope soaked in nitrate (called the 'match') to ignite the fine gunpowder charge the soldier has poured from his powder flask into the priming pan on the outside of the barrel. Sparks from the exploding priming powder then pass through a hole in the side of the barrel to ignite the coarser powder charge the soldier has inserted down it. The consequent detonation propels out the spherical shot, which he has pushed home on top of the charge with the aid of a ramrod. For anyone accustomed to the spare simplicity of the procedures involved in loading and firing a modern gun, it seems incredible that twenty-eight distinct actions were required to discharge a single shot from an arquebus. Yet so it was, and soldiers were repeatedly drilled until they could perform them mechanically.

Nevertheless, at his best a matchlock man could seldom manage more than a shot a minute. During the stress of combat it was all too easy (despite proper training) to botch the fine motor skills required for loading, or to forget the necessary precautions against accidents. The powder in the firing pan might detonate without igniting the main charge, the so-called 'flash in the pan'. Unless the matchlock was kept tilted up the bullet might roll out of the barrel before being fired. The match, which was lit at both ends in case one went out, and was kept glowing by constantly blowing on it, had to be held well away to avoid inadvertently igniting the gunpowder before loading was complete, or detonating the pouches of powder charges dangling from the soldier's shoulder strap. With too little powder in the barrel the ball when fired would fall short of the target; too much and the barrel would blow up in the soldier's face. During repeated firing in a heavy engagement the barrel risked becoming clogged and exploding. And moisture was always the matchlock's enemy: damp powder will not detonate and rain puts out the match.

With its slow rate of loading and constant misfires (nearly half of the shots fired) the matchlock was no competitor in fire delivery for the old-fashioned, hand-drawn longbow that shoots twelve arrows to every musket ball, and was on a par with the crossbow, whose bolt or quarrel was drawn back by a mechanical ratchet device. But the matchlock's advantage was that it could penetrate armour at the far greater range of up to a hundred paces, and on penetration caused much greater physical damage than an arrow or bolt.*

Even so, a matchlock ball, which was an inch in diameter, had not nearly the destructive, bone-shattering effect of a high-velocity bullet shot from a modern rifle. Such a bullet leaves a massive exit wound once it has smashed straight through the body, whereas a ball was turned easily aside from its straight flight on encountering a bone, or might even run along its length. Thus, if it did not simply lodge in the body, it might make its exit through a modest hole at a considerable angle from its point of entry. The worst danger for the victim was that on its course it might sever an artery or pierce a vital organ. If it did not, there was some hope of recovery.

Army doctors, who had considerable experience in dealing with horrific wounds, were adept at probing for embedded bullets and extracting them, or cutting out arrows and other projectiles. They were also accustomed to sewing up gashes and stabs inflicted by sharp-edged weapons. When a limb was badly broken or crushed, however, they had little alternative to amputating it and drastically cauterising the wound. In an age before anaesthetics many a patient died of shock, if not from loss of blood. Moreover, since doctors had no knowledge of germs and took no precautions against infection in the chronically unhygienic conditions of the age, there was always a considerable chance that the wound would become infected (especially if cloth or dirt had been driven into the wound), and the patient would die. Indeed, death in crowded and insanitary camps and billets from infectious diseases – whether typhus, smallpox, plague, typhoid or dysentery – constantly threatened soldiers even more than battle wounds, especially when they were weakened by under-nourishment and the difficult physical conditions of military life.

The matchlock was undoubtedly the deadliest projectile weapon available at that time, even if it was painfully laborious to load. In accuracy, however,

---

* The light arrow from the composite Asian bow was generally not able to penetrate armour.

it could not compare to the various forms of bow and arrow. There were no grooves inside the barrel (what we know as 'rifling') that give a predictable spin to the bullet, and a ball fired from a smoothbore spins randomly in flight. Moreover, the ball, manufactured more or less expertly in the field by the soldier himself from the piece of lead and the small bullet mould he carried with him, was inevitably loose and ill-fitting in the barrel and not necessarily quite spherical. These imperfections caused it to tumble inaccurately through the air. Even for the musket, whose heavier shot was less subject to deviation than was that of the lighter arquebus, at a range of 200 feet a ball could stray more than five feet from the target being aimed at. As a result it was accurate up to only fifty yards or so, although a lucky shot that found a target could kill at double that distance.

In practical terms, such inaccuracy meant an arquebusier or musketeer could seldom hit an individual target being aimed at. So, to be effective, matchlock men had to be packed closely together to deliver volley fire against equally large and tight formations. This too had its drawbacks. The noise made by multiple, simultaneous discharges was ear-shattering, making it difficult to hear verbal commands or even trumpet calls. And black-powder detonations gave off dense clouds of dirty white smoke. On a damp or windless day smoke entirely obscured the battlefield, making it almost impossible to identify whether the troops looming up through the murk were friend or foe. Yet, for all their many drawbacks (not the least being that exploded powder had to be replenished and could not be reused like an arrow or spear), gunpowder weapons had an undeniable winning edge in battle if deployed effectively in mass formation – and if rain did not douse them.

The Portuguese fighting in Morocco found to their cost that they could not keep the military advantages of the gunpowder revolution to themselves for long. Thanks to the inevitable process of what is known as 'technology transfer', by the end of the fifteenth century Moroccan rulers, cities, mountain tribes and Bedouins were all acquiring firearms and cannons of their own from intrepid entrepreneurs and the enemies of the Portuguese. More than that, they were being instructed in their effective use by international soldiers of fortune and Christian *renegados* (renegades) in their pay, and especially by Muslim and Jewish refugees from the Spanish conquest of Granada. And to train a man in the effective use of a matchlock took only a few days compared to the months required before a bowman became proficient.

By the early 1520s the Portuguese also began to feel the effects of much stiffer Moroccan resistance as the *jihad* of the Sa'adian *sharifs* rolled north. Sensibly, King João III the Pious decided it was prudent to put dreams of further expansion in Morocco into abeyance, and to concentrate instead on consolidating the Portuguese hold over the fortified enclaves they already possessed. Leading members of his court were mortified by what they regarded as their king's craven abandonment of their dearly held crusading dream. Nevertheless, João's defensive strategy was eminently sensible, particularly since a new and powerful player had entered the arena in North Africa.

In 1453 the Ottoman Turks stormed and sacked Constantinople (now Istanbul), the last forlorn bastion of the Byzantine empire, and proceeded to gather under their dominion all the lands ruled a thousand years before by the Eastern Roman Empire. The Ottomans were essentially dependent on Christian *renegados* for knowledge of advances in the technology of the gunpowder revolution, but this did not prevent them from adopting it enthusiastically. So when, in 1517, the Ottoman army conquered Egypt from the ruling Mamluks it was the most professional and best equipped in the world at that time. Its expertise with siege and field cannon was the terror of all the sultan's enemies, and the disciplined firepower of its infantry swept all before them.

Following rapidly on their conquest of Egypt, the Ottomans extended their sway right across *al-Maghrib*. They seized all its Mediterranean ports, which they proceeded to administer with a light and distant hand through the *Beylerbey* (regent) of Algiers, who exercised sovereignty in the sultan's name over the *pashas* (governors)* of Tripoli and Tunis. Their conquering gaze fixed next on Morocco. A three-cornered struggle ensued there between the Ottoman *beylerbey*, the Sa'adian *sharifs* and the enfeebled Wattasid sultans. The Portuguese stayed out of the fray and watched from their fortified enclaves. Thrice over the course of two decades of war the Moroccans repulsed invading Ottoman armies in battles in which firearms played the decisive role. Finally, in 1554 the Sa'adian *sharifs* emerged as the undisputed rulers of Morocco and

---

* *Pasha* was an honorary, non-hereditary title in the Ottoman political system granted to generals or governors.

established their capital at Marrakesh close to their power base in the south of the country. The Ottomans, conceding that furthermost northwest Africa was geographically beyond their effective military reach, decided to call it quits over Morocco. In 1573 Sultan Selim II (unforgettably known as Selim the Sot because of his excessive – albeit forbidden – consumption of alcohol) wrote to Abdallah al-Ghalib, the Sa'adian Sharif of Morocco, calling for a truce and a common front against the infidel.

Yet Morocco was still denied peace. When in 1557 Abdallah al-Ghalib had succeeded his father (assassinated by members of his own suborned guard acting under Ottoman instructions), he had consolidated his rule by executing as many of his brothers as he could lay his hands upon. Several escaped to Ottoman territory, and two of them – the sixteen-year-old Abd al-Malik and his younger half-brother, the eight-year-old Ahmad – would survive to ascend the Moroccan throne in the years to come.

Abd al-Malik and Ahmad both served their military apprenticeship in the Ottoman army. Abd al-Malik spent much of his exile in Algiers, where he married the daughter of an Ottoman official, and where he enjoyed a close friendship with the *beylerbey*. This wealthy, cosmopolitan port, impregnable behind its fortifications, was then the main base for the Muslim corsairs of *al-Maghrib* and Morocco, who preyed remorselessly on Christian shipping right across the western Mediterranean and eastern Atlantic. They struck as far north as Iceland and Ireland, the Channel Islands and southern England, and virtually depopulated the coastal regions of southern Italy and Mediterranean Spain as they raided for booty and slaves. At the height of their activities there were on annual average about 35,000 Christian captives held as slave labour in *al-Maghrib* and Morocco. Serving regularly on the *beylerbey*'s swift galleys rowed by these enslaved unfortunates, Abd al-Malik had ample opportunity to hone his military skills against the infidel.

On 7 October 1571 Abd al-Malik fought in the great sea battle of Lepanto in the gulf of Patras in western Greece. It was a stunningly spectacular victory for the Holy League* over the Ottoman navy and one that permanently reduced the Ottoman naval presence in the western Mediterranean. Considering that

---

* The Holy League comprised the fleets of the crown of Spain, the papacy, the republics of Venice and Genoa, the Knights of St John and other Christian states under the command of Don Juan de Austria, the bastard son of the Emperor Carlos V.

15,000 of the Ottoman forces perished, Abd al-Malik was fortunate to be among the several thousand survivors the Spanish took prisoner. While in captivity he employed his leisure to perfect his Spanish, probably originally learned before his exile from the slaves and concubines of his father's court. Besides his native Arabic, he was also fluent in Turkish and seems to have had some knowledge of Italian, French and German too. Christian captives in Algiers reported that he followed their custom of sleeping in a bed and eating at a table. That was most unusual, because in Muslim North Africa even the houses of the great had but little furniture. Woven mats and precious carpets covered the floors on which plump cushions were strewn for seating. The elite slept on bedding laid on the floor and ate clustered on their cushions around large trays placed on low stands, served by their domestic slaves.

Abd al-Malik was indeed remarkably cosmopolitan. He enormously admired the Ottoman style of government and administration, and always wore Ottoman rather than Moroccan dress. At the same time, he nourished a genuine and informed interest in Christian customs, music and intellectual life that disturbed more orthodox Muslims, like his own brother Ahmad, who was a profound Islamic scholar, delighting in religious debate. On the other hand, Abd al-Malik's westernised interests could not fail to impress Christians. Miguel de Cervantes, the famous Spanish novelist and poet who was captured by Algerian corsairs in 1575, admiringly described him as 'a great soldier, generous, wise, self possessed, endowed with a thousand virtues'.[1]

Once ransomed from Spanish captivity, Abd al-Malik took service once more with the Ottomans, and in 1574 performed prodigious feats of valour and leadership in the campaign that wrested the fortress of La Goletta and the port of Tunis back from short-lived Spanish occupation. His mother, Shaba al-Rahmaniyya, living in exile in Istanbul, is said to have brought his deeds to the personal attention of the newly enthroned sultan, Murad III, who saw how he could make use of him to bring Morocco closer into the Ottoman orbit without much cost or effort.

When his brother, Abdallah al-Ghalib (the ruler of Morocco who had driven him into exile) died in 1574, he was succeeded as *sharif* by his son and designated heir, Muhammad al-Mutawakkil. Uncomfortably for the new ruler, the reputation of his exiled uncle, Abd al-Malik, quite overshadowed his in the eyes of his subjects. From Algiers Abd al-Malik had assiduously cultivated his connections in Morocco over the years, and his brother Ahmad had regularly gone in disguise to Morocco to make contact with his leading adherents. His supporters eagerly built up Abd al-Malik's public image as a military hero and a champion of the *jihad*.

Sensing his nephew's insecurity, Abd al-Malik saw that the moment had at last struck for him to seize the throne. He applied to his patron, the sultan, and in return for pledging himself Murad's vassal, in 1575 he received an Ottoman loan with which to raise troops to invade Morocco. As a far more able and experienced commander than Muhammad al-Mutawakkil, in July 1576 Abd al-Malik crushed his hated brother's heir in battle. The defeated Muhammad al-Mutawakkil fled Morocco to wash up as a suppliant at the court of King Sebastião of Portugal.

King Sebastião Invades Morocco

At the tender age of three, in 1557, Sebastião had succeeded his grandfather, João III, as King of Portugal and the Algarves.* This last male sprig of the House of Aviz-Beja was born on 20 January, the feast day of St Sebastian, and was named with unfortunate prescience after this martyr who (according to tradition) had been transfixed by arrows. Until he achieved his majority in 1568 and commenced his personal rule as a teenager of fourteen, his great uncle – the necessarily childless Cardinal Henrique – acted as regent for him.

Jesuit fathers raised Sebastião in isolation and educated him strictly in the spirit of the Counter-Reformation, so that all his short life he remained exceedingly devout and ostentatiously chaste. He was no milksop, however, and grew up to be a strong, very tall, lively young man with blue eyes, close-cropped blond hair and a perky little moustache and goatee. Raised and deferred to as king from the cradle, he had perhaps not unnaturally developed a decided mind of his own that his detractors characterised as arrogant, self-opinionated, obstinate and impulsive. Above all things he delighted in every form of knightly activity, and mercilessly subjected himself to a sort of military asceticism that involved swimming and riding, practising the use of arms and devoting hours to spiritual exercises.

---

* His father died a few weeks before his birth.

Sebastião burned with obsessive zeal to go on crusade and to reactivate the *Reconquista* in Morocco. He shared this ambition with his *fidalguia* (service nobility), who like him were still obsessed with the chivalric ideals of their knightly caste and were determined to prove their military prowess in battle. For years Morocco had been the military proving ground for noble youths who aspired to earn their knighthoods serving with the Portuguese garrisons stationed there.

Thus, when Muhammad al-Mutawakkil appeared as a suppliant seeking Christian help for his restoration to the throne of Morocco, it seemed to Sebastião that God was presenting him with a golden opportunity to put himself at the head of the holy and high adventure of a fresh crusade in Africa. To his mind, the cause was a doubly legitimate one as he regarded himself as a rightful heir to the Christian Visigoth kings who had once ruled over parts of northern Morocco. More prosaically, a determined invasion would permit Portugal to consolidate its control of the Moroccan wheat lands, its rich seaboard and the glittering trans-Saharan gold trade.

Consequently, while his uncle, the famously prudent King Felipe II of Spain,* sensibly turned down Muhammad al-Mutawakkil's initial request to support him in his doubtful attempt to regain his throne – and indeed tried to talk Sebastião out of embarking on such a foolhardy venture – the young king ardently embraced the opportunity as irresistible. Seeing that Sebastião was not to be dissuaded, Felipe – in the interests of Catholic and Iberian solidarity – promised to contribute soldiers to the cause as well as logistical support in the form of ships and supplies. Furthermore, in a gesture of well-intentioned but dubious symbolism, he presented Sebastião with the precious helmet and silk tabard worn by the latter's renowned grandfather, the Holy Roman Emperor Carlos V,† who forty years before had led the ultimately doomed Spanish struggle against the Ottomans in North Africa. In return, Felipe stipulated only that as a first step Sebastião must direct his expedition against Larache. This Atlantic port was strategically situated very close to the Strait of Gibraltar. It commanded the vulnerable sea route to the Spanish possessions in the New

* King Felipe of Spain was the brother of Joanna, Sebastião's mother.

† The Habsburg Holy Roman Emperor was also King Carlos I of Spain and King Felipe's father.

World, along which passed the regular infusion of American silver that fuelled the enormous Spanish war machine.

With money borrowed from merchants and bankers, and even Jews (to the scandal of the devout), Sebastião set about assembling an army that in the end numbered about 18,000 men, of whom some 16,500 were infantry. Contingents of foreign soldiers of fortune constituted a good third of this number. A papal force of Italian and Irish Catholic volunteers under the English Catholic *condottiero*, Thomas Stukeley, was one. Another was made up of Walloons from the Spanish Netherlands and (surely inappropriately for a Catholic crusade) Protestant Germans from the Holy Roman Empire with their own Lutheran pastors. King Felipe's contribution took the form of a contingent of 2,000 of his valuable Castilian veterans.

The Portuguese forces made up the bulk of the infantry but were its least professional element. The ordinary soldiers were peasants and labourers who could not afford to buy military exemption and were more often than not pressed into service by their lords. They had only the most rudimentary military training and little practice in the handling of their weapons. Their officers were young nobles and gentlemen who, for all their swaggering braggadocio, often lacked much practical experience in real campaigning. But their king had left them with no option but to serve in the Moroccan campaign. Sebastião was determined that all his nobility would accompany him on his great and holy venture, and he threatened them that, if they held back, their lands, rents and privileges would be forfeit.

Veterans of the wars in North Africa argued in Sebastião's war council held in Lisbon for a large force of cavalry to counter the swirling swarms of horsemen they expected to face in Morocco. But cavalry was an exceedingly expensive arm to equip and maintain. Each horseman riding into battle, armed with lance and sabre, required a hugely dear warhorse as well as several spare mounts and a team of support personnel to maintain them. Most cavalrymen still wore armour because it deflected missiles at fairly long range and edged weapons in hand-to-hand fighting. It was usually limited to steel breast- and backplates, gorgets (steel or leather collars to protect the throat), tassets (the articulated armour that protected the upper legs), various pieces to protect the hands and arms, and closed helmets with visors. The full cap-à-pie suit of plate armour that weighed around seventy pounds was heavy and unwieldy, and more suitable for the tilt yard than to a campaign. Nevertheless, because it was so expensive and prestigious, it continued to be worn by those who could afford it, such as the king and his great nobles. Battle armour, though, was normally not the highly decorative chased and damascened parade armour familiar to us from many a formal and bombastic portrait, but plain and unornamented.

As was appropriate to their knightly pretensions and to their wealth, it was noblemen who made up the small force of some 1,500 cavalry that Sebastião was finally able to muster under the command of the Duke d'Aveiro. This did not nearly meet the number of horsemen the North African veterans thought essential, but Sebastião was content to make a virtue of necessity. He decided that it was in any case preferable to rely on the modern configuration of a Spanish-style army in which the infantry, mustered into large combined-arms formations, greatly predominated.

The *tercio*, as this versatile infantry formation was known, nominally consisted of 3,000 men (although it inevitably suffered varying degrees of attrition from illness, desertion, mutiny, wounds and death). The members of a *tercio* bore a variety of weapons that allowed them to meet every contingency on the battlefield. Half the men carried steel-tipped pikes between fifteen and twenty feet long, and were drawn up in a square like a bristling hedgehog. Another large contingent, armed with swords and daggers, javelins and halberds,* was positioned inside the pike square. Several hundred arquebusiers, known as the 'sleeve', were stationed outside the square in mobile groups, primarily at the corners, to enfilade an approaching enemy force with their crossfire. Field artillery, if it was available, was usually lined up to the front of the *tercio*.

Because the arquebusiers of the 'sleeve' would otherwise be left defenceless while going through their complicated and lengthy reloading procedures after firing a volley, they retired behind the ranks of pikes to do so. The pikemen thus provided them with the sort of solid defence otherwise offered by walls or field entrenchments.† When repelling cavalry, a pikeman placed the butt of his weapon against his heel to buttress it and presented the steel point

---

* A wicked weapon consisting of a wooden shaft five to six feet long topped by a long spearhead with an axe blade on the front and a hook on the back that was very effective in grappling horsemen.

† Handguns were used in conjunction with pikes until the adoption of the socket bayonet, developed in the 1690s, made the pike redundant. It finally disappeared from the battlefield *c*.1705.

diagonally at the chest of the charging horse that invariably (and sensibly) shied away. Nor was the rider inclined to urge on his reluctant steed, because a pike outreached any lance carried by cavalry. A pikeman, when advancing to the attack against enemy infantry (cavalry on the move could always stay out of range of a lumbering *tercio*), held the pike horizontally and pointed it straight ahead to jab his enemy in the face. Yet, because a pikeman needed both his hands to wield his weapon, he then became vulnerable to the darting blades of enemy swordsmen, and even the butts of discharged arquebuses wielded like clubs.

Tercios could be devastatingly effective when sufficiently disciplined and well drilled, and when they had developed strong group solidarity. But these dense, tightly packed blocks of infantry made large targets, vulnerable even to chronically inaccurate artillery and arquebus fire, let alone bolts, arrows and javelins. This is where iron discipline was indispensable. The moment a *tercio* began to break up under fire and lose its tight formation, it became easy prey to flank attacks by cavalry and to a determined push by the enemy infantry, when it faced annihilation in a desperate hand-to-hand mêlée.

Portugal had adopted the Spanish *tercio* in the sixteenth century, calling it the *terço*. When Sebastião raised his army for Morocco he set the size of the *terço* at 2,000 men, only two-thirds the size of the Spanish model. Unfortunately, his four *terços* of raw recruits lacked the necessary experience and training, and were not nearly of the same calibre as his papal, imperial or Castilian *tercios*. It was anticipated that the fifth Portuguese *terço* would approach their standard because it was made up of *aventureiros* (poor nobles who lacked the money to equip themselves appropriately for cavalry service). Their accoutrements for service in a *terço* were relatively cheap, although they were not necessarily able to afford all the pieces of armour customarily worn by pikemen for protection. These comprised a breast- and backplate, tassets, pieces to protect arms and shoulders, and an open helmet, which almost always took the form of a morion with swooping brim and metal crest. Officers wore ornate, engraved morions to assert their status, and all morions sported plumes secured in the holder at the back of the helm.

Except for some elite corps such as royal bodyguards, soldiers did not yet wear uniform. They would really begin to do so only in the later seventeenth century, and by the eighteenth century uniforms and soldiers were synonymous. But in the sixteenth century soldiers chose their own doublets and breeches of whatever cut or colour they preferred because it was held that they fought more bravely and cheerfully that way. For identification on the battlefield soldiers might agree to wear plumes, armbands or sashes of the same colour, or some other common emblem such as a cross.

On 14 June 1578 Sebastião 'attended by all the Nobility and Gentry, rode to the cathedral [in Lisbon], where his standard was Blessed, on which was the Figure of our Saviour Crucifyed'.[2] He then embarked immediately on his brigantine,* which joined the gaudily bedecked but motley armada of 500 or so ships of every variety that was to take his army to Africa. At about midnight on 6 July, after a leisurely voyage that allowed for much ostentatious junketing at various ports of call, the fleet anchored before Tangier in Morocco, which was held by a Portuguese garrison.

The fleet carried more than soldiers, however. It was perfectly normal at that time for a huge number of camp followers and all their baggage horses and carts to accompany an army. More often than not, as was the case with Sebastião's expeditionary force, the rabble of non-combatant soldiers' 'wives', who looked after their material needs (and who would change hands every time their mate was killed or died of disease), their children, chaplains, pages, musicians (including the royal choir), sutlers,† cooks, launderers, grooms, lackeys and slaves almost equalled the actual fighting force in numbers. Indeed, Sebastião deliberately brought enough civilians with him to found a city should he fail to conquer one. But it is clear that he expected to capture a great many. In his overweening confidence he carried a gold crown in his extravagant baggage train along with the rich clothing, magnificently appointed portable chapel and other extravagant trappings necessary to assert his royal state, for he planned to be proclaimed Emperor of Morocco once he had defeated Abd al-Malik.

Picking up some 500 trained arquebusiers, known as *fronteiros*, from the garrison of Tangier, Sebastião's army, encumbered by its baggage train of 1,000 wagons and dragging along its field artillery (which numbered between ten and twenty pieces) lurched southwards along the coast to the port of Asilah.

---

* A brigantine was a small ship that carried both sails and oars, and which was much favoured by the Barbary corsairs.

† A sutler is a camp follower selling provisions to the troops.

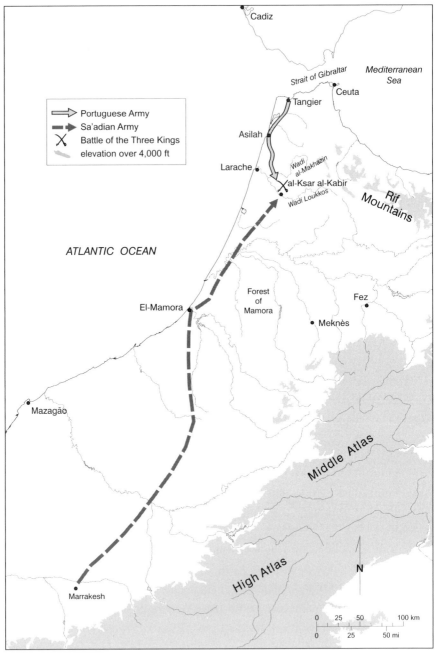

MAP 1 *The Moroccan campaign, July–August 1578*

The governor of the place was still loyal to Muhammad al-Mutawakkil and surrendered the town to the Portuguese. Muhammad al-Mutawakkil himself joined Sebastião at Asilah with what forces he had managed to raise. To Sebastião's considerable disappointment they numbered less than 2,000 men, half of whom were mounted arquebusiers and the remainder cavalry.

It was also while bivouacked outside the walls of Asilah, where his disgruntled and squabbling troops began to come down with the dysentery so prevalent in crowded and filthy army camps, that Sebastião presided over a stormy council of war. The assembled commanders could not agree on the best way to advance on the Atlantic port of Larache, the army's first objective. The fleet was available to transport the army there by sea, but because of the dangerous shallows before the port, and on account of its strong fortifications, some argued with good reason that an amphibious assault was too risky. The alternative was to take the overland route to Larache. The direct coast road required the hazardous crossing of the tidal Wadi Loukkos at its mouth, so Sebastião decided to take the inland route towards al-Kasr al-Kabir. At a distance of about fifty miles south of Asilah the army would cross an upstream ford across the Wadi Loukkos and then turn northwest for Larache, an estimated two days' march away. The distance did not seem too great, but the uncertain whereabouts of Abd al-Malik's forces presented a distinct threat.

Sebastião, deluded by his own wishful thinking, impatiently discounted the report of a French *renegado* who had deserted from Abd al-Malik's army – a report that additional intelligence correctly corroborated – that a large Sa'adian force was rapidly mustering near enough to bar his way overland. So, sticking to his belief that Abd al-Malik was still safely at his capital of Marrakesh hundreds of miles away to the south, he brusquely overrode the cautious reservations of his commanders, for good measure gratuitously impugning their courage in the process. These experienced and much older soldiers were so filled with dismay at Sebastião's rash decision that it is said some of them even treasonably contemplated taking him into custody to prevent his leading the army to disaster. That they did not do so speaks to the unshakable rigour of their code of honour, which required their absolute loyalty to their sovereign.

On 29 July the Portuguese struck camp and began their fatal march south from Asilah. The soldiers took the lead in a relatively compact body. The artillery, ox wagons carrying biscuit, water and gunpowder, the rest of the baggage train with its loads of tents, court luxuries and other equipment, and the rabble of camp followers made up its draggled tail, which stretched over many miles of sweltering coastal plain. Some of the great nobles did not ride, but took their ease in the elaborate coaches they had brought with them. The late summer sun beat remorselessly down, reflecting viciously off body armour that became intolerable to wear. Provisions for people as well as the host of draught animals and cavalry horses began to run out and water was hard to come by in the parched countryside. Soon swaggering military noble and camp follower alike were dehydrated and exhausted. The pace of their march slowed and morale fell. As the Portuguese dragged themselves along, Abd al-Malik's mounted scouts hovered threateningly on their flanks and reported their halting progress back to their canny commander.

After five days of marching and a few minor brushes with the enemy, who either strongly held or destroyed the bridges over the rivers along their path, on Sunday 3 August the Portuguese reached a narrow ford across the tidal Wadi al-Makhazin with its steep banks. It took the army much of the day to negotiate it. But at least the next, crucial ford across the Wadi Loukkos was now only three miles away across a baking plain, through which ran a little stream, the Wadi Warur. Once over the Wadi Loukkos, the army would turn right for Larache and the succouring fleet.

The Battle of the Three Kings

The utterly spent Portuguese encamped at the confluence of the Wadi al-Makhazin and Wadi Warur with the ford they had just struggled across directly behind them. But they would barely sleep that night. Their scouts had come pelting back with the awful intelligence that waiting ominously for them, and barring their way to the ford across the Wadi Loukkos, was Abd al-Malik and his serried host. With no time to fall back across the narrow ford they had taken all day to cross, Sebastião realised there could be no retreat for his unsupplied, exhausted army and its reproachful officers. No tactical, honourable or chivalric option remained for him but to pick up the gauntlet Abd al-Malik had flung down. The next day, 4 August, he offered battle where he stood.

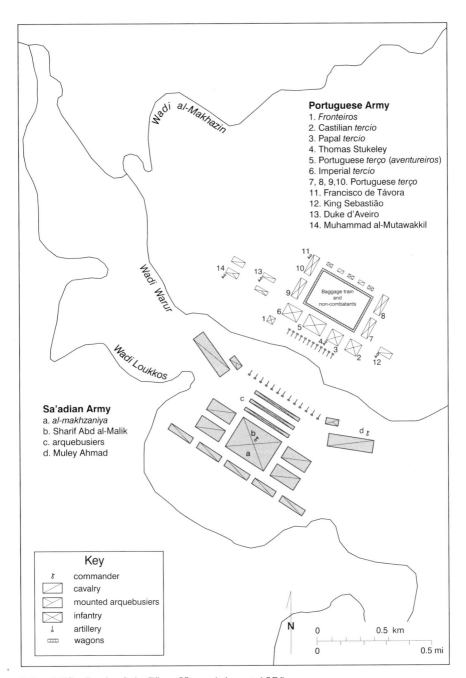

Portuguese Army
1. *Fronteiros*
2. Castilian *tercio*
3. Papal *tercio*
4. Thomas Stukeley
5. Portuguese *terço* (*aventureiros*)
6. Imperial *tercio*
7, 8, 9,10. Portuguese *terço*
11. Francisco de Távora
12. King Sebastião
13. Duke d'Aveiro
14. Muhammad al-Mutawakkil

Baggage train
and
non-combatants

Sa'adian Army
a. *al-makhzaniya*
b. Sharif Abd al-Malik
c. arquebusiers
d. Muley Ahmad

Key
commander
cavalry
mounted arquebusiers
infantry
artillery
wagons

N

| 0 | 0.5 km |
| 0 | 0.5 mi |

MAP 2 *The Battle of the Three Kings, 4 August 1578*

Still only in his late thirties, Abd al-Malik was a very ill man that morning. He had been vomiting for days and was running a high fever. It seems from the description of his Jewish doctor, Joseph Valencia, that he was suffering from acute dysentery following a meal of fish and fruit, although either plague or deliberate poisoning was also mooted. Whatever the cause, he was too weak to trust himself in the saddle, so while his army deployed for battle after morning prayers, he remained reclining in his litter. Even so, he insisted on being dressed in the resplendent golden brocade robes of dignity conferred on him by Sultan Murad III, with a bejewelled and plumed turban on his head and his most precious rings on his fingers. Around his waist he girded his favourite Ottoman sword and dagger, richly studded with rubies and turquoises. His flamboyantly apparelled courtiers and officials clustered around him, as did his bodyguard with their gilded pikes. Five mounted standard bearers, each with the green banner of Islam, stood ready to precede him into battle.

The Portuguese invasion had caused initial consternation in Morocco. Many of the inhabitants of Fez had fled in panic to the nearby Middle Atlas mountains, and in the south the *sharif* had set about urgently improving the fortifications of Marrakesh. At the same time he and his thirty-year-old brother and designated heir, Muley (or Lord) Ahmad, had begun efficiently to raise and supply an army, taking fullest advantage of the breathing space the Portuguese gave him while they dallied at the coast. By the first days of August he probably had as many as 70,000 men under his command from every corner of Morocco. On 2 August he moved this force forward through al-Kasr al-Kabir to take up the position of his own choosing twelve miles to the northwest, where the open plain gave his cavalry ample room to manoeuvre against the advancing Portuguese.

About half of Ahmad's force was made up of the elite units of *al-makhzaniya* (his standing army). Abd al-Malik paid them a regular salary taken mainly from his revenues from the sugar industry, and barracked them in some splendour at his capital, Marrakesh. The *sharif's* power as ruler depended upon these troops of state, and he selected his personal guard from among them. They accompanied him at all times, including the battlefield, riding beautifully caparisoned horses of the finest bloodstock and flaunting magnificent silk attire of every colour. Their weapons were of the very best and were beautifully worked with quivers and sword scabbards plated in gold.

The members of *al-makhzaniya* came from many different backgrounds. Some were the *sharif's* own Sa'adians, while others were his military slaves. Embittered refugees from Granada made up an important element because they were at the cutting edge of gunpowder technology and formed specialised units of marksmen. There were also Christian *renegados*, or *'uluj'* – captives or fortune-seekers who had embraced Islam and sold their up-to-date military skills to Muslim masters. Further mercenaries came from all over the Muslim world to serve Abd al-Malik. Because none of these foreigners had developed much local support for a possible revolt, and gave their loyalty to him alone, the *sharif* was content to entrust them all with the battle-winning firearms he kept out of less reliable hands.

Besides *al-makhzaniya*, Abd al-Malik had at his disposal troops of lesser weight. There were large numbers of *jaysh* (fighting men from the privileged Arab nomad tribes of the north of the kingdom). They owed the *sharif* military service in return for exemption from taxation for the lands granted them, but where they had the right to levy taxes of their own on the peasantry. Typically, they wore helmets and chain-mail armour, and carried shields of antelope hide, sabres and long spears. They were among those the *sharif* did not permit to carry firearms because he remembered only too well how readily they had rebelled or changed sides during the recent civil wars. Because the Portuguese invasion was an emergency, the *sharif* also called on the relatively untrained and poorly armed levies and militias raised by the more reliable notables and towns of the plain. On top of all these forces, Abd al-Malik had also collected about thirty field guns drawn by mules or camels, some of them cast only just in time for the battle and serviced by his trained Andalusian or *renegado* gunners. The Moroccan army was also distinctly in advance of the Portuguese in terms of its medical support. Well-equipped surgeons accompanied it on campaign with their own hospital tents.

In its command structure, Abd al-Malik modelled his army on the Ottoman one where he had learned the military trade. He was the commander-in-chief, but his deputy was the *wazir*, a position held by his energetic and charismatic brother Muley Ahmad, who was notably handsome too, with rounded cheeks and a golden-brown complexion. Under him were the other high officers, all of them his Sa'adian relatives, who commanded the important elements of the army: the *sharif's* personal guard, the arquebusiers, artillery and cavalry.

This heterogeneous army was colourfully dressed in every form of garment known to the western Mediterranean world, from flowing white Moroccan *djebellas* with their hoods and wide sleeves to the doublets and breeches of Christian mercenaries and the flashing silks and brocades of the elite horsemen. Chain mail was much in evidence, as were spiked helmets, great turbans and high caps.

Crucially, and in complete contrast to Sebastião's foot-slogging army, only a third of this great host was infantry, but a very high proportion of both infantry and cavalry were armed with arquebuses. Critically, although an arquebus with all its finicky loading procedures was very difficult to manage on horseback, Moroccan horsemen (unlike European cavalry of the time) seemed to have mastered the art. They were particularly adept at their version of the *caracole*, a manoeuvre that required a line of cavalry to fire at the enemy from point-blank range while riding by, and then to turn abruptly about to reload while another wave took their place in the firing line.

Sebastião and his commanders, knowing only too well that they were outnumbered by three to one, but counting on the tenacity of their disciplined infantry formations to withstand the cavalry charges they anticipated Abd el-Malik would hurl at them, decided to stand on the defensive until the Moroccan attack had broken itself against their ranks. Then would be the moment to go over to the attack and drive the demoralised Moroccans from the field.

With this intention, Sebastião drew up his army in a great hollow square with its back to the Wadi al-Makhazin. He ranged his dozen or so cannon* in front of his position and posted the *fronteiros* (the arquebusiers from the Tangier garrison) and a detachment of cavalry forward to defend them. Behind them was the vanguard that would face the enemy head on. That is where Sebastião placed his best troops. The imperial *tercio* was on the right of the line, and the papal and Castilian units on the left. The king gave the place of honour in the centre to the *terço* of Portuguese *aventureiros*. The baggage train, draught animals and all support personnel and camp followers were placed behind them with many of the wagons drawn up around them to form a rudimentary barricade. A Portuguese *terço* took up position on either side of this *laager*. These were the weakest units in the army, poorly trained, unmotivated and

---

* Some of the Portuguese cannons had been abandoned on the march south from Asilah.

demoralised by the privations they had suffered. To their rear, and to complete the fourth side of defensive formation, Sebastião positioned a mixed force of cavalry and arquebusiers flanked on either side by the two remaining *terços*.

The Wadi Warur ran diagonally in front of the Portuguese position and was at its closest on their right, giving that flank some natural protection against encirclement. However, it was too far away on their left to form any appreciable obstacle across the open plain. Anticipating that Abd al-Malik would attempt to outflank him with his overwhelming numbers of horsemen, Sebastião divided his perilously small force of cavalry and placed a detachment on either flank of the infantry square. Unaccountably, he made the detachment on the right twice the size of that guarding his more exposed left flank and placed his mounted *fronteiros* of the Tangier garrison there. Moreover, he despatched Muhammad al-Mutawakkil and his Moroccan horsemen, about half of whom were mounted arquebusiers, to support them. Perhaps he was hoping that would make them strong enough to effect a successful counter-attack when the time came.

As was usual in the Muslim world, Abd al-Malik drew up his army in a great crescent with his cannon lined up in front. But in his deployment of individual units he followed the typical plan of the now-defunct Moorish kingdoms of Spain that had become the norm in Morocco too. He left gaps between his guns to allow his infantry to flow through them to the attack, rather than following the much more static Ottoman practice of lining up field guns interspersed with wagons and chaining them all together to form a barrier against cavalry charges. In his vanguard, immediately behind the guns, he placed some 10,000 arquebusiers in three extended lines, one behind the other, each only a few ranks deep. He mixed up his more reliable units with those whose loyalty was less assured, thus guarding against the compromising, sudden desertions at the height of the fighting that had bedevilled Morocco's recent civil wars. Behind the long ranks of his vanguard, Abd al-Malik drew up the bulk of *al-makhzaniya* in a giant square of halberdiers, pikemen and arquebusiers and planted his great banner in their midst. He was laid down next to it in his litter, surrounded by his bodyguard.

The Moroccan cavalry took up position on either flank of the infantry. Two lethal units of mounted arquebusiers were ranged forward on both sides of the line of cannons to catch any Portuguese advance in their crossfire and to mount a speedy counter-attack. Abd al-Malik placed some 10,000 light cavalry armed with lances and swords immediately to their rear to give them support. Muley Ahmad, who would succeed him that fatal day to become the greatest Moroccan ruler of the age, commanded the cavalry on the right, which faced the weaker of the two Portuguese cavalry wings. Smaller cavalry units guarded the flanks of the huge infantry formation at the centre. Finally, Abd al-Malik stationed dependable and experienced troops to their rear to deter any of the unseasoned levies and militias who might panic and try to quit the field.

Because many of the units that made up his conglomerate army were unreliable, and the loyalty of others dubious, Abd al-Malik understood well that he could not afford to stand back and wait for the Portuguese to try and break through. He had to win quickly and decisively. So, in the interests of maintaining morale, and taking advantage of his numerical superiority, especially in cavalry, it was essential to take the initiative in outflanking, squeezing together and pinning down the Portuguese. That achieved, he planned to use his arquebusiers and better troops to push the contained enemy back upon the Wadi al-Makhazin, and once their formation broke up under the unremitting pressure, to annihilate them.

By the same token, in order to win Sebastião had only to keep his embattled army together under the Moroccan assault. This was a matter of maintaining discipline as his tight formations of infantry were pounded by cannon and arquebus fire, stung by arrows and pierced by lances and flung javelins. If he succeeded in his defensive strategy, the disheartened enemy would begin to break away, and many units could then be expected to defect to the winning side and to al-Mutawakkil's cause. That would be the moment for the *tercios* and *aventureiros* to advance, crash into the wavering Sa'adian centre and drive Abd al-Malik from the field.

It was normal to hold a religious service before combat, especially when an army (or, at any rate, its commanders) believed it was engaged in God's work. Victory was therefore divinely ordained and death in battle a holy sacrifice. So, once the young king in his splendid armour had finished drawing up his anxious army to face the Moroccan host that had already deployed after its own diligent morning prayers, it was the turn of the bishops of Coimbra and Oporto. A forest of crucifixes preceded them, held high and glinting in the fiery sunlight that shone in the eyes of the troops and was already making their armour unbearable. With the voices of the throng of priests and choristers raised in solemn chant, the bishops (neither of whom would live to see another day) processed in a cloud of incense along the Portuguese ranks blessing the troops and giving them final absolution. It is well that both sides prayed, for many would never see the sun rise again over the lowering Jebala mountains on the eastern horizon.

With a great shout of '*Bismillah!*' by which those who uttered it offered themselves as vehicles for the glory of God, the Sa'adian gunners opened the battle at about nine o'clock in the morning with a devastating volley of cannon fire. The densely packed Portuguese ranks were severely shaken as the iron balls ploughed through them, crushing abdomens and tearing off limbs and heads. One cut down the experienced and competent Thomas Stukeley, the commander of the papal *tercio* who also had charge of the Portuguese vanguard. To encourage the shocked infantry, a Jesuit priest raised a great crucifix above their heads in blessing and many sank briefly to their knees in prayer. When they rose they joined in chanting the Portuguese battle cry, '*Aviz e Christo!*'

Simultaneously with the cannonade, Abd al-Malik's cavalry, with the mounted arquebusiers in the lead, charged both of the Portuguese flanks. Pikemen could usually be confident they could repel cavalry. In a charge cavalry inevitably fanned out as swifter horses and more courageous riders outpaced the rest, thus greatly limiting the shock effect of their impact – even if they could be spurred on to a wall of bristling pikes. But on this occasion the Portuguese were consternated and severely disrupted by the unexpected effectiveness of the Moroccans' expertly conducted series of *caracole* manoeuvres that poured arquebus fire into their flanks. Meanwhile, the cavalry supporting the mounted arquebusiers swept forward to threaten the Portuguese rear. The outnumbered Portuguese artillery, already thrown in disarray by the opening Moroccan salvo, returned fire as best they could. However, as Mustapha Jannabi wrote at the time, 'by Divine favour, the cannonballs all flew harmlessly over the faithful'.[3] The arquebusiers on both sides then opened fire, and the advancing lines of Moroccan arquebusiers rapidly overran the unarmed Portuguese gunners and the arquebusier *fronteiros* from Tangier, who were supposed to defend them. It seemed that Abd al-Malik would gain the rapid victory his tactics required.

Battle is a test of nerve and will, and no victory is ever assured until the enemy flees; nor is victory quite as inevitable as the eventual outcome might suggest, for battles are subject to wild and unexpected fluctuations of fortune. The Battle of the Three Kings was no exception, and was far more closely run than has often been credited. For despite being severely rocked in the initial encounter, the Portuguese fought back furiously. King Sebastião was at first left stunned and speechless by the fury of the Moroccan attack, but he quickly recovered his nerve. Generals at that time had little chance in the noise, confusion and poor visibility of the battlefield of synchronising the operations of their subordinate commanders who were expected to fight on as they best saw fit. All a general could do was personally take command of one part of the army or gallop about the battlefield to encourage his troops where the fighting was the hottest. Sebastião chose the latter course. His mettle now up and with no regard for his personal safety, he repeatedly exposed himself to enemy fire as he rode forward with his escort to urge his men on by his intrepid example.

Sebastião had three horses shot from under him that day, and paused in his efforts only to allow his squires to pour water into his suit of plate armour to cool it down as the scorching sun rose towards its zenith and the temperature reached forty degrees Celsius (104 degrees Fahrenheit). Survivors of the desperate fighting later talked about a 'dark hour'[4] when so overwhelming was the appalling combination of the airless heat, the dust and acrid smoke, the din of gunshots and clashing weapons, the shouts and screams of wounded men and animals, the terrible, remorseless confusion and fear of it all, that men entirely lost their bearings.

When it became clear that the Portuguese were not going to collapse as at first seemed likely, Moroccan militias and other less experienced troops began to lose heart and, as Abu al-Malik had feared they would, began to trickle away from the battlefield in such numbers that his numerical superiority was appreciably reduced. Sensing that the initiative was passing to them, the soldiers of the Portuguese vanguard lowered their pikes to charge the thin ranks of Moroccan arquebusiers, overwhelming their cannons as they went. When the pikemen crashed into the Moroccans, the Portuguese swordsmen ran out between them to attack the Moroccan arquebusiers and gunners who, with nothing more than their daggers and arquebus butts to defend themselves, had distinctly the worse of the hand-to-hand fighting. At the same time Sebastião rallied his cavalry and led a charge that threw the light Moroccan cavalry back in disarray.

Moroccan arquebusiers and horsemen alike fell back behind their great infantry square or fled the field. Some of the Moroccan troops (*renegados* in particular) began to change sides and join the Portuguese. As Abd al-Malik's Jewish physician, Joseph Valencia, remembered the situation at that point: 'our horse and foot retired until they were behind al-Malik's banner . . . When the Sharif saw his people overcome, he looked every way to see none behind him, some had fled for fear of the gunshots.'[5]

At this critical moment, the ailing Abd al-Malik was helped out of his litter, mounted his warhorse and rallied his men by personally leading a furious cavalry counter-attack against the Portuguese right. His charge forced the Duke d'Aveiro's overextended cavalry back upon the right flank of the imperial *tercio*, severely disrupting its formation. Meanwhile, the Moroccan infantry pushed forward again to recapture their cannons. At that triumphant moment Abd al-Malik fell from the saddle in a faint – whether from the effects of his food poisoning, a stroke or a bullet is uncertain. His attendants helped him back to his litter where he expired (the first of the three kings to die that day). Swift thinking by some of those closest to him preserved Moroccan morale, which might otherwise have collapsed if his death had become widely known. They spent the rest of the battle shuttling between the curtained litter and Muley Ahmad, now in actual command, pretending they were relaying orders from the *sharif* who lay dead within.

Even so, the Moroccan attack began to falter, and once again the experienced troops of the Portuguese vanguard pushed forward. Yet their very success was their undoing. As they exultingly advanced against the wavering Moroccan arquebusiers, the *tercios* and *aventureiros* began to open up a fatal gap between themselves and the inexperienced Portuguese *terços* to their rear. These began desperately to shout at the vanguard to fall back and maintain the defensive formation of the square. But it was too late. The Moroccan centre that had maintained its cohesion and morale surged forward to reinforce their faltering lines of arquebusiers, and to its dismay the Portuguese vanguard found it had become too heavily entangled with the enemy to its front to disengage and retire.

Adroitly seizing the sudden advantage, the Moroccan horsemen determinedly spurred again at the outnumbered Portuguese cavalry and Muhammad al-Mutawakkil's horsemen, breaking through their desperately scattering ranks to burst into the spaces left open between the vanguard and the rest of the Portuguese square. They also fell on the flanks held by the inexperienced and severely rattled *terços*, and their mounted arquebusiers once again sowed panic in their ranks with their galling fire. One of them shot down Francisco de Távora, who commanded the *terço* that held the right rear corner of the Portuguese formation. His terrified troops instantly broke up, some fleeing towards the river behind them and others trying to take refuge behind the barricade of baggage wagons in the centre of the disintegrating Portuguese position.

By now the elated Moroccans were surging through the many gaps they had succeeded in prising open in the Portuguese formation. They fell upon the desperate, screaming camp followers in the centre, who were trampling each other to death in their vain attempts to escape, and upon the demoralised troops who had run back among them. Others proceeded systematically to destroy the now isolated and surrounded separate elements of the Portuguese army. The knots of the professional *tercios* and the *aventureiros* resisted staunchly as comrade stood by comrade, loyal to each other to the bitter end. They fought on with their swords and daggers when their pikes were broken, but many Portuguese tried to flee the field. Only about a hundred made it safely to the coast. Muhammad al-Mutawakkil, the second of the three kings to perish, drowned attempting to swim his horse across the Wadi al-Makhazin, where the tide was up. The victors recovered his corpse, and Ahmad ordered it to be flayed, stuffed with straw, paraded in derision among the cities of northern Morocco where his support had been strongest, and finally hung on the walls of Fez.

The Portuguese Defeat and its Consequences

As a true knight, King Sebastião disdained flight and brushed aside the pleas of his surviving commanders to surrender. He was last seen with a small band of noble companions and the remnants of his bodyguard galloping furiously into the encircling enemy ranks in a final, forlorn bid to turn the tide of battle. He was the third of the three kings to die. Uncertain whether or not the king had survived the battle, his fleet waited for some days outside Larache until they were convinced his body had been found. It would seem that after the battle two of his captive pages identified Sebastião's bloodied corpse, naked and stripped of its glorious armour by the looters who had scoured the field, with a mortal wound in the head and an arm almost lopped off. They brought it to the dead Abd al-Malik's pavilion, where the captured Portuguese nobles were being held. They sorrowfully confirmed the identification and immediately offered an extravagant ransom for the body so that it could be brought back to Portugal for interment. But Ahmad proudly refused and had it buried in a coffin filled with lime in the grounds of the house of the Governor of al-Kasr al-Kabir.

Many Portuguese nevertheless insisted that Sebastião's body had been falsely identified. They believed their king had been spirited away from the battlefield to be healed of his grievous wounds by Prester John, the mythical Christian king who lived beyond the Nile. For centuries the legend of his mysterious survival persisted, and people continued to look yearningly forward to the promised return of the blonde young king, *Sebastião o Desjado*, the Longed-For, who, in the Last Days, would return to lead Portugal to its triumphant destiny.*

The bitterly fought Battle of the Three Kings lasted about four terrible hours. At last, some 15,000 surviving Portuguese soldiers, accepting that it was hopeless to fight on any longer, and tortured by thirst and untreated wounds (crushed and splintered bones, stab and slash wounds, bullets and other missiles embedded in the howling flesh) laid down their arms. Captivity was also the lot of the wretched surviving camp followers, huddled defenceless and despairing among the wagons and panicking draught animals. At least 8,000 Portuguese lay dead about them, intermingled with as many fallen Moroccans.

The booty that fell into the victors' hands was stupendous. Strewn about the wrecked wagons and coaches was the gold and silver plate of the households of the king and his nobility, luxurious bedding, rich clothes of silk and velvet, and all the other expensive trappings of a royal court on progress. That evening parties of Moroccans, each with its quota of lamenting prisoners and loot, made off exalting to their towns, villages and encampments.

The flower of Portugal's nobility had died alongside their king. Still, a hundred or more of them fell alive into Moroccan hands, some of whom had been found huddled in panic in their resplendent coaches or had proved

---

* This messianic belief, which persisted into the nineteenth century, is known as 'Sebastianism'. In many ways it was analogous to the British legend of King Arthur.

only too eager to throw down their arms with shaming promises of the rich ransoms they would pay. Muley Ahmad kept them all for himself, demanding enormous ransoms for their release.* For years to come, scraping together enough gold to redeem them would drain the wealth of Portugal's greatest families and swell Ahmad's coffers, earning him the nickname of *al-Dhahabi*, the golden. Less exalted prisoners could also be ransomed, and finding the money would soak up nearly all the remaining bullion and coin in Portugal.

Nobles might expect a reasonably comfortable captivity until released, but ordinary prisoners were all enslaved and had to labour for their captors until their ransoms came – if they ever did. The more fortunate were incorporated into the *sharif's* army as slave soldiers (which at least allowed them to retain their honour). In this category were several hundred boys under the age of fifteen who had fought in the Portuguese ranks or who had been among the camp followers taken prisoner. Ahmad ordered them to be circumcised, converted to Islam and put into Moroccan dress. Some served in his palace as his personal pages and the rest became soldiers. Other captives were taken into relatively easy domestic service, the more attractive entering their masters' harems as concubines. Many duly converted to Islam, which eased their lot and made them appear more trustworthy to their masters. The most unfortunate found themselves in chains and held in appalling conditions while they were set to rowing the galleys, working the fields or labouring on construction sites and the roads. Worst off were those who suffered in the mines and quarries. All were subject to brutal beatings and other punishments at the whim of their masters.

One grateful, if indirect, beneficiary of the battle was King Felipe of Spain. Sebastião's old great uncle had succeeded him as Cardinal King Henrique I, known somewhat derisively as the Chaste. Overwhelmed by the insuperable problems Sebastião's fatal adventure had bequeathed him, Henrique sank under their weight and died in 1580. Felipe swiftly made good his dynastic claim to the throne of Portugal† at a brief, little battle at Alcântara bridge outside Lisbon, after which his victorious troops went on undiplomatically

---

* In 1581–1582, when Felipe II of Spain was making good his claim to the Portuguese throne, he bought the support of many of the Portuguese nobility by helping provide ransoms for their relatives still held in Morocco.

† Felipe's claim to the Portuguese throne came through his mother, Isabella, the sister of King João III of Portugal. His most determined rival was Antonio, the Prior of Crato, who was the illegitimate grandson of King Manuel I the Fortunate. In April 1581 the Portuguese officially accepted Felipe as their king.

to put the city thoroughly to the sack. For the next sixty years, until their successful revolt in 1640, the Portuguese and their possessions overseas would be ruled from Madrid as part of the worldwide Spanish empire.

The other more immediate beneficiary of the battle was Abd al-Malik's brother, Muley Ahmad, whom the Moroccan soldiers hailed on the battlefield as their new ruler. He became known as Ahmad al-Mansur, the Victorious, for the crucial part he played that day. He went on to drive the fatally weakened Portuguese from their Atlantic ports in Morocco, and also to succeed in keeping the Ottomans – now wary of his military power – in diplomatic check.

With their utter defeat at the Battle of the Three Kings, the Portuguese once and for all abandoned any lingering thought of extending the *Reconquista* in Morocco. They hung on grimly to three coastal fortresses at the entrance to the Mediterranean – Ceuta, Tangier and Mazagão – because in the past these ports had been the natural launching pads for Muslim invasions of Iberia, and it was important to deny them that role in the future. Otherwise, the three ports served as strategic naval bases against the Barbary corsairs. They were also convenient garrison posts where young Portuguese soldiers could learn their honourable, if savage, trade in raids and skirmishes against the *Mouros* – practical experience that prepared them for active service elsewhere overseas.

CHAPTER TWO

Ravaging the Swahili Coast

Outflanking the Muslims

From the Mosteiro dos Jerónimos in Belém on the north shore of the wide mouth of the river Tagus in Portugal, the monks of the Order of St Jerome* could gaze out and admire the stout caravels as they sailed up the river laden with all the treasures of the Indies. Their sails were emblazoned with the red, squared cross that was the emblem of the Order of Christ.† The order's grand master had been Prince Henrique the Navigator (1394–1460), the fifteenth-century patron of Portuguese exploration down the west coast of Africa, who had invested his order's revenues in the grand enterprise. It was a venture that paid off 10,000-fold, and one for which the monks had every reason to be thankful. In about 1501, following the triumphant return in 1499 of Vasco da Gama from his voyage around Africa to Calicut in India – the culmination of all those dangerous and frustrating decades of exploration – King Manuel I the Fortunate (r.1495–1521) commissioned the building of their monastery in thanksgiving. He financed it from the 'pepper tax', a royal levy on the spices, precious stones, gold and other commodities caught in Portugal's enormous commercial net that now spread from the Atlantic to the Pacific Ocean.

Da Gama died of malaria in the Portuguese-held port of Cochin (Kochi) in southwestern India in 1524, and in 1539 his body was brought back to Portugal. It was interred with great honour in the nave of the church of the

---

* Known as the Hieronymites, they cared for the monastery until 1834, when all the religious orders in Portugal were disbanded. The monastery is now a museum open to the public.

† Following Pope Clement V's suppression in 1314 of the powerful Order of the Knights Templar, King Dinis of Portugal founded the Order of Christ in 1319 and endowed it with the riches and privileges of the Templars.

Jerónimos monastery, Santa Maria de Belém, with its six slender, octagonal piers rising up like palm trees, their foliage of stone fanning into the complex net vaulting of the shadowy roof far above.* Santa Maria was built in the flamboyant Late Gothic style of architecture known as 'Manueline', with its typical, all-over decoration full of maritime motifs that fittingly celebrated the Portuguese voyages of discovery and the paramount part da Gama had played in them.

In the soaring south transept of the same church, with its many references to the sea, there is another tomb: gold and grey and many-tiered, surmounted by a royal crown. The tapering structure is supported on the backs of two sturdy, black elephants, which bring to mind exotic India or sub-Saharan Africa. Yet within the sarcophagus repose what are purportedly the remains of King Sebastião, that rash young man who perished on a parched Moroccan plain with neither the sea nor an elephant in sight. King Felipe, as a goodwill gesture to his new subjects once he had ascended the throne of Portugal in 1581, had successfully negotiated with Ahmad al-Mansur to return his nephew's remains from al-Kasr al-Kabir for Christian reburial in Portugal. The *sharif* magnanimously handed them over without accepting a ransom in return, and in 1582 Felipe had them placed in that fine tomb prepared for them in Santa Maria. But who can ever be truly certain that the poor bones were really those of the headstrong young king?

One must wonder too if any contemporary grasped the superb irony that Sebastião's presumed bones should be laid to rest in an edifice built specifically to celebrate Portugal's empire in the Indies. After all, eighty years before the fatal Battle of the Three Kings, any sound strategic or economic justification for further Portuguese conquest in Morocco had already evaporated, leaving only the valueless residue of ideological and vainglorious motives that had lured Sebastião to his death. Surely, should not Sebastião have kept more firmly in mind his own royal style that King Manuel had pointedly adopted on da Gama's triumphant return from India: 'By the grace of God, King of Portugal and the Algarves, of either side of the Sea in Africa, lord of Guinea and of conquest, navigation and commerce of Ethiopia, Arabia, Persia and India'?

---

* The tomb we see today with its effigy of Vasco da Gama was erected only in the nineteenth century. The engineering of the church was so advanced that it was one of the few buildings to survive the Lisbon earthquake of 1755.

These sonorous titles made it abundantly clear where Portugal's greatness and prosperity lay: Africa south of the Sahara and the lands surrounding the Indian Ocean.

Ever since the Arab conquest of the late seventh century AD, the Muslim states of North Africa had decisively cut Christian Europe off from direct trade with the lands south of the Sahara or with the Indian Ocean. If Europeans wished to procure gold (a mighty lure because Europe's gold deposits were so scanty), slaves, ivory, spices, silks, jewels, porcelain or other oriental luxuries, they had to do so through Muslim middlemen. And these despised enemies of Christ were prospering on the proceeds.

Moreover, North African merchants, slavers, teachers of religion and raiding soldiers were venturing ever deeper southwards into Africa. From Egypt they quested up the great waterway of the Nile, clambering past the many cataracts that interrupted its course to find slaves, ivory and gold in the very heart of Africa. Hoisting sail in the Red Sea ports, they scudded down the east coast of Africa to found a necklace of trading cities within the coral reefs. Exploiting the dependable prevailing monsoon winds and currents that between May and October propelled their ships northeast to the Persian Gulf, India and the Spice Islands beyond, and that reversed their direction from November through April to send them back home again to the African coast, these North Africans prosperously linked up with all the rich trade routes of the Indian Ocean.

From Morocco and *al-Maghrib* they picked their way from oasis to oasis across the burning wastes of the Sahara, carried on the swaying backs of the Arabian camels that were so well suited to bearing heavy loads and surviving the harsh conditions.* On the further side of the desert wastes they encountered the *Sahel* (shore), as they termed the dry, scrubby savannah lands along the southern margins of the Sahara. There, close to the banks of the Niger river, they made direct contact with ancient African kingdoms and city states that from time immemorial had maintained a thin trickle of trade with North Africa. Through them, they gained access to the gold-rich kingdoms of the deep tropical forests far to the south. Gold, slaves and salt flowed north

---

* Arabian camels, or dromedaries, have one hump. They were introduced in great numbers into North Africa with the Arab conquest and made it much more feasible to cross the desert than it had been previously with horses or oxen as draught animals.

across the desert in return for the fine Barb horses of *al-Maghrib* that the proud aristocracy of the *Sahel* states so delighted to ride.

The Christian rulers of Iberia, who were still firmly enmeshed in the world view of the *Reconquista*, chafed at being cut off by the Muslim foe from direct access to this lucrative trans-Saharan trade. Following their conquest of Ceuta in Morocco in 1415, the Portuguese set about outflanking the Muslim rulers of North Africa by finding an alternative route south by sea. Thanks to ever-improving ship design and navigational techniques, their little vessels pushed further and further down the Atlantic coast of the bulge of Africa.

This commercial and strategic enterprise received welcome religious sanction when in 1452 Pope Nicholas V issued a papal bull authorising the Portuguese to attack, subdue and enslave all Muslims, pagans and other enemies of Christ they encountered, thereby justifying the seizure of their lands, goods and trade. This was nothing other than the Christian equivalent of the Islamic dogma of the *Dar al-Harb* (Lands of War), which sanctioned the identical treatment for all unbelievers found outside the bounds of the *Dar al-Islam*.

Pursuing their ideal of the international crusade against Islam, the Portuguese hoped to find an ally in that mysterious Christian potentate Prester John, who was supposed to live somewhere beyond the Nile. This belief reflected a shadowy knowledge of the existence of the ancient Christian kingdom of Ethiopia. However, its precise whereabouts, and that of Prester John, remained uncertain. So, wherever they landed in Atlantic Africa, Portuguese sea captains enquired after him, and optimistically mistook great rivers such as the Senegal and Gambia for branches of the Nile. Eventually, as their steady exploration southwards revealed the immensity of the continent, they had to accept that Prester John must dwell far away to the east, and that they would not find him until they had rounded the tip of Africa.*

Wherever they set foot on Africa's Atlantic shore, the Portuguese tried to tap into the thriving internal trade routes. These became increasingly prosperous in Upper Guinea, which is what the Portuguese called the region south of the Senegal river where the desert wastes gave way to richly cultivated agricultural land. Rounding the western bulge of Africa to sail cautiously eastwards along its southern shore, in 1471 the Portuguese mariners reached an extensive

---

* See Chapter 3.

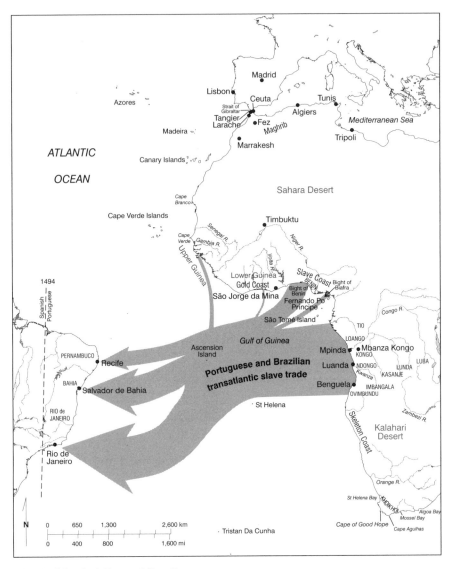

MAP 3 *Atlantic Africa and Brazil*

stretch of coast they dubbed Lower Guinea. Its western reaches would become known as the Gold Coast because of the gold dust and gold ornaments traded there. The source of the gold remained elusive, lost in the endless tropical forests that stretched away to the horizon. Still, what was important for the Portuguese was that they could get their hands on the precious metal. So in

1482, right on the seashore, they built a *feitoria* (factory), which is what a fortified compound where foreign merchants both lived and traded was called. They named it São Jorge da Mina (known for short as El Mina, or The Mine). It was constructed of dressed stone brought all the way from Portugal, and thinly garrisoned by sixty Portuguese soldiers and by African auxiliaries stationed in the surrounding villages. The profits from El Mina were prodigious. Over the next two decades they were nearly double the revenues of the Portuguese crown and paid for the expensive and hazardous voyages of discovery further south down the coast of Africa.

In the following decades the Portuguese planted a string of *feitorias* along the African coast east of the Volta river as far as the Niger delta. These bases opened up a barter trade with the coastal kingdoms, notably the powerful conquest state of Benin. In exchange for European goods such as brass bowls, bracelets, beads and textiles the Africans tendered gold, ivory, pepper and a commodity that gave the shoreline washed by the waters of the Bight of Benin its fearsome name: the Slave Coast.

Slavery was an ancient practice in Portugal. It went back to the twelfth-century wars of the *Reconquista* when Muslims were enslaved, but was fading away until revitalised by Portuguese contacts with Africa in the fifteenth century. The Portuguese had no more compunction than their Muslim enemies in enslaving pagans and non-believers, and it would be centuries before the institution of slavery became a moral issue. The first West African slaves were brought back for Prince Henrique the Navigator in 1441, and by the 1470s Lisbon had developed into Portugal's main slave port. By the mid-sixteenth century there were more than 32,000 African slaves in Portugal, mainly the property of the nobility and the religious orders. They were set to work as labourers on the great estates and in the towns where many were in domestic service. Once the Portuguese began to settle Brazil in the later sixteenth century and to require slave labour for the plantations there, the huge transatlantic colony completely overtook Portugal as the main destination for slaves.*

The West African slave trade would not reach its hideous crescendo until the eighteenth century, when six million Africans would be shipped across the Atlantic, three times more than had been taken in the previous two-and-

---

* See Chapter 6.

a-half centuries combined. The sheer horror of this mounting catastrophe can blind us to an unpalatable reality that many are still reluctant to accept: those heartless European slavers, succumbing (justly, one might prefer to believe) to tropical diseases in their sweltering coastal forts, were usually only the ultimate purchasers of human goods delivered to them along trade routes that stretched back into the very bowels of Africa. Slavery took many complex forms in Africa,* ranging from personal bondage to pay off a debt, through backbreaking, remorseless labour in the fields and mines, to military slavery, its most honourable form. It was also an ancient institution, practised since at least the Egyptian Old Kingdom nearly 5,000 years before. Throughout Muslim Africa the enslavement of non-Muslims was legitimate according to Islamic sharia law and was universally practised.

Because it was Africans who typically obtained the slaves at source, the Portuguese (and other slavers from half the countries of Europe who followed after them) had little motivation to conquer, occupy or rule the territories beyond their coastal forts and their scattering of dependent villages nearby. Forts might serve to protect their trade from other European rivals, but they were built there in the first place only on the sufferance of local African rulers, who found them useful outlets for trade, but were also powerful enough to make sure that the white aliens occupying them played by their rules. So the Portuguese early on understood that for the successful conduct of the slave trade little more was required than harmonious relations with surrounding African rulers, spiced by occasional shows of force to ensure favourable commercial terms.

More perniciously, because they also knew full well that warfare produced slaves from among the defeated, the Portuguese and their European successors sometimes deliberately fomented wars and civil conflicts to keep up the supply, and lent their military assistance to the side they favoured. Such was particularly the case from the late fifteenth century in what is now Angola, further down the west coast of Africa beyond the Niger delta. It was from this vast, troubled region that the Portuguese would eventually draw the bulk of their slaves.†

---

* Slavery was at its least prevalent as an indigenous institution in southern Africa.

† See Chapter 6.

Doubling the Cape of Good Hope

Sailing on beyond the twentieth parallel south, Portuguese explorers left the lush regions of equatorial Africa behind them. They found the coast becoming ever more desiccated as they touched land on the foggy and inhospitable Skeleton Coast of present-day Namibia. Nevertheless, it began to dawn on these dauntless explorers and their excited patrons back in Portugal that they were on the verge of finding a route by sea right around the southern tip of Africa. That meant that sooner, rather than later, they would break into the Indian Ocean with the most momentous of likely consequences. Not only would they reap fabulous commercial profits, but they would gloriously further the crusading cause by ruining the prosperity and resilience of the Muslim world by seizing the sources of its trading wealth.

Galvanised by this glittering prospect, King João II the Perfect Prince (r.1481–1495), put together an expedition under Bartolomeu Dias (c.1451–1500), a skilled navigator, Knight of the Order of Christ and member of his royal household, to make the final exploratory push. Dias sailed from Lisbon in August 1487 with a little fleet of three caravels. They were absurdly small to modern eyes, but they were of the latest design. Shipwrights in fifteenth-century Spain and Portugal had begun to build their vessels around a complete skeleton, with ribs and braces, fitting the planks 'carvel' style. Previously they had followed the 'clinker' style with caulked, overlapping planking around a simple shell. The added strength of the new technique made possible a more complex rig: three or four masts that could carry a variety of sails, either square to provide motive power, or triangular to assist lateral movement. Two of Dias' vessels were only of fifty tons, but they were of the small and highly manoeuvrable type, the *caravela latina* (lateen-rigged caravel), that had proved so useful for earlier explorers by performing well both in-shore and on the high seas. The third ship was probably a *caravela redonda*, a larger vessel with mixed triangular and square rig designed with a great hold to carry supplies and a heavier weight of cannons.

Making two landfalls on the Namibian coast, Dias then stood out to sea to cope with contrary, southeast trade winds and the strong, northward-flowing Benguela current. For thirteen days his little flotilla was driven southwards under half-furled sails before a furious gale. When the storm died down, Dias steered eastwards to find the west coast of Africa. But the Portuguese had rounded the southernmost tip of Africa without even realising it. Eventually guessing this is what they must have done, they turned north to find land. In February 1488 the storm-tossed sailors finally made landfall at what is today Mossel Bay in South Africa, but Dias called it Bahia dos Vaqueiros after the herds of Nguni cattle espied grazing there.*

Dias and a party of sailors landed by boat on the white sands of the sweeping beach, overlooked from afar by high mountain ranges shimmering blue in the summer haze. They tried to open up communication with herdsmen they encountered still lingering in amazement on the shore, some of whom (as was common) were riding their cows. These were Khoikhoi pastoralists whose ancestors had migrated into southern Africa from the north a thousand years before. They spoke no language known to any in the party of the Portuguese, whose appearance was inexpressibly alien to them. Rapidly losing their nerve, the Khoikhoi turned tail and urgently drove their cattle inland.

The Portuguese would not have been much surprised at the Khoikhois' terrified response to their unexpected arrival. No Africans south of the Sahara would ever have met people quite so unnaturally, if not disgustingly, pale skinned as the Portuguese, nor any wearing such outlandish garments. Moreover, their alarming ships with their towering masts and spreading sails were of totally unknown design. No wonder, then, that Africans were inevitably astounded at the sight. They were often deeply fearful, too. With superstitious dread they suspected the visitors were from the land of the dead (whose inhabitants were believed to be white, the colour of supernatural beings) or from another world entirely, and that they had mysteriously flown in on the sails of their ships. Only with time would curiosity overcome fear or repugnance, and familiarity breed contempt or indifference, mingled with a self-interested desire to trade or acquire novel objects.

It was different for the Portuguese. During their voyages of exploration along the African coast they had always expected to encounter black-skinned people, who, after all, had been familiar in the Mediterranean world since

---

* The Nguni cattle breed is indigenous to southern Africa and is a hybrid of indigenous cattle and those introduced 1,400 years ago from further north in Africa by migrating Bantu-speaking peoples. There are many different skin patterns with a variety of horn shapes, but their noses are always black tipped.

earliest antiquity. Besides, the Portuguese had been fully accustomed to the many slaves from sub-Saharan Africa held by the Muslims of North Africa before they began to acquire them themselves. They easily distinguished African slaves from their masters, the *Mouros* (who looked only slightly different from swarthy southern Europeans), on account of the blackness of their skin. Thus, to Dias and his party, the Khoikhoi they watched scampering off towards the safety of the surrounding hills appeared not very different from such slaves, or from the people of the Guinea coast encountered previously.

The Khoikhoi were not a particularly warlike people, even if their name means 'men of men'; they were admired, successful hunters rather more than warriors. Yet they did on occasion fight among themselves when roused, hurling spears, stones and small sticks, as well as firing arrows. On that thundery summer's day in 1488 they recovered from their initial alarm and resolved that the unwelcome pale intruders should be driven off. So when the Portuguese began taking water into their barrels from a freshwater perennial spring close to the shore, they started to shower them with projectiles from the nearby hills. Dias' royal instructions strictly stipulated that he was to cause no harm to the Africans he encountered. But mentally exhausted after days of riding the storm, vulnerable and very far from home, he reacted furiously. He took aim with his crossbow and transfixed one of the stone throwers with a bolt. The others immediately fled. Thus the very first encounter between Europeans and Africans east of the tip of Africa was marked by bloodshed. It was a dreadful omen of things to come.

Sailing on for some way after this skirmish, Dias encountered the warm Agulhas current that flows powerfully down the east coast of Africa and realised he must have reached the Indian Ocean. But with supplies dangerously low and no end to the voyage in sight, his men decided they had had enough. At modern-day Algoa Bay they compelled Dias to turn back for home. On the voyage they sighted Cape Agulhas, the southernmost tip of Africa. On a fine day soon afterwards they scudded past a great peninsula dominated by an enormous, flat-topped mountain. Overwhelmed by the awesome sight, and turning north there for home, Dias dubbed it the Cape of Good Hope.

Sailing to the Swahili Coast

Dias triumphantly returned to Lisbon in December 1488, but it was only under the patronage of King João II's successor, Manuel I, that the Portuguese felt in a position to take full advantage of his discoveries. In 1497 Manuel gave command of an expensively and carefully fitted-out flotilla to Vasco da Gama, a young service nobleman still in his twenties. He was a member of the chivalric Order of São Tiago, and had some military and naval experience in North Africa. Yet there was nothing particularly distinguished about his record to explain why he was chosen as admiral.* Most likely, he was known for the necessary ruthlessness and determination that would mark his leadership.

Two of the ships in the flotilla – the *São Gabriel*, captained by da Gama, and the *São Rafael* – were both 200-ton *caravelas redondas*, square-rigged for ocean sailing and with lateen sails for manoeuvrability. The third ship was an ordinary caravel with only lateen sails, called the *Berrio*, while the fourth was a *nau* (larger store ship), also called a carrack. Carracks were three- or four-masted, ocean-going ships, both square-rigged and lateen-rigged. They had a high, rounded stern topped by a large aftercastle as well as a high forecastle. The complement of the tiny fleet numbered only about 170 men, all of them well armed with sword and dagger and an assortment of crossbows, arquebuses, lances and axes.

Between them, da Gama's ships mustered only twenty small pieces of artillery. All were short, light, breech-loading swivel guns mounted on the gunwales of his caravels, and while they might have been good enough for ceremonial display and basic defence, they could hardly compare with the heavy guns carried by subsequent Portuguese fleets sailing into the Indian Ocean. The stone shot they fired weighed less than a pound and had a maximum range of only 200 yards, because the gunpowder charge had to be kept small for fear of bursting the barrel or blowing off the breech block. Consequently, they could do little damage to an enemy vessel (except perhaps to one of the flimsiest of Indian Ocean craft), let alone sink it. But these little swivel guns could be reloaded quickly and proved ideal in combination with

---

* It has been suggested that his appointment came as the result of political deal-brokering between the various factions at Manuel's court.

small-arms fire from arquebuses and crossbows in dissuading enemy crews from coming close enough to board.

On account of Portugal's strict social hierarchy, the captain of a ship was always a *fidalgo* (a gentleman by birth with a coat-of-arms to prove his illustrious lineage). Thus, because professional competence or naval experience was less important than gentle birth as the criterion for command, sea captains usually left the technical side of sailing to the master, a professional sailor under their command. That freed aristocratic officers to concentrate on the glorious business of fighting, which was more appropriate to their knightly status.

The fundamentally maritime nature of Portugal's expansion overseas meant that fighting took the form either of battles at sea or of amphibious operations. When the Portuguese went on shore to negotiate, trade or later settle, they also had to be prepared for combat. Yet it was not until well into the sixteenth century that ships regularly carried trained soldiers who were sailing to reinforce Portugal's far-flung garrisons. Until then, sailors often had to be prepared to fight on land. The problem was that, while many crew members were expert in fighting with edged weapons in the undisciplined, hand-to-hand, rough-and-tumble of boarding an enemy ship when agility and initiative counted for most, they had no experience of land warfare. Furthermore, most sailors possessed little training in firearms, which explains why the crossbow remained a favourite weapon at sea long after the arquebus or musket had made it obsolete on shore. Nor did they have the drilled, disciplined steadiness to wield a pike which, as we have seen, was the vital adjunct of the handgun in the military formations of the period. Unlike officers, who always wore plate armour (or at least a steel breastplate) as a symbol of social superiority as much as for protection, sailors were quite unused to bearing its weight and inconvenience. Instead, they wore leather jackets for protection, or sometimes coats of mail, as well as the ubiquitous open helmet.

As a result of their poor discipline and training, when Portuguese sailors landed in enemy territory (and many soldiers were no better) they seldom waited to form up properly in close formation. Instead, they rushed in headlong to get at the enemy. They did so partly because the Portuguese, being always outnumbered, hoped that the enemy would be thoroughly daunted by the sight of so much cold steel bearing down on them. The other reason lay in the *fidalgos'* military ethos of 'do or die', and in their overweening confidence.

While on occasions this could lead to unexpected victories over great odds, on others it would result in unnecessary disasters of the same variety (although not nearly of the same scale) as the Battle of Three Kings.

In victory, habitual ill-discipline resulted all too often in dispersal to plunder and pillage, and in deplorable massacres. Such merciless savagery had its roots in the bloodthirstiness and xenophobia of the crusading ethos that still remained very much in force; but it also had much to do with the nature of the men on board the Portuguese ships. They were habituated by the hardships and perils of shipboard existence to under-value life, and were always ready to break out violently when loot and rape beckoned. And among the crews was a particularly lawless element of rogues and criminals – the *degredados*. These were jailbirds and convicted criminals given a chance (when not forcibly recruited) to serve out their sentences in a shorter time – or to escape the death penalty – by sailing on missions which, like da Gama's, were too hazardous for most ordinary subjects to contemplate. Usually, if they survived the voyage, they remained exiled in the most forlorn, disease-ridden and distant posts of the empire.

Da Gama's flotilla set sail in July 1497. Shortly after rounding the bulge of Africa, it riskily struck out southwestwards into the unchartered wastes of the deep Atlantic to avoid the contrary winds and currents off the Namibian coast. After sailing out of sight of land for three months, da Gama at last reckoned the moment had come to steer east for the tip of Africa. In November 1497 he skilfully made landfall a scant hundred miles north of the Cape of Good Hope, anchoring in the frigid waters of what is now called St Helena Bay. The ships' crews disembarked on the arid shore to recoup and repair their vessels.

Their stay on shore extended over several weeks, during which time they were eager to avoid a repetition of Dias' earlier fracas at Mossel Bay in 1488. They did their best to convince the dubious hunter-gatherers they encountered that they came in peace and wished to initiate trade. However, the people, who were dressed in skins and wore copper ornaments and who lived a little way inland, subsisting on the flesh of washed-up whales, roots and honey, soon enough decided that they preferred the menacing and unruly strangers to depart. Their warriors suddenly attacked the boats drawn up on the beach and, as the contemporary historian João de Barros recorded: 'such was the showers of stones and arrows upon the boat that when Vasco da Gama went to pacify them he was wounded by an arrow in the leg'.[1] Three others were wounded along with him. The incensed Portuguese retaliated with their powerful crossbows, shooting several of their assailants and driving the others back in fright at the effectiveness of this unfamiliar weapon.

Back on board the *São Gabriel*, da Gama next led his flotilla around the monumental Cape of Good Hope and then followed the coast as it unrolled eastwards before him. After a while the Portuguese realised the land was beginning to veer northwards, so that they were now sailing up the eastern coast of Africa where no Christian ship had ever ventured before. As they went, they made several more landings for water and found that, as before, the people's suspicious reluctance to trade more often than not turned into open hostility against the intruders.* What the Portuguese could not have known was that, most likely, they were the first aliens ever to have landed on those shores. Indian Ocean traders never ventured that far south because it was beyond the reliable system of monsoon winds. Moreover, in the Moçambique Channel between the east coast of Africa and the enormous island of Madagascar the Agulhas current runs against the prevailing direction of the wind, which, as the Portuguese would discover, makes sailing extremely hazardous.

In February 1498, in the sweltering heat and breathless humidity of a summer's day at the eighteenth parallel south, da Gama's flotilla put in at the broad estuary of the Quelimane river in what is now central Moçambique. Unknowingly, they had sailed past Sofala, just down the coast, the southernmost terminus of the East African coastal trading system. At the Quelimane the Portuguese encountered for the first time the typical sailing craft of the region, the dhows that plied the coast and the deeper rivers such as the Zambezi. With a capacity of up to fifty tons, they were open without decks and carried a single mast with woven palm-leaf mats for sails. Coir† ropes bound together their superstructures of cane and their hulls of wooden planks, which were caulked with pitch.‡ Such vessels seemed absurdly flimsy to sailors who had braved

---

* In late November da Gama and an armed party landed at Mossel Bay, where Dias had earlier skirmished with the Khoikhoi. They started to barter with the people on the shore before panicking and opening fire on the beach with two swivel guns mounted on the poop of their longboat.

† Coir is the prepared fibre of the husks of coconuts.

‡ The planking in European ships was held together by iron spikes, but the Arab world was short of metals, and ropes also had the advantage of not being subject to corrosion.

the tempestuous, open waters of the Atlantic. As the Portuguese were to find, the coast provided few natural harbours for larger vessels. But that was not a problem for the dhows. The long coral reefs sheltered endless sandy beaches, where they could beach at high tide. When the tide went out dhows could make repairs and unload their cargoes, and then float off when it rose again.

On shore at Quelimane the Portuguese discovered a thriving commercial settlement eager to trade. Most of the people were African, but some, as the Portuguese guessed by their appearance, seemed half-Arab. In contrast to the nearly naked peoples they had encountered further south, these, according to de Barros 'had cotton cloths dyed blue hanging behind them, and others wore turbans and silk cloths, and even caps of coloured camlet*'.[2] Moreover, they betrayed no surprise at the Portuguese ships. Alongside the local dhows, they were already familiar with ocean-going craft every bit as big or bigger than da Gama's ships (albeit of much flimsier construction) that sped before the monsoon winds to trade in the far-flung ports of the Indian Ocean.

To the excitement of the Portuguese, some of the people of Quelimane could communicate a little in Arabic. Da Gama was now certain that he had entered the thriving waters of the Indian Ocean trading system. Gleaning from the Quelimane traders that a great port city called Moçambique lay north up the coast, he pushed energetically on. The encounter there would be crucial, for he was not simply the admiral of a small Portuguese fleet. He was also King Manuel's ambassador, charged with establishing good relations and favourable trading contacts with the rulers he visited on his voyage. Whether he possessed the diplomatic skill to do so was another matter.

The People of the Coast

In that momentous summer of 1498 the Portuguese were blundering into the ancient and sophisticated world of the Swahili coast that stretched for 2,000 miles between the port towns of Sofala in the south and Mogadishu in the north. For more than 500 years Muslims had been settled there in their thriving, little towns, sandwiched between the sea and the hostile peoples of the interior, making their fortunes from the Indian Ocean trade. The people

---

* Camlet is an oriental fabric made of camel's hair or Angora wool.

of the land of Zanj (as it was known in the Muslim world) acknowledged no single political authority or outside power.* Instead, each of the towns had its own ruler and all were chronically in competition for local dominance.

Such rivalry seldom took much of a military complexion in what was primarily a mercantile civilisation. Towns were usually built on off-shore islands to protect them from the sometimes hostile Africans of the interior, and were normally left unfortified. A few of the largest might possess a few cannons, but otherwise the gunpowder revolution had not yet reached these shores. Weapons still took the form of javelins and bows and arrows. These were primarily in the hands of the bodyguards maintained by some of the rulers, the best of whom were slave soldiers. On occasion, rulers hired mercenaries from the mainland to fight their little wars. None was the least prepared for the military challenge the Portuguese would hurl down.

The Swahili, or 'people of the coast',† shared a complex but common culture, the Muslim faith and the Kiswahili language. They were a cosmopolitan amalgam of the descendants of merchants from the Red Sea, Persian Gulf and East Indies who had cohabited with local African women, as well as of local African men who had adopted the prevailing Swahili culture. Hindu and Jain money lenders and retailers from Gujarat in northwestern India were settled there too, and the Portuguese at first mistook these Indians for the Christians they were seeking. Visiting traders regularly spent part of the year in the Swahili towns as guests of the local merchants while they waited for the monsoon to reverse and send them home again. Indeed, the coast was a great, prosperous melting pot of peoples, and in about 1518 the Portuguese mariner Duarte Barbosa wrote of the inhabitants of Mombasa: 'The men are in colour either tawny, black or white and also their women go very bravely attired with many fine garments of silk and gold in abundance.'[3]

The closed elite of the Swahili coast were the *waungwana* (patricians) with their emphasis on civilised, gentlemanly conduct. Many *waungwana* insisted on their Arabic or Persian ancestry, the most aristocratic of all being the *sharifs*

---

* Zheng He's great maritime expedition of 1417–1419 from Ming China reached Malindi on the northern Swahili coast, and in 1431–1433 he voyaged to Mogadishu on the Horn of Africa. It is possible some Swahili cities were forced into a tributary relationship as a result, but this did not endure beyond the late 1430s.

† 'Swahil' is a Bantu word, rooted in the Arabic *sahel*, meaning coast or margin.

who claimed descent from the Prophet. Their wealth came from trade, for they were the middlemen for the gold dust, slaves and ivory of the African interior, as well as the mangrove timber of the coast, that the foreign merchants carried away. As a class that prized refinement above all things, the *waungwana* desired luxury trade items in return. Decorative niches set in the walls of their elegant houses displayed their valuable collections of Chinese porcelain and perfumes held in flimsy glass vessels. Persian rugs covered the floors they swept with their robes of Gujarati textiles and across which their wives trailed their Persian silks. Keeping large numbers of domestic slaves of both sexes set the *waungwana* apart from ordinary town dwellers such as retailers and labourers, as well as from the poor fishermen in the creeks and river estuaries, and from the peasants working their plots outside the towns.

On 2 March 1498, da Gama's ships anchored off a low, swampy, narrow, little island they called Moçambique, lying in the broad mouth of a river estuary. At its northern point were a harbour and small town. De Barros wrote contemptuously of it that: 'all the houses were of straw,* except a mosque and the dwelling of the sheik, which were of mud'.[4] Its situation was nevertheless typical of most Swahili towns in that its off-shore position protected it from the people of the mainland, while the headlands that closely embraced it on both sides sheltered its harbour from the open sea.

Warily, the Portuguese did not attempt to enter the port where four seagoing merchant ships from India were moored, but waited outside to see how its inhabitants would receive them. These da Gama described in his logbook as 'of a ruddy complexion and well made' and the *waungwana* as wearing linen or cotton robes with 'variously coloured stripes, and of rich and elaborate workmanship' along with turbans with 'borders of silk embroidered in gold'.[5]

Da Gama opened negotiations with the *maliki* (local ruler),† who owed allegiance to the great city of Kilwa Kisiwani further up the coast. He was typical of Swahili kings in that he embodied the sacred and magic qualities of his town in his person. He headed the town's bureaucracy and was entrusted with conducting diplomatic relations. As any Portuguese familiar with North Africa would have recognised, in his negotiations with them the *maliki* adhered

---

* The 'straw' houses would have been of palm-leaf matting with thatched roofs.

† Swahili rulers were known as *maliki* on the southern coast and *mfalane* on the northern coast.

to the complex and showy royal rituals common to other Muslim courts, but which were intriguingly overlaid by local African practices.

A decorous, diplomatic to-ing and fro-ing commenced between the ships and the town, with da Gama remaining cautiously on board his ship. It was not long before the Portuguese noted for future reference that Moçambique had no defences and that the *maliki* had no soldiers to speak of. For his part, the *maliki* initially welcomed the Portuguese, mistaking them for Turks, and therefore Muslims. But it rapidly dawned on him that the intruders were Christian, not least because of the red cross of the Order of Christ emblazoned on their sails. The Muslim-dominated Indian Ocean trading area was until then free of sectarian strife, and open to Hindus and Jews. But Christians, especially rough and well-armed ones such as these, suggested the need for extreme caution.

The Swahili began to obstruct the Portuguese efforts to provision their ships. Realising this might lead to retaliation, they belatedly started to throw up a makeshift palisade of wood, banked up by earth, to defend their town. Then, while the Portuguese were loading the supplies they had commandeered, they tried to seize the initiative. Seven boatloads of armed men set off from the shore and attacked the interlopers with arrows. The Portuguese easily chased them off with crossbow and arquebus fire and, by now thoroughly angered as well as frustrated, bombarded the town as best they could with their small cannons. The Swahili panicked, and many of them, particularly the *waungwana*, tried to flee to the mainland in boats packed with all their valuables. The Portuguese had much satisfaction in intercepting and looting many of these craft, including the *maliki*'s own. Altogether, this was a very bad beginning for Swahili–Portuguese relations, and it soon became apparent that da Gama intended to go on as he had begun.

Unfavourable winds took the Portuguese past the city of Kilwa, as well as the islands of Zanzibar and Pemba. But on the eve of Palm Sunday, 7 April 1498, the Portuguese vessels, battered and leached by months at sea, cast anchor in the tepid ocean at a cautious distance from the town of Mombasa, which, in recent years, had overtaken its rival Kilwa as the dominant city on the Swahili coast.

Like Moçambique, Mombasa was sited on a small island in an estuary with coastal headlands protecting it from the achingly blue, open sea that faded to turquoise at the shore. From on-board the Portuguese could make out that its busy harbour, guarded by a low-lying fort, was thronged with shipping, all dressed with flags for a Muslim holiday. As they would come to recognise, it was also a typical 'stone-built' town (*mji*, as it was called in Kiswahili), although the 'stone' was actually coral rag from the long coastal reefs, bonded with lime mortar. The terraces of double- or triple-storeyed, flat-roofed 'stone' houses were dazzlingly white-washed and neatly aligned in narrow streets set back at right angles to the shore. Inside were sheltered courtyards that opened through delicately carved and painted, double doors* on to porches facing the street. Benches were placed there for conversation and business. To the Portuguese, such a layout was eerily reminiscent of the Moorish towns some had seen in southern Spain. Rather different, though, were the haphazard suburbs surrounding the town with their houses of palm-leaf matting with thatched, pitched roofs set amid vividly green plantations of coconut palms and cultivated gardens.†

Another familiar but distinctly unwelcome feature of Mombasa could not escape the Portuguese. These were the minarets that bristled throughout the town. True, they were of an unusual cone shape that was unique to the Swahili coast, and very different from the tiered, square towers of Morocco, but were unmistakable for all that. The largest was attached to the great Friday Mosque in its open communal space in the middle of the town; while others belonged to the smaller, neighbourhood mosques dotted about the town's wards. Visible too were the thatched tombs of holy men visited by devout pilgrims, for like all the other towns of the coast Mombasa was the seat of an *umma* (community of true believers), a place of consciously cultivated civilisation and urbanity among the surrounding African pagans. To the deeply disappointed Portuguese, who had vainly hoped to discover Christians on the east coast of Africa, all this marked out the Swahili as despicable *Mouros* of the same perverse religion as their ancient foes in Iberia and Morocco. This stigma made them infinitely worse than the merely ignorant Africans close inland, even if (according to Duarte Barbosa) the latter were so degraded that they 'went nearly naked, smeared with red clay and with bored lips'.[6]

---

* The heavily carved doors now associated with Zanzibar became common only in the nineteenth century.

† The distinctive clove plantations of the Swahili coast were introduced in the nineteenth century.

1 *A map of Africa, along with its inhabitants and towns as they were known to the Dutch in the early seventeenth century.*

2 *A late sixteenth-century panoramic view of Lisbon.*

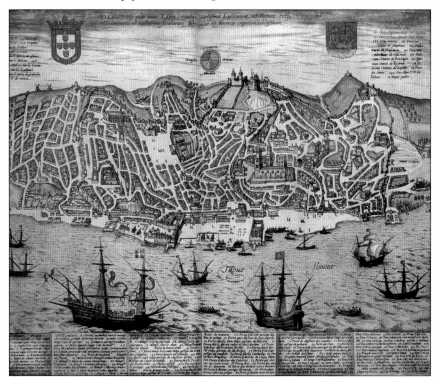

3 ABOVE *A Portuguese map of Africa c.1558 with armoured horsemen depicted pursuing Moors north of the Atlas mountains. The fortress of São Jorge da Mina is shown on the Gold Coast surrounded by palm trees. A Christian church in Kongo can be seen in the right-hand, bottom corner with a Portuguese standard and a cross.*

4 ABOVE *The Koutoubia mosque in Marrakesh, Morocco, built in the late twelfth century. The design of the magnificent, square-towered minaret, 225 feet tall and topped by its graceful lantern storey, is typically Moroccan.*

5 LEFT *A portrait of King Sebastião (1554–1578) of Portugal, painted c.1571.*

6 ABOVE *A gate in the late seventeenth-century fortified walls of Meknès, a city below the Atlas mountains in northern Morocco.*

7 RIGHT *Vasco da Gama (c.1460–1524), who opened the way to India for Portugal and subdued several cities along the Swahili coast, from an early sixteenth-century manuscript.*

8 LEFT *Francisco de Almeida (c.1450–1510), the first Governor of the* Estado de Índia, *who in 1505 sacked both Kilwa and Mombasa and captured Sofala, thus establishing Portuguese hegemony along the Swahili coast, as depicted in an early sixteenth-century manuscript.*

9 *A schematic representation of the Portuguese defeat by the East India Company in November 1612 at Suvati (Swally) off the coast of Gujurat. Note the five Portuguese carracks, and the supporting fleet of oared barques carrying no cannon. Terços of pikemen and arquebusiers are engaged on shore. The Portuguese fort guarding the entrance to the nearby port of Surat can be seen at the top of the picture.*

10 *A modern view of the massive, thirty-nine-foot-high, seaward curtain walls connecting the great bastions of Fortaleza de São Sebastião. Commenced in 1546 on the northern tip of Moçambique Island to guard the entrance to the harbour, it was completed in 1558. The Gate of Arms can be seen at the bottom of the picture.*

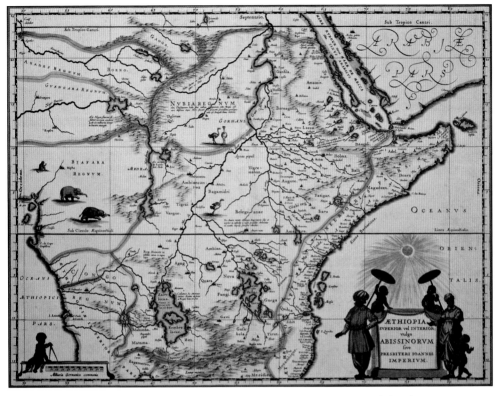

11 *A Dutch map published in 1660 showing the Swahili coast, Ethiopia and Angola.*

12 *Fortaleza de Jesus de Mombaça was begun in 1593. Its construction was essentially completed three years later, although additions continued to be made into the mid-seventeenth century. The view is from below the walls of the São Matias bastion facing south towards the rectangular bastion commanding the harbour.*

13 *Fort al-Jalali, one of the twin fortresses guarding the narrow entrance to the harbour at Muscat, was built by the Portuguese in 1587–1588 and originally called Fortaleza de São João. It fell to the Omanis in 1650, and its present form dates from the early 1800s.*

14 *The town of Tete and the fort from the north shore of the Zambezi, 1859.*

15 *An early twentieth-century illustration (reflecting the colonial mindset of the period) of the
battle in 1572 between the Portuguese, led by Francisco Barreto, Captain of Moçambique,
and the Tonga people, which took place by the Zambezi river upstream from Sena. It depicts the
Tonga female spirit-medium being shot while performing a ritual dance.*

16 *Chart of the South Atlantic by Diego Homem, 1558, showing the west coast of Africa and Brazil in South America.*

17 *A captured slave gang of Coimbra, a Portuguese mulatto slaver of Bihe, Angola.*

Alarming intelligence of the Portuguese bombardment of Moçambique had preceded them along the Swahili coast, and the people of Mombasa were anxious to see them speedily depart. But the Portuguese required water and a pilot to guide them across the ocean to India, and were not ready to leave until they had procured both. Delegations passed between the ships and the shore and mistrust steadily grew. The Swahili were incensed by the infinite disdain and discourtesy of the Portuguese, whereas the Portuguese suspected that the Swahili intended treachery. They became convinced of it once they had extracted a confession to that effect from two Swahili with the assistance of burning oil. And true enough, at midnight several boats put out from the town. Swimmers tried to cut the cables of the *São Rafael* and the *Berrio* while others boarded the vessels and climbed the rigging with the intention of damaging the sails. The alarm was given and the Portuguese repelled the boats with gunfire.

So it was that on 13 April a distinctly disgruntled da Gama quit treacherous and unwelcoming Mombasa and sailed on, still in search of a pilot. He was more fortunate at his next port of call. On Easter Sunday, with all the ships decked in flags, he anchored in the open sea outside Malindi. The town's lofty, white-washed houses lay along a bay on the mainland, surrounded by palm groves and maize and vegetable gardens. The evil reputation of the Portuguese had sped ahead of them, and at first no one from Malindi dared approach the ships. As an anonymous Arab historian later explained: 'When the people of Malindi saw them, they knew they were bringers of war and corruption, and were troubled with very great fear.'[7]

But this time da Gama behaved as well as he knew how in order to secure a reliable pilot. Over nine days the Portuguese put on displays of sham-fights, fireworks and music intended to entertain as well as overawe the Swahili on shore. The *Mfalane* of Malindi took the point, and at length received da Gama in his palace. In his journal, da Gama left a description that gives a vivid impression of the royal state kept on the Swahili coast:

> The king wore a robe (royal cloak) of damask trimmed with green satin, and a rich *touca* [turban]. He was seated on two cushioned chairs of bronze, beneath a round sunshade of crimson satin attached to a pole. An old man who attended him as page carried a short sword in a silver sheath. There were many players on *anafils* [long brass horns] and two trumpets of ivory

richly carved, and the size of a man,* which were blown from a hole in the
side, and made sweet harmony with the *anafils*.[8]

Fortunately for the Portuguese, the people of Malindi proved to be ancient
rivals of Mombasa, where the Portuguese had been ill received, and the *mfalane*
was only too pleased to gain potential military support against Kilwa, which
was claiming suzerainty over neighbouring cities. So he decided it was politic
to work with the Portuguese and, with every expression of undying friendship,
found da Gama a suitable pilot. On 24 April the Portuguese weighed anchor
and set sail for Calicut.

Da Gama returned to Malindi in January 1499 *en route* to Lisbon, his mission
to reconnoitre a route to India triumphantly concluded. He left behind on
the apprehensive Swahili coast a fearsome impression of boorish Portuguese
behaviour, cruelty and military aggression. The Swahili certainly hoped that
with their departure they had seen the last of the Portuguese infidels, but they
were to be sadly disappointed. The 'bringers of war and corruption' would be
back only too soon, and in ever-growing strength.

The Sack of Kilwa

In Lisbon, many courtiers around King Manuel remained strongly committed
to the ideal of the crusade. They continued to encourage him in his ever-
smouldering ambition to recover the Holy Places in Palestine from the
Mamluk rulers of Muslim Egypt. Da Gama's total misconception that the
Hindus he had encountered in India were actually Christians misled them into
persuading their willing monarch that the great explorer's divinely inspired
voyage to India heralded the formation of a great, trans-oceanic Christian
alliance against Islam. So that the momentum should not be lost, the king
immediately fitted out more naval expeditions destined for the Indies.

In order that the ships which made up these expeditions could defend
themselves effectively against any warships they might encounter in the Indian
Ocean, the Portuguese steadily improved their fighting capacity by increasing
their tonnage and fitting them with more and more larger guns. But to get to
India in the first place they required convenient ports to make repairs and take

---

* These were *siwas*. As symbols of royal authority they were put to ceremonious use on public occasions.

on supplies. Because outbound vessels took the mid-ocean route and did not make landfall in Atlantic Africa, such havens had to be beyond the Cape of Good Hope. The cities of the Swahili coast were ideal for the purpose, for not only were they wealthy trading ports but also da Gama reported that they were weak and divided, and would not be capable of much resistance. Moreover, they were Muslim and predominantly hostile, so their subjugation was entirely justified in Portuguese eyes.

During da Gama's voyage of 1498 to India, and again during Pedro Alvares' subsequent expedition in 1500, the Portuguese used Malindi as their port of call because initially it alone of all the Swahili towns was prepared to welcome them. But in fact it was too far north for a convenient passage to India, and a better situated port to the south was required. In 1502 da Gama himself led a well-armed force of fourteen ships to the Swahili coast to make a demonstration of force and secure the necessary bases before proceeding to India to bombard the prosperous port of Calicut into submission. Overawed, Moçambique made peace and permitted the Portuguese to found a *feitoria* to supply their ships. Further north, da Gama extracted tribute from the island state of Kilwa Kisiwani, the dominant city on the coast and full of tempting riches, by treacherously seizing the *maliki* when he came out to the ships to parley, and threatening to drown him if he did not comply.

Thus the Portuguese began to enforce a monopolistic mercantile system on the Swahili coast through which they squeezed the rich seaborne trade already there by extorting what was in effect protection money. Ultimately, they would impose this system on all of the *Estado da Índia*. That was the name the Portuguese applied collectively from the early sixteenth century to all their cities, fortresses and territories in East Africa and maritime Asia, as well as to all the coasts, islands and waters east of the Cape where the Portuguese crown maintained a presence or vague overlordship.

The operation of the Portuguese monopoly on the Swahili coast was straightforward but effective. Only the Portuguese themselves were permitted to carry the really valuable goods exported from the coast, namely gold and ivory. Swahili merchants were allowed to deal in other specified items so long as their ships were licensed by the Portuguese and carried the required *cartaz* (pass). These coastal traders were also required to pay custom duties and were forbidden from trading with Portugal's enemies of the moment.

Portugal's aggressive and ever-growing presence in the Indian Ocean, combined with King Manuel's very evident plans to wage a global war against Islam, were beginning to raise real alarm in the *Dar al-Islam*. The Mamluk rulers of Egypt consequently made preparations to send a fleet to aid the people of Kerala, as the southwestern Indian coast was known, against the Portuguese. King Manuel caught wind of the Mamluk intentions, and resolved to thwart them by sending the most powerful Portuguese fleet yet into the Indian Ocean.

By March 1505 Manuel had assembled a fleet of fourteen carracks and six caravels carrying 1,000 sailors and 1,500 soldiers. He gave the command to Dom Francisco de Almeida (1450–1510), whom he also appointed the first governor of the *Estado da Índia*. De Almeida was a loyal service nobleman of ancient and impeccable lineage, whose father was the Count of Abrantes. Among his brothers he numbered two bishops and the Portuguese ambassador to Rome. His portrait that hangs in the National Museum of Ancient Art in Lisbon depicts him as fair and balding, with a sharply chiselled nose, a broad forehead and a long, forked beard hanging down to his chest. Both his gaze and his stance are open and steady, that of a man habituated to command.

De Almeida's orders could not have been clearer, for King Manuel presented him on 5 March 1505 with detailed and uncompromising instructions that ran to 30,000 words. De Almeida was to establish fortresses on the Swahili coast and that of Kerala, by force if necessary. In the true spirit of the *Reconquista* embraced by the king, he was to attack Muslims wherever he found them. Thus, for example, when he took Sofala, the southernmost of the Swahili ports and earmarked for a fortress because of its rich gold trade with the interior, he was to seize any Muslim merchants he found there. Following that, his instructions specified that he must inform the people of Sofala that: 'in ordering those Moors to be made captive and their property taken, we do so by reason of their being enemies of our holy catholic faith and because we wage war continually upon them'.[9]

Therefore, for the Swahili, the arrival in July 1505 of de Almeida's fleet in their waters heralded a new and miserably regretted age of iron, when their cities would be looted and their treasure plundered, and when they would be compelled to obey infidel overlords and trade according to their monopolistic rules.

And indeed, de Almeida and his subordinates set about their mission with grim efficiency, embracing the opportunity to overawe the coast by condign acts of terror. Their major targets were the two richest and most powerful cities of the coast: Kilwa, where the *maliki* had provocatively ceased paying the tribute imposed by da Gama in 1502; and proud, hostile Mombasa, whose ruler had been warned by Indians from Calicut of the barbarities the Portuguese had recently visited there.

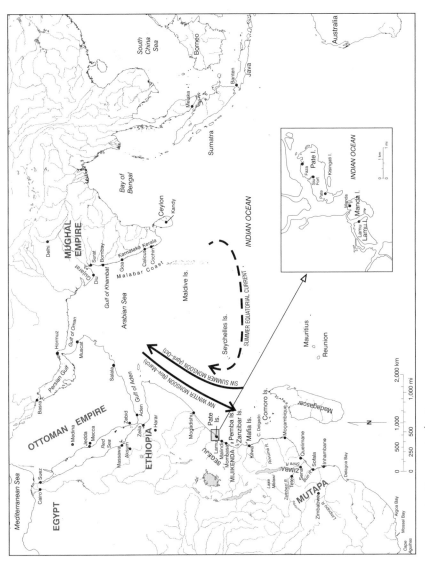

MAP 4 *The* Estado da Índia

After reuniting his fleet, which had been scattered in a storm in the Moçambique Channel, de Almeida made straight for Kilwa. When viewed from the sea, the beauty of the town on its off-shore island, with its fine houses, several storeys high, set in orchards of palm trees, ignited the cupidity of the Portuguese on board who saw its many mosques as a provocation that justified their sacking it. De Almeida announced his arrival on 22 July with volleys of blank fire intended to terrify the people into immediate compliance. The next day he followed up this show of force with a pretence at diplomacy accompanied by much pomp. De Almeida went on shore, as described by the historian de Barros in 1552, in 'a boat under a canopy of scarlet silk, with numerous flags bearing his device . . . surrounded by the boats of all the noblemen, amid the sounding of trumpets and booming of artillery'.[10] The *Maliki* of Kilwa understood perfectly what de Almeida was about, and did his best to fend the Portuguese off with polite but feeble evasions. They were hardly persuasive, least of all his excuse for refusing to meet de Almeida: a black cat had crossed his path, his emissary explained, and that was a bad omen. But with overwhelming force to back him up, de Almeida was not prepared to shadow-box.

Before dawn on 24 July, the Vigil of the Feast of São Tiago, or St James the Apostle, of whose chivalric order de Almeida was commander, as many who could of the Portuguese assault force crowded aboard his flagship to make a general confession and received a plenary absolution from the Vicar-General of India. Amid the booming of artillery and the shrilling of trumpets, and under the standard of the Cross of Christ, about 700 Portuguese landed on the shore. With the larger part of his force de Almeida stormed into the town. His son, Lourenço, took command of the remainder and made straight for the *maliki*'s palace, which was on the outskirts of Kilwa, facing on to the harbour quay.

The people of Kilwa barred their doors, and from their high houses desperately rained stones and arrows down on the Portuguese, who were tightly jammed in the narrow streets. The Portuguese arquebusiers and crossbowmen fired back with such effect that they soon cleared the defenders from the windows and flat roofs where they were stationed. Pushing on in this manner through the town, de Almeida's force at length joined up with his son's in the wide square in front of the palace, which was built like a fortress with defensive towers. There, several hundred of the *maliki*'s best warriors had sallied out to attack Lourenço's troops with showers of arrows and stones, and were holding them at bay. But now, with their great superiority in firepower, it did not take the reunited Portuguese forces long to drive the *maliki*'s men back into the palace fortress.

The triumphant Portuguese, their blood well up, were already lustily breaking down the palace doors when a herald appeared at the top of a tower. He was waving a flag, and with many urgent gestures and loud shouts made it clear the garrison wished to surrender. De Almeida thereupon took off his helmet and halted the attack. But he was being duped. What he did not realise was that the herald was creating a diversion to allow the *maliki* to escape through a small door of the palace to a nearby grove of palm trees. There his wives and treasure were already waiting for him, and all successfully made it by boat to the mainland and safety. Most of the *waungwana* fled with the *maliki* in their own small craft, carrying off with them as much of their property as they could.

Once the Portuguese had secured Kilwa, the vicar-general, accompanied by Franciscan monks chanting a *Te Deum*, walked solemnly in procession through the prostrate town to the palace, two crosses raised high in righteous triumph over the vanquished infidels. As part of the celebrations de Almeida knighted many of his officers in recognition of their gallantry. But, in truth, the battle had not been a particularly hard-fought one. Few Portuguese had died in the assault, although many had been lightly wounded. It would seem that the inhabitants of Kilwa had not suffered too many casualties either.

However, the worst was still to come. Before their noble officers could bring them back under control, de Almeida's men, inflamed by their successful assault, began to rape and loot all across the defenceless town. They plundered the rich houses and warehouses, which were stashed with ivory, carpets, sandalwood, camphor and other valuables, and stripped the people of their clothes and jewellery. We know from Duarte Barbosa's description of the inhabitants of Kilwa a dozen years later, once the town had recovered from the sack, what they wore upon their persons was worth a small fortune: '[The Moors] are finely clad in many rich garments of gold and silk, and cotton, and the women as well; also with much gold and silver in chains and bracelets, which they wear on their legs and arms, and many jewelled earrings in their ears.'[11]

Order somewhat restored at last, de Almeida appointed the fugitive *maliki*'s adviser, Muhammad Ankoni – who had opportunely turned his coat – as his successor. The price the new ruler paid for his elevation was to swear fealty to the crown of Portugal. Next, following his king's specific instructions, de Almeida erected a strong, square fortress at the harbour entrance on the western side of the island. It was provided with three projecting bastions designed to provide flanking fire from twenty pieces of heavy artillery and many lighter guns. Rubble from demolished houses on the site was used for building material, and several surviving houses were incorporated into the structure. De Almeida named the fort São Tiago after the saint under whose protection the Portuguese had seized Kilwa, and assigned it a garrison of a hundred men.*

Portuguese forts on the Swahili coast would become ever more impregnable over the years as design followed the baroquely elaborate trend in Europe.† They would be garrisoned by trained soldiers regularly shipped out from Portugal to a likely death from tropical disease, and by local levies of uncertain military skill and loyalty. Therefore, right from the beginning, with the establishment of Fort São Tiago, these forts seem always to have been held by absurdly small garrisons whose discipline and morale were generally poor. But such garrisons enjoyed the negative but very real advantage of being like rats in a hole: they had to fight courageously because they had nowhere to run. Furthermore, they were defending sophisticated bastioned fortresses that maximised their ability to resist. Of course, fortresses could always be lost to disease or treachery, but the ability of small garrisons to hold out was always greatly enhanced whenever the Portuguese navy was able to command the sea at their backs. That allowed supplies, ammunition and reinforcements to be brought in almost indefinitely until the enemy, who (fortunately for the Portuguese) were seldom united or sufficiently determined, gave up the siege.

The Sack of Mombasa

Leaving a subdued but sullen Kilwa in its wake, de Almeida's fleet anchored threateningly before Mombasa on the afternoon of 14 August, the Vigil of the

---

* The Portuguese lost Kilwa to Arab mercenaries in 1512, but regained control in 1597.

† See Chapter 4 for a discussion on the design of bastioned fortresses.

Feast of the Assumption. Mombasa was smaller and less influential than Kilwa, with a possible population of about 10,000, but its people remembered their previous edgy encounter with da Gama only too well. They had, moreover, already learned with horror of Kilwa's sorry fate. So they were determined to resist. In preparation the *mfalane* brought in 1,000 or more auxiliaries, all African archers from the mainland, and forbade anyone to leave the town on pain of death. Hans Mayr, an eyewitness with the Portuguese fleet, recorded that one of the defenders was later to yell from the shore at the Portuguese crews that: 'Mombasa was not like Kilwa: they would not find people with hearts that could be eaten like chickens as they had done in Kilwa.'[12]

When de Almeida sent two ships forward to fathom the bar to the harbour, a small, poorly fortified shore battery of seven or eight guns fired on them, and a ball went clean through one of the ships from stem to stern. The Portuguese returned a heavy volley. A lucky shot exploded the battery's powder store and the garrison fled. The fleet then entered the harbour and the *mfalane*, now thoroughly intimidated, decided it was best to attempt to negotiate after all. However, de Almeida was not prepared to haggle with the *mfalane*'s envoys. He peremptorily informed them that their master must subjugate himself to the King of Portugal and pay tribute. Frightened as he was, the *mfalane* found this demand too much for his pride to stomach. He balked, and de Almeida prepared to attack the town that very evening.

The ships in the harbour subjected Mombasa to an intense bombardment, concentrating on the ruler's palace. In several places they breached the city's walls, which faced only landwards because all previous threats to the town had come from the people of the mainland. Return fire from the town was paltry and ineffective. De Almeida's next step was to land two small forces during the moonless night, despite showers of stones and arrows from the defenders, with the purpose of burning down the town to make the main assault next day less difficult. Most of the town was built of coral rag, but there were still enough houses and outbuildings constructed of timber or wattle and daub, with roofs thatched with palm leaves, for the blaze set by the landing parties to take violent hold. Great sections of the town went up in lurid flames that engulfed several ships in the harbour along with a wealth of merchandise.

The devastating fire had barely died down when, a few hours before dawn on 15 August, the Feast of the Assumption, the Portuguese troops received general absolution. They then landed in force. With crossbowmen and arquebusiers firing to clear the enemy from the houses, as they had in Kilwa, they advanced through the town in two columns, led as before by de Almeida and his son Lourenço. The desperate and infuriated people of Mombasa resisted fiercely. As the Portuguese pushed only two abreast through the narrow lanes, which were further blocked by the stone benches in front of the houses and by hastily erected wooden palisades, the inhabitants showered them with stones, arrows and spears from their windows and house tops, and rolled great rocks down the steep streets at them. The Portuguese suffered few casualties from these missiles because of their armour – although that would not have saved them from severe bruising – and were able to take shelter from them underneath the overhanging balconies. Still, such was the intensity of the barrage and the exertion required to clamber past endless obstacles in the suffocating heat that the exhausted soldiers could make little headway through the town.

Eventually accepting that the assault was getting nowhere, de Almeida ordered his men to retire to the ships and regroup. While they rested, he set his ship's carpenters to making long, wooden ladders. These the Portuguese carried with them when they resumed the assault. They set the ladders up against the sides of the multistoreyed houses and swarmed up them to clear the flat roof tops of defenders. The Swahili downstairs at the windows were now trapped between them and the soldiers in the street, and the Portuguese set about systematically clearing houses with much heartless butchery. Perhaps as many as 1,500 defenders perished.

During the height of the carnage the *mfalane* made desperate efforts to negotiate a truce. He had already abandoned his palace, which was seized by the Portuguese, and had retired to a palm grove outside the town. While his emissaries sought out de Almeida, he hovered disconsolately among the palms with his courtiers, all still in their sumptuous robes and turbans. About 500 African archers took up position with them for their protection. They were the *mfalane*'s bodyguard of slave soldiers and, as was common among such units, remained intensely loyal to his person. He could not have been much surprised, however, when de Almeida contemptuously rebuffed his overtures. Accompanied by the elite of the town, the *mfalane* thereupon made good his escape to the mainland.

Once resistance was at an end, de Almeida gave the town over to a thorough sack, which he permitted to continue over two days. To make it all the more systematic, and to maintain better control over his troops than at Kilwa, he allotted specific districts of the town to each of his captains for their men to loot. As Barbosa described it, Mombasa was: 'left ruined and plundered and burnt. Of gold and silver great booty was taken here, bangles, bracelets, earrings and gold beads, also great store of copper and other rich wares in great quantity'.[13] The Portuguese lost only thirty or so soldiers in the assault and sack, mainly of wounds from arrows with burnt wooden tips, soaked in poison.

It took the Portuguese fifteen days to load their immense booty before de Almeida could sail on to India. The bulk of it was supposed to go to the crown with only a twentieth part to the soldiers. Nevertheless, it is clear that many of them, particularly noble officers, kept back many valuable items, especially gold or silver objects, to sell for their own profit once they landed in India. Of the 1,000 captives they took in the sack there was room on board to carry away only 200. These, in de Barros' words, de Almeida 'divided among the noblemen, and the remainder he set at liberty, being women and other weak creatures'.[14]

Before finally departing, de Almeida ordered his men to set fire to what was left of the 'city of abomination',[15] as de Barros was pleased to call it, doubtless on account of Mombasa's many mosques. De Almeida left no garrison behind to hold the charred ruins of the town, which was still sending up clouds of acrid smoke when he set sail. There was no need. Malindi up the coast was already the ally of the Portuguese and Kilwa their tributary. Sofala would soon be theirs as well.

The Capture of Sofala

The subjugation of Sofala, the southernmost of the Swahili cities, was assigned to the smaller squadron of six ships under the Castilian Pedro de Añaya. It was part of de Almeida's command, but had sailed out from Lisbon only in May 1505. When de Añaya arrived at Sofala in September 1505, he did not immediately storm the town. Instead, he cautiously entered its harbour in the broad estuary of the Buzi river and proceeded to negotiate with Sheik Ysuf, its blind and eighty-year-old *maliki*. The greed of the freshly arrived Portuguese was immediately raised (as it was all along the Swahili coast) by the Indian silks, rich furnishings, ivory and gold that adorned his court. But for the moment they restrained themselves because their peaceable approach seemed to be working. The *maliki* permitted the Portuguese to build a fortress, only stipulating in a commendably businesslike fashion that they pay compensation to the owners of the buildings on the site they selected. By the end of November de Añaya's men had completed their fort, but, for lack of stone or adobe, they had no choice but to settle for a poor affair constructed of parallel stockades filled up with sand.

The Portuguese would soon regret their fort's weakness, for the people of Sofala rapidly tired of their uninvited but overweening guests. In allowing them to erect their fort, the *maliki* had been slyly banking on the Portuguese quickly succumbing to malaria and other fevers of the coast. Many were indeed already very ill, or had died, but those still active were rapidly cutting into the trading profits of the town with their monopolistic techniques. So the war faction on the *maliki*'s council persuaded him to join those plotting to surprise the fort and expel the Portuguese.

De Añaya learned of their plans from an informant on the council trying to curry favour with the interlopers. So, despite being fever-ridden, the forty-odd surviving Portuguese were ready when 1,000 men of Sofala, reinforced by inland Africans, charged the fort discharging flaming arrows, spears, stones and other missiles. The Portuguese held their fire and discharged a volley only at point-blank range. It threw the Swahili into complete disarray, and after another devastating volley the Portuguese sallied out of their fort over the heaps of dead and dying. Their counter-attack brought them right into Sofala where they set about butchering all the inhabitants who had not fled. De Añaya himself forced his way through the defences of the *maliki*'s palace, scattering his panic-stricken courtiers, and stormed on until he and his men arrived at the inner chamber where Sheik Ysuf was sitting. In his book, *Ethiopia Oriental*, published in 1609, the Dominican friar João dos Santos described what happened next. The fierce, old man, 'though blind, endeavoured to sell his life at the price of that of his enemies, by hurling at them the *assegais* [spears] which lay beside him, by which he wounded some of the Portuguese'.[16] De Añaya was one of his victims, and when he fell back with a slight wound in the neck, a companion leapt forward to decapitate the ancient *maliki*. The triumphant Portuguese displayed his head on a lance around Sofala, its white beard matted with dark blood.

The Portuguese immediately set about strengthening their fort as best they could, and appointed their useful informant on Sheik Ysuf's council the new *maliki* of the stricken town. His elevation, as with that of the new ruler of Kilwa, proved that with the Portuguese treachery always paid good dividends. As for de Añaya, he fell sick and soon died, quite possibly from poison on the blade of the spear Sheik Ysuf had hurled at him.

The Swahili Coast and its Place in the Portuguese Empire

Having settled the Swahili coast to his satisfaction, de Almeida sailed on to India and glory. On 3 February 1509, in the waters of the Gulf of Khambat in the Arabian Sea, just off the port of Diu in Gujarat, he won a swingeing naval victory over the much larger combined fleets of the Mamluks, Ottomans, the Zamorin of Calicut and the Sultan of Gujarat.* His great carracks sailed past the enemy fleet in line-ahead formation and blasted off broadsides from up to 200 yards away that shattered the oared galleys and other flimsy Indian Ocean craft opposing them. Indeed, these Indian Ocean warships were helpless against the veritable floating gun platforms of the interlopers. Their tactics depended on ramming and boarding, but they were kept at a distance by the hail of Portuguese cannon fire. Nor could they reply in kind by fitting comparable guns to their vessels because the recoil would have shaken their lightly built craft to pieces. So, for the foreseeable future, the Portuguese had established their naval dominance in the waters of the Indian Ocean.

True to his convictions, de Almeida saw his victory over this international Muslim fleet as another step towards the ultimate recapture of Jerusalem that would crown Portugal's worldwide crusade. More prosaically, the battle instantly secured Portugal's dominance in eastern waters because both the

---

* The Catholic maritime republics of Venice and Ragusa gave this Muslim fleet logistical and technical assistance to help deny the Indian Ocean to their commercial rivals, the Catholic Portuguese.

Mamluks and the Ottomans, stung by the scale of their defeat, withdrew their fleets from the Arabian Sea.

Diu might have crowned de Almeida's career,* but in that same year King Manuel sent out Alfonso de Albuquerque (1453–1515) as governor to replace him. De Albuquerque was a middle-aged, service nobleman with a frowning mien and huge, white beard down to his waist, well seasoned in the soldier's trade by decades of bloody warfare in Morocco, Italy and Spain. A highly educated man, he was steeped in the history of the military heroes of antiquity, such as Alexander the Great and Julius Caesar, whose deeds he hoped to emulate. Nevertheless, he shared the world view of his king and of the man he was superseding as Governor of the *Estado da Índia*. Like them, he saw himself as waging the universal struggle against Islam.

However, his strategy differed significantly from de Almeida's. Whereas de Almeida put his faith in great sea battles to eliminate rivals, de Albuquerque was convinced that what a maritime empire most required was a network of permanent naval bases. Strongly fortified against enemies, they would provide secure havens for small, trouble-shooting naval squadrons to provision and refit. To be fully effective, these strongpoints had to be situated at the main choke points around the Indian Ocean to dominate the major trade routes.

De Albuquerque resolutely pursued this strategy. By the time his command expired in 1515, and the king had rewarded him by making him the first viceroy of the *Estado da Índia* and Duke of Goa, he had established almost complete naval superiority in the Indian Ocean from his chain of fortified bases. The main bases were Goa on the coast of Karnataka in India, seized in 1510, Melaka [Malacca] commanding the straits between the Malay peninsula and Sumatra, which was captured in 1511, and Hormuz at the northern entrance to the Persian Gulf, taken in 1515. In 1512 Albuquerque designated Moçambique Island on the Swahili coast as the westernmost base of this far-flung network.

The Swahili coast was vital for the effective operation of the Portuguese trading system. Portugal itself produced few trade goods desired in the

---

* On his way home to Portugal in 1510, de Almeida perished in a pointless skirmish with the Khoikhoi on the beach of Table Bay at the southern tip of Africa. Floundering in the deep sand, and weighed down by their armour, some fifty Portuguese died before their boats, which were waiting beyond the line of breakers, could get in close enough to take them off.

sophisticated world of the Indian Ocean. So, to pay for the valuable spices the Portuguese shipped back to Europe, they required the gold dust and ivory of the East African interior traded through the Swahili ports. It was the Portuguese dream to control these precious commodities at source. But that would mean the dauntingly difficult conquest of the mysterious Mutapa empire and its subsidiary kingdoms, where the gold and ivory were mined and hunted. Eventually this quest would become their major priority in East Africa, but for the moment the Portuguese held off.* Instead, they made do exploiting the huge international system of trade they now monopolised. Portuguese ships brought Indian silks, cottons and glass beads to the Swahili coast. Swahili coastal and river vessels trans-shipped these goods to the trade fairs held deep in the interior, where Swahili merchants exchanged them for the gold and ivory that the Portuguese then shipped on to Goa.

Thanks to de Almeida, by 1509 the Portuguese had subdued much of the Swahili seaboard and had their choice of anchorages for centralising this vital trade. But they could never focus on more than one or two bases at a time because they simply did not have the manpower and resources to hold them. A major reason for this was their high mortality rate. In contrast to the Americas, where the contemporaneous arrival of the Spanish *conquistadores* and other Europeans unleashed disastrous pandemics among the indigenous populations, the people of the Swahili coast had developed some immunity to Eurasian endemic strains through centuries of trade across the seas. In a complete reversal, it was the Portuguese interlopers in East Africa who had no immunity to local diseases. They arrived weakened by months at sea, with no chance to develop antibodies to local microbes, and fell prey to malaria, dysentery and other tropical diseases that took a cripplingly heavy toll of any garrison, debilitated further by their inappropriately thick European clothing and unhealthy diet.

The alternative to stationing garrisons in coastal forts was to attempt to control the Swahili cities indirectly through allies or puppet rulers. This was never a particularly successful ploy because the history of the Swahili coast had long been one of dissension, intrigue and palace plots. This did not change

---

* See Chapter 5.

simply because the Portuguese were there, and they found that no sooner had they found a compliant ruler than he was overthrown or murdered.

Consequently, for moving out the gold dust and ivory, the Portugese were left with no alternative but to concentrate on a single port. Moçambique with its fair harbour, situated on its small island just off the coast, seemed the likeliest candidate. Since da Gama's voyage of 1502 it had been an ally, and a *feitoria* and naval base had been established there.* Unhelpfully, it lacked fresh water and supplies of food, which had to be brought in from the mainland, and was also notoriously unhealthy. When the Portuguese began to erect a fort there in 1507, they also found it necessary to build a large hospital. Over the coming years hundreds of unfortunates were destined to perish there in misery and squalor – many more, in fact, than died on the voyage from Portugal. Nevertheless, Moçambique was better situated for the interior trade than Kilwa, its only possible rival as a depot. When in 1512 the Portuguese lost control of Kilwa to a local revolt given muscle by Arab mercenaries, de Albuquerque plumped decisively for Moçambique. It consequently became the main port of call for all vessels plying between Lisbon and Goa. Kilwa, which had been dependent for its wealth on the gold trade from Sofala, now definitively diverted to Moçambique, was ruined economically.

Once the Portuguese had concentrated the Swahili gold trade in their *feitoria* on Moçambique Island, they did not much concern themselves with the affairs of the rest of the coast. They contented themselves with maintaining friendly relations with allied cities such as Malindi and Zanzibar, and with making occasional piratical naval raids against others to loot their wealth. Otherwise, for much of the sixteenth century they did not consider it worth their while to maintain garrisons along the East African coast north of Moçambique – for as long, that is, as they could continue to dominate Muslim shipping in the waters of the Persian Gulf, Red Sea and off the Horn of Africa.

---

* The Capelle de Nossa Senhora do Baluarte, built in the first decades of the sixteenth century in the vaulted Manueline style and located on the northeastern tip of the island overlooking the sea, is probably the oldest extant European building in the southern hemisphere.

CHAPTER THREE

Coming to the Aid of Prester John

The Christian Kingdom of Prester John

The rain-sodden Portuguese camp at Debarwa was pitched high on the escarpment of the Ethiopian plateau with the distant Red Sea glinting fitfully thousands of feet below. On a chilly day in July 1541, the Portuguese commander Cristóvão da Gama was preparing to welcome the Dowager Queen of Ethiopia with all the pomp due her exalted rank. He was himself 'a great gentleman' in the eyes of his officers such as Miguel de Castanhoso,* who witnessed the scene, because his father was the celebrated explorer Vasco da Gama and his elder brother was the Governor of the *Estado da Índia*. De Castanhoso breathlessly described how, as befitted his lofty station, da Gama was 'clothed in hose and vest of red satin and gold brocade with many plaits, and a French cape of fine black cloth all quilted with gold, and a black cap with a very rich medal'.[1] His captains and *fidalgos* strutted about him in the most brilliant attire they could muster, and the arquebusiers under their command were drawn up in neat ranks behind them. Banners of blue and white damask with red crosses flapped damply above them all, the royal standard of the crimson Cross of Christ on its white ground in the forefront.

When Queen Sabla Wengal ('Harvest of the Gospel') and her retinue approached, the Portuguese trumpets shrilled and the soldiers saluted her twice with peeling fire from all their artillery and matchlocks. The queen and her ladies were all mounted side-saddle on mules, for in Ethiopia the unshod

---

* Little is known of de Castanhoso except that he was a Spaniard of noble birth and a Knight of the Order of Christ, who served at sea as a captain in the Portuguese service and throughout the campaign in Ethiopia. His eyewitness account was published in Portugal in 1564, but was already in manuscript by 1544.

horses were reserved for battle or for ceremonial occasions when they were led without riders. The solemn men who attended the queen were dressed in the typical Ethiopian attire of loose, cotton breeches with oblong, cotton cloaks draped around their bare shoulders.* Their fine but curly hair was soaked in unrefined butter and tortured into plaits and horns and sprays. A number of them carried a swaying silk canopy above Sabla Wengal, its curtains falling all the way to the ground and leaving only a narrow opening in the front for her to see through. Sabla Wengal was elegantly dressed in a capacious robe of white cotton, over which was draped a cloak of black satin embroidered with flowers, edged with fringes of fine gold. Her head was so muffled up that only her eyes could be seen.

The *bahrnagash*, who was the Ethiopian governor of the coastal province in the far northeast of the kingdom where the ceremony was taking place, and whose title meant the 'Ruler of the Sea', led her handsome, black mule by the bridle. As etiquette demanded, he was on foot and naked to the waist as a sign of submission in the royal presence. A *lemd* (lion skin), worn only by distinguished warriors of high rank, was draped across his shoulders.

Sabla Wengal was patently astonished by the sight of the Portuguese, the likes of whom she had never seen before, and whose dress and military array were utterly strange to her. Nevertheless, she knew how to comport herself as a queen. She made sure the assembly caught sight of her delicately signalled joy and relief when da Gama's welcoming speech was translated for her. He declared that he was responding to the embassy sent by her son, Negus Galawdewos (or King Claudius), begging the Portuguese then operating in the Red Sea against the Ottomans to aid him in the name of God against their common Muslim foes. As da Gama stoutly concluded: 'All the Portuguese who were there had come ready to die for the faith of Christ and the salvation of that kingdom.'[2]

The presence of this crusading expeditionary force in remote Ethiopia might well appear an extraordinary corollary to the recent Portuguese subjugation of the Swahili coast. In fact, it was a logical consequence of the grand strategy devised by Alfonso de Albuquerque, the first viceroy of the

---

* The poor often wore tanned skins instead of cloth garments. Their abbreviated dress was sufficiently scanty to offend the modesty of the Portuguese Jesuit missionaries, who compared it unfavourably to the concealing robes of the elite.

Estado da Índia, which was propelling the Portuguese ever further up the east coast of African towards the Horn of Africa and the Red Sea.

By the time de Albuquerque's command expired in 1515, only one major strategic choke point remained to be secured if the Indian Ocean were to be secured as a Portuguese lake. This was the entry from the Gulf of Aden to the Red Sea, the Strait of Bab el-Mandeb. If the Portuguese could establish a base close by and block the straits, they would be able to deny the Red Sea to Muslim shipping. Yet there was more to it than that.

De Albuquerque, that intemperate crusader, reckoned that if a Portuguese fleet could wrest control of the Red Sea from the Mamluk rulers of Egypt, then it would be in a position to capture the port of Jedda in the Hejaz (as the western shore of the Arabian peninsula is known). Jedda was where Muslims on the *hajj* (the pilgrimage to Mecca, an act that is one of the five pillars of Islam) disembarked for the holy city. With Jedda in their hands the Christians would be able to storm inland, sack Mecca and then hold it for ransom against the restoration of Jerusalem to the Christians – or so de Albuquerque feverishly calculated. To help fulfil this ultimate crusader's fantasy, de Albuquerque seriously considered forging an anti-Muslim alliance with the Christian kingdom of Ethiopia, the fabled realm of Prester John. The difficulty with this plan was that his actual knowledge of Ethiopia went not much further than the wild and unconfirmed traveller's tales then current.

Ethiopia's mystery, as well as its tenacious survival over the centuries, lay in its inaccessibility to the outside world. Inland from where it just touches the Red Sea coast,* the country stretches southwards for more than 1,000 miles across a series of high plateaus, the most extensive being the Amhara massif. These highlands are diagonally bisected by the Great Rift Valley with its series of volcanic lakes. The valley is an unstable region of earthquakes and droughts, through which the Awash river flows down to Lake Abbe, seventy miles from the sea. The highlands on the eastern, or seaward, side of the Great Rift Valley drop away into the arid Ogaden desert of the Horn of Africa. They are less extensive that the main Ethiopian massifs to the west of valley that rise abruptly, overwhelmingly, to more than 8,000 feet above the scorchingly hot Danakil desert at their northern extremity.

---

* This is a region that is now the independent country of Eritrea.

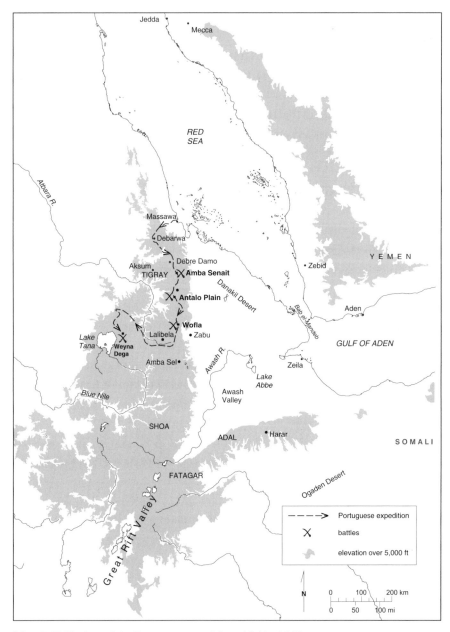

MAP 5 *Ethiopia and the Portuguese expedition, 1541–1543*

Ranges of mountains, many of them huge, flat-topped *ambas* with precipitously scarped sides, rear thousands of feet high out of the already lofty plateaus. The wide tablelands of the *ambas* are well watered and extensive enough to grow food for a monastic community or garrison, and to pasture flocks and herds. Consequently, these *ambas* made natural fortresses, especially since access was often restricted to a single, easily defended path, and sometimes not even that. Some have such soaring cliffs that the only way to the summit was for the monks or garrison to hoist a visitor, huddled precariously in a basket, up by stout, leather thongs.

The western slopes of the Ethiopian massifs are somewhat gentler than the beetling, eastern ones, but daunting enough as they merge with the spreading plains of the Sudan. Many rivers flow westwards through spectacular gorges, brutally incised deep into the rocky terrain. They drain into the Blue Nile, which rises in Lake Tana on the northwestern high plateau and thunders over soaring waterfalls to its eventual rendezvous with the White Nile at Khartoum.

Despite its proximity to the equator, because of its great altitude the Ethiopian plateau is temperate grassland and thorn-bush country. It enjoys generally good rainfall, which falls from June to September. The Portuguese, accustomed to a Mediterranean climate with its winter rainfall, always referred to this rainy summer season as 'winter'. Forests grow on the mountain slopes and along the riverbanks. In the sixteenth century, wild animals of all varieties still abounded: lions, leopards, civet cats,* elephants, hyenas, rhinoceroses, giraffes, monkeys and antelopes of all descriptions. For fear of them people never ventured out at night and slept in trees if overtaken by the dark.

A favourable climate, combined with the rich volcanic soils, has meant that for untold ages the highlands have sustained industrious, settled peasant communities. For their staple diet of spongy, sour flat bread the Ethiopians grew their cereal crops of tiny-grained teff, millet, wheat and barley on every piece of land level enough to put under the wooden ploughs noted by the Portuguese, each one drawn by a pair of oxen. Unfortunately, most regions were prey to periodic plagues of locusts, which stripped every living plant bare. In the early sixteenth century, Father Francisco Alvares† described such

---

* The Ethiopians used the perfume extracted from the anal glands of the civet to scent their clothes.

† Father Francisco Alvares was the chaplain to the Portuguese embassy of 1520–1526 to the *negus*. Alvares's account was first published in Lisbon in 1540.

a locust swarm: 'Their multitude, which covers the earth and fills the air, is not to be believed; they darken the light of the sun.'[3] Cattle with great, spreading horns constituted the main form of wealth for the people, but they also kept sheep and goats that grazed on the mountain pastures, along with the donkeys and mules that carried their coffee, cotton and honey to market.

Ethiopian villages, built very close to each other in the more fertile regions, consisted of clusters of round huts with steep, thatched roofs, always within easy reach of a similarly constructed church, where the faithful worshipped on Sundays. The people slept on ox hides strewn on the floor or on low, trestle beds, covering themselves with their cloaks or, if rich, with fine coverlets. Otherwise, neither the rich nor poor possessed much furniture besides their cooking and eating utensils. Likewise, the mansions of the elite differed more in scale than in quality from the huts of peasants. Each mansion was made up of eight or more single-storeyed, thatched rondavels with walls of stone or packed earth. They were grouped in a capacious enclosure surrounded by high drystone walls topped by thorn-tree branches. At night watchmen drove the livestock inside the enclosure and kept fires burning to deter the wild predators roaming outside.

Surrounding these fertile, cultivated, densely settled highlands, but far below them, are the arid lowlands with their poor soils, searing heat and reluctant rain. They are suitable only for nomadic pastoralists, who in the sixteenth century subsisted off the milk and meat of their camels. Those living on the seaward side of the lowlands traded the salt they collected in the coastal saltpans with the farmers of the highlands.

Ominously for the peasants of the high plateau, the peoples of the lowlands shared one thing in common, regardless of how they eked out a precarious living: they all gazed enviously upwards at the rich lands presently denied them, but which they always planned to raid or settle if they could. For their part, the highlanders were constantly on their anxious guard against any such attempt.

Ethiopia, then, was like some great fortress, determined to protect its prosperity from those without. The Portuguese knew, however, that although otherwise inaccessible from the sea, sixteenth-century Ethiopia controlled a narrow, forty-mile corridor of coastline on the southwestern shore of the Red Sea, where the port town of Massawa was situated. Just like most of the Swahili cities, it was built for defence on two off-shore islands,* and the Portuguese saw that it would make an ideal naval station for projected operations within the Red Sea. To secure its use, however, would first necessitate making diplomatic contact with the remote and secretive Ethiopian court and winning its goodwill.

The origins of the Ethiopian kingdom are as old as time. Nearly 1,000 years before Christ there were already trading and cultural links between shadowy kingdoms on the Ethiopian highlands and the people of southern Arabia. These contacts gradually extended to embrace the Egypt of the pharaohs and later the Hellenistic and Roman worlds. In about AD 100 the kingdom of Aksum arose in what is now the Tigray province of northeastern Ethiopia and Eritrea. Its people appear to have been a combination of Sabaeans, settlers from southern Arabia, and local Africans whose language was Ge'ez. Aksum flourished as the greatest power in the region. Secure in its military muscle, it traded far and wide, minted its own coin and built fortified cities. To this day, the carved, monolithic stone stelae (some nearly 100 feet tall) that were erected over the graves of its kings and nobles still have the power to amaze.†

Somewhere between 320 and 350 King Ezana converted to Christianity, a new faith that was becoming established as the state religion in the Eastern Roman Empire, Aksum's major trading partner. However, what precisely was meant by 'Christianity' remained problematic, because early Christianity was much vexed by competing theological interpretations. The most divisive issue concerned the nature of Christ, and therefore that of the Holy Trinity. The orthodox and majority position was (and still is) that Christ maintains two natures – the divine *and* the human. Monophysitism, which was widespread in Egypt and the Levant, asserted that Christ is of one nature, in which the human is wholly absorbed by the divine.‡

In 451 the Council of Chalcedon declared Monophysitism a heresy. Most Egyptians nevertheless stuck to the Monophysite doctrine and formed what

---

* Massawa is today the main port of Eritrea. In 1990 the old town was very badly damaged in the war of independence against Ethiopia.

† In 1937, after the Italian conquest of Ethiopia, Mussolini ordered the removal of one of the giant stelae to Rome. Finally, after decades of foot-dragging negotiations, it was returned and re-erected in Aksum in 2005.

‡ Another contemporary variant, adopted by many of the Germanic peoples who overwhelmed the Western Roman Empire, was Arianism. This doctrine held that Christ was a being created by God the Father, and was therefore different and distinct from Him.

is known today as the Coptic Church. Crucially for Ethiopia's contacts in the centuries to come with Christians from the Latin West, Aksum too embraced Monophysitism under the influence of vigorous, fifth-century missionaries from Syria and Egypt.* This has meant that until today the Ethiopian Church has remained closely attached to the Egyptian Coptic Church. Its hierarchy is subject to the patriarch of Alexandria, who appoints the *abuna* (head of the church in Ethiopia).

Monasticism, another essential characteristic of the Ethiopian Church, also stems from its Coptic roots. Christian monasticism was born in Egypt, where, during the third century, many of the devout began to retire to the desert to live in seclusion and serve God through prayer. By the end of the fifth century hundreds of monastic communities had sprung up. The teaching, writing and example of these desert Fathers have ever since defined the Coptic Church and along with it the Ethiopian Church. The Ethiopian clergy have accordingly always been almost entirely monastic in organisation and, as the Portuguese noted, their patron is St Anthony of the Desert, known as the Father of All Monks. Sixteenth-century Ethiopian monks wore white caps and yellow habits of coarse cotton or tanned goat skin. Nuns were similarly dressed but shaved their heads. They were not cloistered in convents but lived in the villages or the monasteries. Monks and nuns alike strove to inspire lay people by their example to lead lives of great piety in which they regularly prayed, fasted, did penance and sent their children to the monasteries to be taught to participate in the complex church liturgy of music and sacred dance.

While the clergy lived austere monastic lives, they also believed it right to celebrate their faith as befitted God's transcendent glory. So when they led the faithful in worship (all barefooted as required), it was in churches with intricately carved, wooden doors shielded by silk curtains, and with walls wondrously painted with images of Christ and the Virgin Mary, of apostles, patriarchs, prophets and angels, and of St George on horseback slaying the dragon. The officiating clergy were robed in gorgeous, richly embroidered silk and damask vestments. They bore distinctively fretted, silver processional crosses and processional umbrellas, employed finely wrought liturgical vessels

---

* In the seventeenth century the Roman Inquisition identified forty-one propositions of the Ethiopian Church (including keeping the Jewish Sabbath), which it condemned as grossly incorrect.

such as incense burners, and read the word of God from beautifully hand-penned and illuminated parchment bibles and prayer books. To this day the liturgical language, both written and spoken, is Ge'ez, the ancient tongue of the northern highlands of Aksum, where Christianity first took hold.

When Islam suddenly arose in the seventh century, there was no rapid Muslim conquest of Aksum as there was of Egypt in 642. Instead, Muslim merchants from Arabia and nomads of the Horn of Africa gradually infiltrated along the coast of the Red Sea and up the Awash valley. By the 1250s the highlands on the eastern side of the valley were more or less converted to the new faith. A chain of petty Muslim sultanates ran all the way from the port of Zeila (jutting out into the Gulf of Aden on its sandy spit of land) to the southern flanks of the Ethiopian highlands. There the Muslims came into increasing conflict with the Christian kingdom that, having lost control of the coast to the Muslims, and with it its longstanding and prosperous trading contacts with the Red Sea and the Indians, was compensating by steadily conquering the highlands to the south of its original heartland and converting the people to Christianity.

Around the middle of the twelfth century a new dynasty, the Zagwe, arose on the Lasta highlands, 450 miles south of where Aksum had first been built. The Zagwe kings were very devout and worked very closely with the monasteries. Their greatest monuments are the famous, monolithic, rock-hewn churches, chiselled out of the living rock by war captives, which are still the object of pilgrimage. Traditionally, they were created in the early thirteenth century, during the reign of King Lalibela, after whom the complex is named. Under his aggressive generalship, Zagwe rule (along with its monastic culture) spread both westwards towards Lake Tana, and further southwards yet to the Shoan plateau and its Amhara-speaking people.

In 1270 Yekuno Amlak, a lord from recently incorporated Shoa, overthrew and killed the last of the Zagwe kings and founded the new Solomonid dynasty. The dynasty bears that name because its kings claimed legitimacy through their mythical descent via the last King of Aksum to Menelik, the son of the Old Testament King Solomon of Judaea. Menelik was believed to have been born 2,000 years before, of the union between Solomon and the Queen of Saba (Sheba), who returned home to give him birth. When he later visited his father in Jerusalem, Menelik is then supposed to have stolen the

Ark of the Covenant and to have brought it to Ethiopia. This legend not only gave the Solomonids the sanction of the Bible, but also established Ethiopia as the new Zion and their subjects as God's chosen people. Surrounded as Ethiopia was in the thirteenth century by hostile, non-Christian or Muslim states, this belief was crucial in defining its distinctive identity. In token of it, all Christian Ethiopians were expected to bear crosses and signs of their faith on their clothes and even on their ploughs.

The Christianity of the Solomonid kings went hand-in-hand with conquest, and they aggressively uprooted Muslims who fell under their rule and replaced them with Christian settlers. By the mid-fourteenth century the Solomonids had succeeded in taking control of the small Muslim sultanates of the eastern highlands on the far side of the Awash valley, along with their lucrative Red Sea trade in gold, ivory and slaves. Then, in the later fifteenth century, the sultanate of Adal on the Harar plateau, the most powerful of the subjugated Muslim states, clawed back its independence. This development was fraught with danger for Ethiopia. Not only was Adal militarily strong in its own right, but it was also creating a pool of allied warriors from the herders of the surrounding lowlands whom it was busily converting to Islam. More than that, Adal's control of the Red Sea port of Zeila allowed it to import the new gunpowder weapons that from 1515 were becoming available in Arabia through the Ottomans, the rising Muslim superpower, while at the same time denying them to Ethiopia.

For the moment, though, Adal's military threat remained unrealised, and the *negus* (king, ruler) could reign as confidently as if Ethiopia's supremacy were unassailable. Yet his position was shaky, even in his own kingdom. He relied overmuch on his noblemen and the widespread communities of monks to rule and administer his vast lands. They served their sovereign by raising and commanding bands of troops in time of war, and by supplying him with provisions to feed his court and armies. In return the king rewarded them with land grants called *gult*.

This was a system that the Portuguese, with their own feudal practices, could readily comprehend. A *gult* holder was not entitled to cultivate the land himself. The rights to the land stayed with the peasants who could pass it on from father to son, and who forfeited ownership only if found guilty of treason or rebellion. But the tribute or taxes they would otherwise have paid in kind to the state were made over to the *gult* owner. These took the form of agricultural labour, additional services that could range from construction work to preparing a banquet, as well as occasional service such as militia in time of emergency. More often than not, the weight of these obligations became cripplingly burdensome for the peasantry. When it did, they might rise in revolt or give their allegiance to another ruler if he promised to ease their oppressive obligations.

Grants of *gult* estates to important churches and monasteries were virtually permanent because succeeding rulers routinely confirmed them. As a result, immense landed wealth accrued to the already enormously influential Church, whose *abuna* always played a major part in the affairs of state. Noble *gult* holders likewise did all they could to make these royal endowments permanent. The problem for them was that Ethiopian kings ruled by divine right, basing their absolute monarchy on the scriptures, taken (in fact) out of context: 'Render therefore unto Caesar the things which are Caesar's (St Matthew 22: 21). Technically, kings could appoint and dismiss all governors and officials at will, and transfer *gult* estates from them at pleasure. But that was easier said than done.

Many noble *gult* holders operated like professional men-at-arms, maintaining large bodies of loyal, mounted retainers whom the king called up in time of war to serve as the royal army's main striking force.

So kings both feared and relied upon their nobles, and the ability of rulers to enforce their apparently immense powers over them varied from reign to reign. Many a *negus* might shrink from attempting to deprive some noble family of their *gult* lands lest they rise in revolt. This meant that certain great families succeeded in building up hereditary estates and regional power bases, which they reinforced by a network of dynastic marriages and defended against all comers with their armed retainers.

To overawe these great regional nobles who posed a constant challenge to their royal power, and at the same time to inspect and tax their realm, the Solomonid kings remained constantly on the road. They kept no fixed capital and visited the ancient but sadly decayed city of Aksum only for their coronations. Indeed, as the Jesuit missionary Manoel de Almeida* observed

---

* Manoel de Almeida was the Jesuit visitor to the Abyssinian Mission between 1622 and 1633. His

in the early seventeenth century, no Ethiopian settlement deserved the name
of town as they were: 'all villages, some larger, some smaller, but such that
no other name suits them'.[4] By far the largest settlement in Ethiopia was
the *katama* (peripatetic royal encampment), a vast assemblage of tents and
temporary wooden huts close to the current area of military operations where
the *negus* lived as the general in command.

As he shifted his *katama* around his kingdom the *negus* was accompanied by
hundreds of churchmen, officials and courtiers, by nobles with their retinues,
and by military commanders with their troops. All of them were accompanied
by their womenfolk and families, so there were often more women than men
in the encampment. There were also vast crowds of those who served and
supplied them: the cooks, grooms, herdsmen, artisans, merchants, slaves and
prostitutes. Every few months the *katama* had to move on again, not only for
reasons of sanitation but also because of the extreme depredations the huge
encampment made on local supplies of wood for fuel, and on the food stocks
of the wretched peasantry. When on the move along the rough tracks, which
the local peasantry were obliged to clear of undergrowth and obstacles, this
great, straggling column could be quite twelve miles long and required at least
50,000 pack mules and oxen for its baggage, even though the common people
carried their own trifling possessions.

The *katama* invariably followed the same, well-established layout. Because
of its extent it was always situated on an open plain. The royal tents were
pitched on the highest ground, facing away from the rising sun, and protected
by an enclosure with carefully guarded gates. Inside the enclosure, besides the
luxurious tents that formed the royal domestic quarters, there was a large, red
tent for big receptions. Another splendid one sheltered the *abuna*, who, while at
court, wore his hooded cloak of blue silk and his huge, blue turban. Other tents
served as places of worship, and yet more accommodated state officials and
leading officers. A large space was left empty in front of the royal enclosure for
martial displays. Surrounding this parade ground and the royal enclosure, and
stretching as far as the eye could see, were the tents and makeshift huts of the
king's enormous following. All – whether the fine tents of high nobles in their

---

History of High Ethiopia was based on his own experiences and a reworking of the manuscript history of
Ethiopia left unpublished by an earlier Jesuit missionary Pedro Páez, who was in the country between
1603 and 1622.

places of honour in each of the camp's four allotted sections, or the hovels of slaves – were arranged in neat lanes with specified distances between each dwelling. Room was also laid aside for 'public buildings' – the long tent that served as a court of justice, and others that functioned as prisons or markets.

Whether a *negus* were truly powerful or not, the prescribed etiquette underscoring his majesty was always kept up. When seated under his silk parasol of state, high above his subjects on his raised platform covered with rugs and silken cushions, he was being deliberately presented (so Father Alvares noted) exactly 'as they paint God the Father on the wall'.[5] Indeed, in his mantle of gold brocade and wearing his high, many-tiered crown of gold and silver, studded with seed pearls, he was a resplendent figure.

The jostling thong of courtiers heightened the illusion of limitless power. Pages richly dressed in silk closely attended him and mingled with ecclesiastics in their pointy mitres of red silk. Nobles armed with large swords in silver-covered scabbards flanked him. They wore white tunics with girdles of coloured silk, whose long fringes reached to the ground, along with gold collars around their necks and many bracelets – clothes and ornaments strictly forbidden for commoners. Over their shoulders the nobles flung the *lemd*. Armed guards in coats of glittering mail with drawn swords and shields kept close watch. Horses, ceremonially caparisoned with high plumes and rich brocade coverings reaching to the ground, were kept tethered close by to add to the richness of the scene. Most spectacularly of all, four lions – and was not the *negus* the Lion of Judah? – paced and roared in their iron chains.

Even the most powerful of local magnates who wished to pay the *negus* their respects were expected to approach as the humblest of suitors. Francisco Alvares saw Negus Lebna Dengal in all his majesty:

A lord approaches the court with great pomp and takes up quarters at least a league from the court, and there he often stays a month or two without stirring . . . When they [chiefs] get this permission to enter [the royal encampment], they enter it with great pomp, and playing kettledrums and instruments . . . When he [the chief] encamps he does not appear clothed as he does when he makes his entry, but walks about . . . naked from the waist upwards . . . So they say: 'so and so is not yet in favour with our lord, for he still goes about stripped'.[6]

With his rule so absolute and personal, there was always the threat that on the death of the *negus* state authority might collapse. It was thus essential for the *negus'* designated successor to grasp the reins as quickly and firmly as possible. But with so many ambitious lords who could rapidly mobilise their armed retainers, this often proved difficult. It was to avoid succession conflicts that the Solomonids made a practice of imprisoning redundant princes in a monastery atop an inaccessible *amba*. Yet even this precaution could not eradicate the danger that the great nobles might succeed in enthroning a minor they could manipulate and so deny the throne to a less malleable adult prince.

Warfare, therefore, more often than not accompanied a change of monarch. But it must also be understood that in Ethiopia the elite held warfare in high esteem, much as the feudal nobility did in Europe. As in Europe, strongly held Christian beliefs existed comfortably side by side with a highly developed code of personal honour. King, nobles and officers of state were all expected to be *chavas* (active warriors).

They proudly sought visibility in the armed throng through their gleaming accoutrements. A *chavas* girded on a large, double-edged, sickle-shaped sabre with a large pommel. However, it was intended mainly for show. For fighting at close quarters a long dagger – or possibly a club of hard, heavy wood – was preferred. Both weapons were also useful for hurling at an opponent. But it was the spear that was the *chavas'* main weapon. He normally carried a pair of them, one a javelin with a narrow iron blade for casting at the enemy, and the other a lance with a broader blade for hand-to-hand combat. A *chavas* might also carry a bow, although he drew it more when hunting than in combat. For protection he had a round shield, or buckler, that varied in size but could be up to nearly a yard in diameter. It was made of tough buffalo or hippopotamus hide with a raised, central boss and turned-up rim. If it belonged to a *chavas* of high status it might also be covered in ornate patterns in silver or brass. In the sixteenth century some might wear a helmet as well as a long coat of chain mail (which the Portuguese considered of inferior quality). When they did, they might dispense with the shield. A *chavas* would ride to war on his saddle mule and reserve his high-spirited and handsome horse for battle. This precious steed was equipped with a frankly swaggering harness and a saddle with an inordinately high pommel. Like all Ethiopians, a *chavas* rode with his big toe in a stirrup ring, rather than resting his foot on a stirrup iron like the Portuguese or Ottomans.

Every *chavas* aspired to the high ideal of the *tellek saw* (superior man). As a bearer of arms he could never demean himself by touching a plough like a peasant. But at the same time he was under unrelenting pressure to prove his worth and high breeding to inferior people through deeds of valour, generosity and refined etiquette. Thus a *tellek saw* (and every great lord and the monarch most of all) was expected to defend his honour with his blood while at the same time living lavishly, dressing ostentatiously and being open-handed to a fault with his retainers.

An honour code such as this inevitably fostered endemic feuds and vendettas. Yet it also inspired the *tellek saw* and his fellow men-at-arms when they rode to war against Muslims or pagans to regard themselves as Old Testament warriors of God smiting the heathen. In this sense they were no different from European knights on crusade. Like them, from an early age royal and noble youths – unless destined for the church – learned the arts of war and horsemanship besides being instructed in reading, music and the scriptures. Their defining step into manhood was marked by a first kill of an enemy warrior or a noble beast such as a lion. When describing Negus Galawdewos (r.1540–1559), the Royal Chronicles of Ethiopia* perfectly expressed this chivalric ideal in terms a Portuguese *fidalgo* would have related to closely:

> Galawdewos grew up fortified by the grace of the Holy Spirit and learned all the doctrine of the church in his first youth; he was later shown how to ride a horse, draw the bow, and hunt animals; then, as was the custom for the children of kings, he was taught everything concerning the art of war.[7]

Military honour came from horse combat, and cavalry made up of *gult* holders and their mounted retainers dominated the Ethiopian battlefield. A *chavas* identified wholly with his steed. He might even adopt its name as his own when, parading up and down along the ranks before battle, he boasted of his past victories and threw down trophies seized from the enemy in confirmation. In a society that prized the heroic virtues so highly, defending one's honour by

---

* From the thirteenth century Ethiopian scholars had been writing these chronicles in Ge'ez at the command of their rulers to perpetuate and glorify their memory.

overthrowing an enemy champion in single, mounted combat was the surest route of all to honour and office, even for lowly warriors.

Warfare had its strict rules. Honour demanded that armies fight hand-to-hand in the open field with sword, spear and shield, despite the mountainous country's obvious suitability for fortifications and guerrilla tactics. Enemy who attacked from ambush or at night were considered treacherous. Etiquette required commanders to communicate courteously with each other before battle while their troops traded insults.

Opposing armies were typically drawn up with a vanguard closely supported by a rearguard of much the same strength. The army's centre was deployed in close order, and that was where the *negus* would position himself, surrounded by his bodyguards, leading courtiers and sometimes even his womenfolk. Two wings were thrown out in extended formation on either side of the centre. When an Ethiopian army advanced into the fray it did so with ferocious battle cries and with what Father Prutky* described as 'the harsh music'[8] of its long trumpet, kettledrums and outsized cymbals.

Steadfastness to the death in battle was admired in principle, but Ethiopian warriors were also pragmatists. Battles were usually decided at the first furious onset and they saw no point in throwing away their lives needlessly when the day was clearly lost. So it was not deemed dishonourable to preserve one's life by flight to live and fight another day.

The *chavas* constituted the core and striking force of any Ethiopian army summoned out for war by the *negus* or a great lord. Yet he might on occasion be swamped in sheer numbers by peasant levies. The Ethiopian peasants owed their *gult* holders military service, but they were poorly trained and essentially unmotivated. For arms they might carry a poorly made sword, a bow or sling, a spear and a simple buckler. Their lords called them out only at times of major crisis to swell the army's ranks as rather unreliable infantry. In battle, they would normally loose several arrows or slingshots, and then fall back after having ineffectually thrown their spear, inevitably causing confusion in their own ranks. They certainly could never be relied upon to stand fast. Consequently, from the fourteenth century on, it became more usual in routine

---

* Father Remedius Prutky was a Franciscan friar born in Bohemia. He was stationed in Egypt and led a mission to Ethiopia in 1751. He wrote the manuscript of his travels in Latin.

campaigns to supplement the *chavas* cavalry with experienced mercenary recruits taken on for the duration.

Such was Christian Ethiopia and its vainglorious military culture. The question was whether it was really worth Portugal's while to secure Ethiopia's alliance against the Muslims of the Red Sea. De Albuquerque departed the arena before anything concrete could be effected, but in the succeeding decades power shifts in the region prompted a serious Portuguese attempt to bring Ethiopia on board. In making the effort the Portuguese were not proceeding entirely from scratch, because in the past a few tenuous diplomatic contacts had already taken place.

Gran's *Jihad*

Since the fourteenth century the Christian rulers of Ethiopia had been spasmodically seeking a European military alliance against the kingdom's aggressive Muslim neighbours. Embassies had searched out the pope, as well as the rulers of Venice, Milan, Aragon and Portugal, and had brought gifts of leopards, aromatic spices, supposed pieces of the True Cross and offers of dynastic marriage. No assistance had ever been forthcoming, but Europeans were fascinated by these exotic Christians, and increasingly made the identification of the *Negus* of Ethiopia with Prester John.

When in 1453 the Muslim Ottoman Turks captured Constantinople after a memorable siege and so terminated the final, lingering remnant of the Eastern Roman Empire, the Christian rulers of Europe began to rethink possible connections with distant, exotic Ethiopia. With the eyes of the all-conquering Ottoman sultans fixed alarmingly on the rich lands of eastern Europe and on the Mediterranean seaways, any aid in thwarting the threat seemed worth pursuing. To this end, in 1487 King João II of Portugal sent two emissaries to the Middle East in search of the *negus*. One of them, Pedro de Covilham, a veteran of the wars in Morocco, survived years of arduous journeying to reach the court of Negus Eskender (Alexander) (r. 1478–1494). Eskender never granted de Covilham leave to depart his realm, and he lived out the remainder of his life not uncomfortably as a man of influence at the *negus'* ever-journeying court.

Even though nothing came of de Covilham's embassy, his very arrival and continued presence opened the eyes of the Ethiopian elite to the real possibility of relations with Portugal. Therefore, when in 1508 two fresh envoys from King Manuel of Portugal made it to the mountain kingdom, seeking (as de Albuquerque was urging) to gain the use of the Ethiopian Red Sea port of Massawa in their struggle against the Mamluks, they were taken seriously. Power at that time was in the hands of Dowager Queen Eleni (Helena), the widow of Negus Baeda Maryam (r.1468–1478). She was regent for her twelve-year-old step-grandson, Lebna Dengal ('Incense of the Virgin'), also known as Dawit II (r.1508–1540).

Eleni was clearly a ruler of ability and foresight, who had exercised considerable political ability in securing both Lebna Dengal's succession and her regency. She saw how a Portuguese alliance could be of value. Ethiopia lacked a fleet, and Portuguese ships could stem worrying Mamluk naval incursions down the coast. Moreover (as we have seen), to the east of Ethiopia the Muslim state of Adal was growing alarmingly in power, and the Portuguese might help check it.

Since the 1490s the real power in Adal had not been the sultan but Mahfuz, the Amir of Harar. In 1508 Mahfuz declared a *jihad* against Ethiopia and adopted the title of *imam* to symbolise his claim to religious leadership.* At the head of fierce Somali pastoralists and fanatical Muslim volunteers from Yemen and the Hejaz across the Red Sea, he struck again and again at the southern and eastern provinces of the Ethiopian highlands. Cunningly (although the Ethiopians considered his methods decidedly dishonourable) he timed his raids to coincide with Lent, when the Christians were weakened by fasting. By employing equally dishonourable surprise and mobile tactics, and by avoiding pitched battles against the powerful Ethiopian army, he succeeded in carrying off huge quantities of booty, including thousands of Christian slaves. These he sold in Arabia where they were more highly prized than black Africans from what is now the Sudan.

With Mahfuz's exploits against her kingdom infuriatingly turning him into a celebrated, popular hero in the *Dar al-Islam*, the dowager queen decided to proceed with a Portuguese alliance. She despatched Matthew – a pale-skinned Armenian merchant in her service – on a return diplomatic mission that must be one of the most frustrating ever recorded. Matthew went by ship to Goa,

---

* An *imam* leads prayers at the mosque.

the seat of the *Estado da Índia*. The Portuguese there took him for an impostor. Only after subjecting him to great indignities and delays did they finally send him off to Portugal. There too he kicked his heels for year after year, not surprisingly gaining a reputation for roaring like a lion in his many frustrations. At last, in 1520 and twelve years after Matthew had first set out, King Manuel responded to his overtures. He only did so because in the intervening years the Portuguese position in the Red Sea had deteriorated markedly.

The Muslim states of the Middle East had come to regard the growing Portuguese control of the Indian Ocean as a genuine threat to the interests of the *Dar al-Islam*, and worked together to contain the interlopers. They had some success in March 1513, when de Albuquerque failed to capture the port of Aden in Yemen by storm, and so lost his chance to command the entrance to the Red Sea. The situation turned yet further against Portuguese ambitions when in 1517 the Ottoman armies wrested Egypt from its Mamluk rulers. Sultan Selim I the Grim added Egypt as a vassal state to his empire, which now stretched from Belgrade on the Danube to Cairo on the Nile, and posted a garrison there. The Hejaz, and with it Mecca, scrambled to recognise his overlordship, as did most of the Muslim states of the Horn of Africa.

Control of the Red Sea was important to the Ottomans, not only because Selim claimed to be the Caliph – or successor of the Prophet and commander of all believers – and so was obliged to protect the Holy Places, but also because of the valuable Indian Ocean trade. The Ottomans therefore began building ships in Suez and their other Red Sea ports with the objective of consolidating their naval supremacy there and eliminating the Portuguese presence. The Portuguese were not prepared to be pushed out without a fight, and it was this that made them actively seek an alliance with Ethiopia.

Unfortunately for the Portuguese, by the time their embassy under Roderigo de Lima (an insufferably haughty young officer) caught up with Lebna Dengal on the distant Shoan plateau in 1520, the earlier Ethiopian eagerness for an alliance had all but evaporated. It was not just that the *negus*, now a proud and self-confident twenty-four year old, had shaken loose from the control of Dowager Queen Eleni, whose policy it had been to seek Portuguese aid.* More than that, he was still bursting with military pride after resoundingly defeating

---

* Queen Eleni would die in 1522.

Adal in 1517 and, so he believed, removing any real need for Portuguese aid against Imam Mahfuz's depredations. Indeed, the *imam* was dead, cornered by Lebna Dengal at Fatagar on a plain surrounded by mountains when his army was encumbered with booty. According to heroic tradition, Mahfuz had valiantly challenged any Christian to fight a duel to the death with him. A monk called Gabra Endreyas ('Servant of Andrew')* responded, and cut off his head. Be that as it may, Lebna Dengal's crushing victory had reasserted Ethiopia's primacy in the Awash valley and left Adal licking its wounds.

So, with Adal apparently knocked out, Lebna Dengal allowed talks with the Portuguese to languish half-heartedly. Nevertheless, he was not so very different from them in entertaining fantasies of conquering Jerusalem and liberating the Holy Land from the yoke of Islam. He was in any case inflamed against the Ottomans, who in 1518 had massacred Ethiopian pilgrims making their way up the Red Sea to Jerusalem – and who would repeat this bloodthirsty deed in 1525. A war against the Ottomans was therefore not entirely out of the question, and in such operations the Portuguese fleet would be vital. Yet, what the *negus* really wanted most from the Portuguese was military experts and gunsmiths to help modernise his forces and introduce them to the new gunpowder technology that his Muslims neighbours were increasingly employing. He was much less keen on meeting their request to establish naval bases on the Ethiopian coast and to make use of the Ethiopian port of Massawa. Therefore, when de Lima finally left his court in 1526, he carried away rich gifts, but no formal military alliance.

The inconclusiveness of the talks signalled the onset of an ever-deepening crisis for Ethiopia. The presence of de Lima's embassy at the *negus'* court over six long years, and the regular visits of Portuguese flotillas to Massawa to maintain contact with the ambassador, were a constant irritant to the Ottomans and deepened their suspicions about Ethiopian intentions. Worse, the departure of the Portuguese mission served as the signal in Adal for the renewal of war under a new and ferocious leader.

Ahmad ibn Ibrahim al-Ghazi, known as Grañ (*gragn* means left-handed in Amharic), was probably of Somali descent and started life as a common

---

* He was a *chavas* who had become a monk after the *negus*, Naod, had ordered the tip of his tongue cut off for uttering treasonable sentiments.

soldier. His military talents raised him to prominence and caught the attention of Imam Mahfuz, who permitted him to marry his daughter, Bati Del Wanbara. She would be his constant companion on his many campaigns, when she earned a reputation for encouraging him to exercise mercy towards his captives. This marital alliance was vital for Grañ, because after his father-in-law's defeat and death he inherited the *imam*'s support-base of warlords and warriors. They were all eager to renew their looting of the Ethiopian highlands, and looked to him to make it possible. Grañ needed little persuading, and with the connivance of most of the amirs of Adal ruthlessly overthrew the sultan. He then placed the sultan's compliant brother on the throne as his puppet and ruled Adal in his name. With the support of the religious leaders of Adal, Grañ next took the title of *imam*. He then built up a formidable coalition of local Muslim forces that included the warlike Somali nomads of the lowlands. Grañ cemented this alliance by marrying his sister to the most important of the Somali warlords.

His preparations all carefully made, in 1527 Grañ proclaimed a *jihad* against the Solomonic kingdom. Volunteers for the holy war flocked in from the Hejaz. Many of the warriors under his command were far better mounted than the Ethiopians – on large Egyptian or Arab steeds. Some had very good cuirasses in the Spanish style with helmets to match, while others wore coats of mail with full sleeves fitting close to the body. They carried spears, silver-hilted sabres and small battleaxes in the Turkish style and were often splendidly turned out in silks and brocades and other materials and accoutrements imported from Egypt and the Indies. The Pasha of Zebid in Yemen, which the Ottomans had conquered in 1525, saw Grañ as a useful regional ally. He not only supplied him with firearms through Adal's port of Zeila, but also despatched units of Ottoman arquebusiers to lend his army an overwhelming technological edge over the Ethiopians. As the Royal Chronicles recorded, to pay for these firearms and Ottoman troops, Grañ 'sold the jewels of his wives and the furniture of his house without holding back anything for himself, desiring nothing but the reward promised by the very high God'.[9]

Grañ's advance deep into the Christian highlands met with staggering success because of his political and military skills. He harnessed the discontents of the repressed Muslim minority and the exploited peasantry, and played to the ambitions of unscrupulous Ethiopian nobles and men-at-arms who entertained no qualms in changing religion if circumstances required. What soon became clear was that this new *jihad* was not going to stop at a series of raids as the previous one had under the leadership of Imam Mahfuz. This time Grañ was intent on a *futah* (permanent conquest of the Christian kingdom and its conversion into a Muslim sultanate).

Lebna Dengal mustered an enormous host to oppose him. However, for all their bravado, his vaunting nobles and their mounted retainers – let alone the untrained militia that filled the plain – were no match for Grañ's forces. His swooping cavalry was more mobile, and the Ethiopians, who had no firearms to speak of, were terrified by the appalling novelty of the arquebuses with which Grañ's elite infantry units were equipped, and by their several small cannons. Besides, Grañ's forces were fired up by their *jihad*. The Royal Chronicles caught their mood in the *imam*'s purported words uttered to encourage his followers in their holy mission: 'Stand fast, and kill the unbelievers! He among you who dies will go to paradise; he who lives will be happy.'[10]

In March 1529, at the Battle of Shimbra-Kure (the Swamp of Chickpeas) on the Shoan plateau, Grañ shattered the much larger Ethiopian army and pushed on remorselessly north across the Ethiopian highlands. His Muslim forces systematically sacked the numerous churches and monasteries – those irreplaceable stores of Ethiopia's art and culture – and slaughtered all the monks and clergy they could lay their hands on. As the Royal Chronicles lamented, the Muslims:

> . . . were the victors in all fights to the east, west, north and south, and destroyed all the churches whose walls were covered with gold, silver, and precious Indian stones; they put to the sword a large number of Christians and led into captivity young men and women and children of both sexes and sold them as slaves.[11]

In 1535 Grañ occupied Tigray province in the far north and destroyed the church at Aksum where the Solomonid kings were crowned. By 1540 he had to all intents and purposes captured Ethiopia and placed its administration under his own amirs and pliant Muslim Ethiopians. He set about systematically exterminating all the Christian monks and clergy and enforced the conversion of the people to Islam. Those who clung to their Christianity he subjected to a heavy *jizya* (poll tax). Many Ethiopians, who had initially supported Grañ out of discontent with the existing system, realised they had exchanged one tyrannical system for another even worse. Nevertheless, it seemed that nothing could prevent Grañ from succeeding in his objective of transforming Christian Ethiopia into a Muslim sultanate.

As for the *negus*, Lebna Dengal, the Royal Chronicles sorrowfully recorded that he was 'chased from his throne and wandered from desert to desert facing hunger, thirst and cold in complete destitution'.[12] Grañ harried him, along with his immediate family and his few remaining supporters, until they finally found refuge at Debre Damo, a monastery on a huge *amba* in northeastern Ethiopia. It was one of those monasteries accessible only by basket drawn up by ropes, and in past ages had been a prison for redundant princes. Yet, despite defeat and betrayal, Lebna Dengal never lost his pride and his determination to recover his throne. In his extremity he looked again to the Portuguese for military aid against Grañ. So desperate was he that in 1535 he went so far as to promise to subject the Ethiopian Church to the authority of the Roman pontiff, in return for help.

The Portuguese Crusade

By this stage, however, Portuguese ability to challenge the Ottomans had waned drastically. In 1535 the Ottomans captured the key port of Basra at the head of the Persian Gulf. Then, in 1538 the fleet of Suleiman Pasha established Ottoman garrisons in all the ports of the Hejaz and sailed on to seize Aden, the key to the entrance to the Red Sea. Thereafter, the Ottoman galleys effectively commanded the waters of the Red Sea, Gulf of Aden and the Persian Gulf. By 1540 they were beginning to cruise into the Indian Ocean, making any contact by sea between Ethiopia and the Portuguese East Indies distinctly hazardous. Faced with the prospect of being driven right away from this growing sphere of Ottoman naval preponderance, the Portuguese felt compelled to make one last attempt to halt the rot.

In 1541 a large naval expedition from Goa under the command of the Governor of India, Estevão da Gama, the second son of the explorer Vasco da Gama, entered the Red Sea with the aim of destroying the Ottoman fleet based at Suez. The Ottomans proved too prepared and strong to risk a major engagement, so the Portuguese fleet slowly withdrew, sacking coastal settlements as it went. While anchored at Massawa during February 1541, da Gama learned from Ethiopian emissaries what had been happening in Ethiopia since de Lima's embassy had departed fifteen years before. Lebna Dengal had died – or had been murdered – in September 1540, and his eighteen-year-old son, Galawdewos, had succeeded him. His widow, the steadfast Sabla Wengal (d.1568), was still on the *amba* of Debre Damo with surviving members of the royal family. Galawdewos had gamely renewed the campaign against Grañ, but the inexperienced young *negus* was enjoying scant military success. Grañ had driven him off far to the south, to the Shoan plateau, away from his mother in Tigray and potential Portuguese aid from the coast.

Desperate for assistance, Sabla Wengal's ambassadors in Massawa, led by the *bahrnagash*, begged da Gama to save Christianity in Ethiopia from the Muslims. As a sweetener, the *bahrnagash* reiterated Lebna Dengal's offer of six years before – to subject the Ethiopian Church to Rome. Here indeed was an irony. The Christian kingdom of Prester John that the Portuguese had once sought to secure as an ally in its worldwide crusade against Islam was about to be snuffed out by their common Muslim foes. Should da Gama risk coming to Ethiopia's assistance, and was there even any point in doing so?

His men effectively took the decision out of da Gama's hands. Humiliated by the failure of their Red Sea campaign, almost the entire complement of da Gama's fleet volunteered to march to the support of the *negus*. Da Gama could not allow this, but decided he could spare 400 Portuguese soldiers, about 1,000 matchlocks and eight pieces of light artillery. To support these matchlockmen he assigned 130 slaves acquired in India, good fighting men who acted as supports to their masters in battle and carried their extra weapons.

Da Gama entrusted the command of the expeditionary force to his younger brother, Cristóvão, Vasco's fourth son. Cristóvão was only twenty-five years old, and his youth led to some disapproving whispers of nepotism. But he had campaign experience in the East Indies and had repeatedly proved his courage, humanity and seamanship during fights and storms at sea. Indeed, despite the discontented muttering, his appointment would turn out to have been a good choice on the part of his brother. If he proved too bold in action – foolhardy even – that was what was required by the honour code of a *fidalgo*. And to his credit, and unlike many officers of his noble status, he was prepared to share hardship and deprivation cheerfully with his men. As a result, he would earn their deep, personal loyalty and, ultimately, their fierce determination to avenge his death.

On Saturday 9 July 1541 da Gama's fleet set sail out of Massawa for Goa. Less than a year later, in May 1542, da Gama was superseded as Governor of India. His departure meant that there would be no continuing official commitment to the little expeditionary force he had left behind in Ethiopia. That would come as no surprise to Cristóvão da Gama's men. When they began their march inland to the cheery sound of their fife and pipe band, they knew that to all intents and purposes they were being abandoned to their fate. Consciously, they regarded themselves as crusaders, even Christian martyrs, setting forth under the banner of the Order of Christ on a chivalric quest from which there was scant hope of ever returning alive to Portugal.

Da Gama's force was accompanied by the *bahrnagash* as it struggled some sixty miles up the steep and rugged escarpment to the tableland, manhandling its artillery and baggage for lack of draught animals. It halted in rainy weather at Debarwa, the *bahrnagash*'s tumbledown provincial capital, where (as has been described earlier) Queen Sabla Wengal joined them from Debre Damo. Galawdewos was in Shoa, 400 miles to the south, and Grañ was strategically encamped midway between them on the northeastern shore of Lake Tana. The Portuguese had still to grasp how truly desperate the Ethiopian position was, and did not understand how difficult it would be to join up with Galawdewos, whose army they presumed to be much larger than it was.

Da Gama remained encamped at Debarwa for the rest of the rainy season. With the queen residing in his camp with her daughters and attendant courtiers, it clearly had taken on the aura of the *katama*. While at Debarwa, da Gama busied himself preparing for the coming campaign. He had sledges made for his artillery and baggage, and commandeered oxen to draw them through the mud of the practically non-existent tracks. Finally, on 15 December 1541 the Portuguese resumed their march with the objective of joining up with Galawdewos, whom they hoped was moving northwards towards them. Sabla Wengal went with them, attended by her daughters, a retinue of nobles and fifty horsemen, just as she would have accompanied the *negus* when his *katama* moved on.

They headed south, following the eastern rim of the tableland. The going was extremely difficult over the broken terrain, and they had many deep ravines to negotiate without the benefit of bridges. Da Gama was in no hurry, however, because there were political as well as military goals to be won. This was the *katama* on its stately progress, and the queen used the powerful armed presence of the Portuguese to put fresh heart into her subjects along the way, and to persuade the local nobility to transfer their allegiance from Grañ back to the *negus*.

On 2 February 1542 the Portuguese tasted their first blood a hundred miles south of Debarwa, when they captured Amba Senait, held by a small Muslim garrison. Before the assault, Sabla Wengal told da Gama that she thought the attempt too daring for so small a number, but in true bombastic style he replied that 'she should fear nothing, as they were Portuguese'.[13]

When the Portuguese advanced to the attack, the defenders fired arrows at them and rolled rocks down the narrow mountain paths. Realising they had few, if any, firearms, the Portuguese quickly cowed them with their greatly superior artillery and matchlock fire. Then, with da Gama bounding vaingloriously in the lead, they stormed the summit shouting their battle cry of 'São Tiago!' After some sharp hand-to-hand fighting, the Portuguese secured control of the mountaintop with only eight men killed. In earnest of the remorseless crusade he was waging, da Gama then ordered all the *Mouro* prisoners to be killed. On the other hand, he released a number of Christian women being held captive on the *amba*. He was uncertain what to do with the Muslim women taken prisoner, and sent them bound to Sabla Wengal's camp. Like da Gama she was unwilling to show any mercy in this religious war, so she refused even to see the unfortunate women and sent them all to execution.

The Portuguese Victory on the Antalo Plain

Word of the Portuguese victory on Amba Senait rapidly spread round about and encouraged the local peasantry to bring in ample supplies to the Portuguese. But it also roused a furious Grañ to action. Unaware that he was readying to strike, the Portuguese tarried at Amba Senait to tend their wounded and accumulate supplies, and resumed their march south only at the end of February. Progress was slower than ever. Da Gama had sent Francisco Velho and forty men back to the coast on a mission to collect ammunition and supplies from a Portuguese vessel reported to be in harbour at Massawa, and did not want to move on too far before they returned. Consequently, da Gama had marched only as far as the Antalo plain in Wajarat, fifty miles from Amba Senait, when on 1 April he learned to his shock that Grañ was fast approaching with a large army.

Despite his understandable alarm, da Gama believed he could not retreat without losing all the credit he had won thus far in the eyes of the Ethiopians. Rather than throw it away, he decided to make a stand. He therefore pitched camp on a hillock in the plain with the queen and her attendants securely in the centre. There was only just time before Grañ arrived for da Gama to fortify his position lightly with a surrounding *zariba* (palisade of timber). To defend it, da Gama had a mere 350 Portuguese, 100 or so of their armed slaves, and perhaps 200 Ethiopians. Approaching them, according to hyperbolic Portuguese estimates, were 15,000 infantry, all either archers or buckler men with sword and spear, and a striking force of about 1,500 cavalry. In all essentials, this host was still a typical Ethiopian army, but for an additional element that made it lethally different. Grañ always retained 200 Ottoman arquebusiers in his service. In the past their firepower had always proved sufficient to rout any gunpowder-less Ethiopian force that dared stand against them, and their presence in the field would pose the Portuguese with their greatest challenge.

On 3 April Grañ's host came on with tumultuous cries and deafening martial music to invest the Portuguese camp tightly. The defenders easily spotted Grañ himself when he rode forward to scout their position. A bodyguard of 300 glittering horsemen swirled about him and displayed his personal banners: two large, white ones with red crescent moons and a red one with a white crescent.

In keeping with chivalrous local custom, before he unleashed his attack Grañ sent a herald to the Portuguese camp. This individual, whose person was regarded as sacrosanct, offered the Portuguese Grañ's clemency if they abandoned Sabla Wengal and the Ethiopian cause, and came over to his side. Grañ had instructed his herald to refer insultingly to the foreigners as 'monks', which in Ethiopia implied they were people of little worth. Swallowing the insult, da Gama dealt courteously with Grañ's emissary. He then despatched his own herald, a slave very richly dressed to impress the *Mouros*, to carry his reply, written in Arabic, to the *imam*. It was couched in proud and uncompromising terms, declaring that da Gama had come to aid the Christian

King of Ethiopia and that he obeyed only the King of Portugal. There was more to da Gama's diplomatic riposte than words. As tit-for-tat for being called a 'monk', he conceived of a singularly provocative gesture aimed at impugning Grañ's manhood before his warriors. He had his herald deliver the *imam* 'small tweezers for the eyebrows, and a very large looking-glass – making him out a woman'. As was intended, this insult (so de Castanhoso reported with considerable understatement) 'did not please the Moor'.[14] Indeed, he neither forgave nor forgot it, and one day would pay da Gama back most grievously.

Stung to a fury, Grañ sprang up from his table where he was eating with his captains, and called his men to arms. His arquebusiers, supported by swarms of horsemen, moved forward to take up position behind stone breastworks and other cover in range of the Portuguese camp. Their fire harried the defenders ceaselessly until the Portuguese dislodged them in a series of sorties, driving them back with push of pike and arquebus fire. Despite this small success, da Gama knew he could not stay where he was. The besiegers had cut off his supplies and he had no option but to attempt to break out.

At dawn on 4 April he marched southwards out of his camp over the Antalo plain with mountain chains hemming it in to the west and south. The mountainsides were covered by hovering Ethiopians under arms who would not join Grañ but dared not commit to the Portuguese because they considered the odds stacked up too heavily against them. Da Gama's arquebusiers were formed in a bristling square with all the non-combatants (including the queen), baggage wagons and artillery carriages sheltering behind them in the middle of the formation. Thirty-six years later King Sebastião would draw up his forces in the exact same way at the Battle of the Three Kings. Da Gama enjoyed more success than he, however.

When Grañ's forces saw the Portuguese advance out of their camp into the open plain, they raised a wild, joyous noise of shouting, trumpets and kettledrums because they believed the small Portuguese square was now at their mercy. They were mistaken. The Portuguese moved forward slowly but deliberately, firing in all directions as rapidly as they could at the crowds of enemy that hemmed them closely about. Their firepower proved enough to clear a path through their foes until they came under effective counter-fire from Grañ's Ottoman matchlockmen. When the Portuguese began taking casualties their square faltered, and came to an uncertain halt. Da Gama himself was lightly wounded in the leg which, de Castanhoso glowingly reported, 'was for him an honour, for, wounded as he was, he behaved himself and acted as we find no examples of any notable captain in ancient or modern histories'.[15] But chivalrous comportment was not enough to turn the tide. It appeared inevitable that Grañ's men must soon break the hard-pressed Portuguese square. Once they did so and the infidels lost formation, it would be over with them.

Happily for the Portuguese, at this critical moment a shot fired by Pero Deça, a *fidalgo* and renowned marksman, wounded Grañ, who was fighting in the front rank. The ball passed right through his thigh and killed the bay horse he was riding. When Grañ's ensigns saw him fall they lowered their three banners thrice as a signal for retreat. His bodyguards then carried him from the field to a hill nearby to have his wound dressed. Seeing their enemies suddenly fall back in confusion, the Portuguese sounded their trumpets and kettledrums in triumph. But they were too exhausted to take proper advantage of their unexpected deliverance, and in any case had not enough horses to mount an effective pursuit. So they encamped where they stood and Queen Sabla Wengal's attendants pitched her tent as a sign of victory.

The queen and her women then set about tending the wounded as best they could. There were more than fifty of them, most, like da Gama, the victims of matchlock fire. Eleven others had been killed. For such a small force, these losses were not negligible. The Muslim forces had suffered worse. Among their dead that lay in untidy, little heaps across the plain were four of Grañ's captains, thirty of his prized Ottoman arquebusiers and forty horses.

The encounter was not yet over, however. The Portuguese position in the middle of the plain was a poor one, and da Gama moved forward several hundred yards to encamp on a more defensible range of hills with a good supply of water. There the Portuguese stayed to recuperate and had to look on impotently while reinforcements poured into Grañ's camp. Realising that to delay further would only make a bad situation worse, da Gama decided to offer battle again on Sunday 16 April. The Ethiopian patriarch, João Bermudez,* recorded that when the queen realised that battle was about to

---

* Bermudez was an emissary of the Ethiopian king to the Portuguese, whom Pope Paul III had appointed the Roman Catholic Patriarch of Ethiopia. He accompanied da Gama's expedition and harboured many pretensions about his dubious status. His often untrustworthy and self-serving account was published in 1565.

be joined again she and her companions 'were seized with such great fear that they did not know what to do: so much so that, although they were eating when they heard of the Moor's approach they wanted to leave their food'. But Bermudez encouraged them by reminding them that 'for as our Lord had given us the past victory He would also give us one now'.[16]

Da Gama drew up his men once again in their defensive hedgehog and marched out to face Grañ's men massing to receive them. Grañ's wound would not permit him to mount a horse, so he led his men from a litter carried on the shoulders of some of his bodyguards. His infantry came on well, somewhat protected by their bucklers from Portuguese fire, and at one stage Grañ's cavalry surged forward, almost breaking the Portuguese square. The Portuguese finally repulsed the cavalry by detonating firebombs and powder pots that caused their horses to bolt over the plain. Finally, unable to penetrate the Portuguese square because of the steady arquebus fire, morale collapsed in Grañ's army. It broke off the engagement and retired in far greater disorder than it had at the end of the first battle twelve days earlier.

As before, the Portuguese could not convert their enemies' retreat into a rout for lack of horses. Nevertheless, this time they advanced to capture Grañ's camp, an act that, according to the recognised customs of warfare, confirmed their victory. However, this time they had suffered slightly more casualties than in the first battle of Antalo; once again, these were mainly from missiles such as arquebus balls and arrows. More than sixty of them were wounded and fourteen killed, including their experienced and popular master gunner, who was a particular loss.

An immediate and heartening consequence followed on the Portuguese victory. Some of the Ethiopians who had been fighting on Grañ's side decided the moment was opportune to defect to the Portuguese camp. As for Grañ, his setback on the plain of Antalo – his first defeat in more than a decade – forced him to retire to a fortified camp at Zabu, ninety miles away and halfway down the escarpment overlooking the Danakil desert to the east. It was a well-chosen position because it commanded the line of communications down to the coast, and on from there across the Red Sea to Zebid, where the Ottoman pasha was the commander of the Strait of Bab el-Mandeb. Zebid was where the matchlockmen in Grañ's regular pay were recruited, and he needed to reinforce them if he were to succeed against the superior firepower of the Portuguese.

The Battle of Wofla

For their part, the Portuguese could not advance further south to link up with Galawdewos and his forces because the advent of the rainy season made travel with all their baggage and artillery impracticable. So they halted in their new camp at Wofla on the plateau, sixty miles south of Antalo. It was an inaccessible spot which the Portuguese had reached by such a narrow path through rocks and crags that their artillery had had to be carried on the backs of porters. Da Gama positioned his camp at the base of a hill and fortified it as best he could with an encircling palisade. His men settled down in huts built of wood and straw by the sympathetic local people, who also brought in supplies.

Much to da Gama's relief, he was reinforced at Wofla by the safe return of the forty men he had despatched months earlier to Massawa. However, their mission had been a failure because they brought back no supplies of arms and ammunition. They had not been able to make any contact with the Portuguese ship reported to be at the port, because Ottoman galleys had driven it away. But even though they replaced the casualties suffered at the two battles on the Antalo plain, da Gama's force was not much to boast about. Besides his 350 or so tough Portuguese arquebusiers (many of them still recovering from their wounds) and their armed slaves, whose numbers were no longer being recorded, he had only thirty Ethiopian horsemen and 500 foot under the *bahrnagash*. He also had Sabla Wengal and her little court in his precarious care.

Da Gama's camp at Wofla was only twenty miles northwest of the *imam*'s encampment at Zabu, but Grañ's position was screened from Portuguese sight by hills, and for lack of scouts they had no means of knowing what Grañ was up to. They had in fact real cause for concern. Grañ fully understood that the recent Portuguese victories had been largely due to their superior firepower, and he was busily engaged in remedying deficiencies in that department.

Over the next few months of the rainy season the *imam* obtained 900 new Ottoman matchlockmen from the Pasha of Zebid, who was concerned by Portuguese military activity in Ethiopia. In return, the pasha required that Grañ pay the Ottoman sultan tribute, an obligation that the wily Grañ believed he could later wriggle out of. Crucially, Grañ's matchlockmen now outnumbered da Gama's by three to one. Moreover, the pasha also sent Grañ ten field bombards that were superior to the Portuguese field artillery. In addition, as many as 600 Arab volunteers crossed the Red Sea to reinforce Grañ, as well as numbers of skilled Persian bowmen. Twenty aristocratic Ottoman horsemen, exotically sporting gilt stirrup irons (Ethiopians rode with a ring for the big toe) and riding iron-shod horses (Ethiopian horses went unshod) also joined the *imam*'s army.

Thanks to these reinforcements, by the end of August 1542 Grañ's force was overwhelmingly superior to da Gama's in both numbers and armaments. To make matters worse for the Portuguese, Cristóvão learned that the units Galawdewos had raised in distant Shoa were too small and weak for him to risk marching north and forcing a passage through Grañ's army to join him. That intelligence finally opened da Gama's eyes to the extreme weakness of Galawdewos' situation. Until then, he had been able to delude himself that the *negus* had considerable forces at his command. Now he understood with a lurch of the heart that his tiny force stood alone against Grañ's ever-growing host.

In late August Grañ's forces advanced from Zabu on the Portuguese camp at Wofla. This time da Gama had little choice but to stand as best he could behind his poor defences. To venture out into the open as he had on the plain of Antalo against such huge odds only invited disaster. At daybreak on 29 August (ominously, it was the anniversary of the beheading of St John the Baptist) Grañ's army closed in on the Portuguese camp. Da Gama's Ethiopian troops took one look at Grañ's new artillery and at his dauntingly large contingent of matchlockmen proudly arrayed in the van and prudently decamped.

Even though their military value had always been in doubt, to lose half his garrison just as the battle opened was deeply unsettling for da Gama. Gamely, he did what he could with his Portuguese arquebusiers. He posted small advanced detachments on three nearby hills and a battery on another to catch Grañ's advancing forces in enfilading fire. Despite their bravery, these 'forlorn hopes' did not prove effective in slowing down Grañ's complete investment of the camp, and were rapidly overrun. The Portuguese then tried sallying out of the palisade surrounding the camp in small groups armed with matchlocks and pikes. Their objective was to drive the Muslims away from whatever stretch of the defences they were particularly threatening. Grañ's men had an effective counter to this ploy. They fell back rapidly before each furious Portuguese rush. Then, when the Portuguese began to withdraw after making little meaningful contact, their matchlockmen rallied to shoot them down from a safe distance.

By evening, after a terrible day of unremitting combat, the surviving Portuguese were in desperate straits. Da Gama had a matchlock ball lodged in his right knee and another in his right arm above the elbow. The shot had shattered his humerus and he was in agony from the wound. Four out of his five captains were dead and more than half his men with them. The Muslims had at last taken the palisade, captured da Gama's standard and were beginning to overrun his camp. The queen and her women were weeping in panic in her house in the middle of the enclosure. They were doing their best to tend the forty or more wounded who had been brought in, but enemy shot was now whistling through the structure, endangering all inside.

Night then mercifully fell for the Portuguese. Da Gama had to be urgently persuaded to abandon his camp and (as he saw it) along with it his honour. But at last the remnants of the garrison withdrew up the wooded hill overlooking the camp. Sabla Wengal got away with them, but most of the wounded in her house were abandoned to their fate. The hill was too steep for pursuing cavalry, but enemy infantry could keep up with the fugitives. Fortunately for them the pursuit was slack, because Grañ's men were too distracted looting the Portuguese camp. The exhausted and panicking Portuguese were nevertheless being harried up the hill in the dark over unseen rocks and gullies and other obstacles when a sudden, huge explosion in the camp distracted their pursuers, and allowed them to break away. It seems that, when the looters entered the queen's house and started slaughtering the wounded lying there, either a Portuguese or one of the queen's women who had not fled (accounts differ) ignited a store of gunpowder and blew up the makeshift hospital and all inside it.

During the desperate and disorganised retreat, da Gama and fourteen close companions, all of them wounded, fell behind and became separated from the main pack of fugitives. Unable to go on, they took cover in some thickets. There Grañ's men captured them at first light, their hiding place betrayed by a local Muslim woman. Da Gama, in terrible pain from his wounds, was dragged off directly to Grañ's tent. There he was thrown down before the *imam*, who was gloating over a horrid pile of 160 Portuguese 'heads' – at least, that is what the Portuguese chroniclers, to spare their readers, called the severed genitals or foreskins Grañ's warriors had cut off their slain foes and brought back in triumph to their general. This custom seems to have been a common one in Ethiopian military society, where, as Father Lobo* witnessed in the 1620s, noses, ears and heads might also be brought back as battle trophies. Some 200 years later, Father Prutky described a scene in which the *negus'* warriors carried their gruesome trophies back in red bundles to lay at his feet. Then, with the whole court looking on, and to shouting and trumpet fanfares, the champions would: 'leap in the air with their weapons, demonstrate their trophies with hands held high, perform gymnastic feats like acrobats, look to the emperor for applause and reward, and in similar manner perform over again their feats of military prowess'.[17]

Grañ forced da Gama to contemplate the loathsome heap of bloodied trophies hacked from his comrades' bodies. The *imam* then had him stripped and scourged before the assembled troops, who yelled insults at him. To humiliate him further, his tormentors next buffeted his face with his own slaves' captured shoes (a supreme insult), and teased his beard into wicks worked with wax, which they set alight. Grañ kept the best for last. Now was the precious moment when he could be avenged for da Gama's calculated insult before their first battle. He ordered Cristóvão's eyebrows and eyelashes to be pulled out with the offending tweezers the Portuguese herald had delivered, 'saying that he had always kept them for him (da Gama), as he and his followers did not use them'.[18]

Satisfied at last that he had sufficiently shamed his tough adversary, who throughout his ordeal had manfully continued to scream back defiance and invective, Grañ beheaded him with his own hand. Ethiopians later affirmed to Father Páez that 'there rose a spring of water from the very spot where his body fell and his blood was spilt', and that washing in the spring miraculously cured various diseases. This they attributed to God 'wanting to honour His servant and to show how much he had pleased Him in life and death' as a martyr.[19]

Grañ had da Gama's body quartered and the pieces sent around his realm with skin from his head to advertise his victory. In 1626 the Jesuit missionary, Father Lobo, relying on local lore, believed he had found da Gama's skull and

---

* The Portuguese Jesuit, Jerónimo Lobo, arrived in Ethiopia in 1625 and spent the next nine years there. He left a manuscript describing his experiences.

some of his bones. He sent them to the viceroy of India, 'and, along with them, Dom Christovão's helmet, which a great lord of the lands had preserved with great esteem along with an image of Our Lady, which had belonged to the same'.[20]

Grañ's victory at Wofla seemed complete. He had killed nearly all the Portuguese leaders and about 200 of the rank and file. He had captured all their artillery, many of their matchlocks and much ammunition. There consequently seemed no further point in retaining so many of his Ottoman matchlockmen, especially since they put him under the obligation of tribute to the Pasha of Zebid. Grañ therefore dismissed all except his usual contingent of 200. These he thought sufficient to finish off young Galawdewos, as they had his father, Negus Lebna Dengal. Thoroughly satisfied by the turn of events, Grañ retired to his favoured headquarters on the northeastern shore of Lake Tana.

Meanwhile, fifty of the escaping Portuguese under Manuel da Cunha had fled north towards Debarwa, where da Gama had first encamped in 1541, hoping to find a ship at Massawa. Another 120 took refuge with Sabla Wengal on Amba Sel, a great mountain seventy miles south of the fatal battlefield. There, in mid-September, these marooned remnants of da Gama's expedition were finally joined by Galawdewos at the head of a contingent of several thousand Ethiopians. Galawdewos, as he later wrote to the Governor of India, 'bitterly wept for the death of so many Christian strangers who had come to help us', and particularly for da Gama who 'died like a very valiant and courageous martyr of Jesu Christ, fighting the Moors'.[21] Cristóvão da Gama himself could not have described his own death better.

The Battle of Weyna Dega

For the forces gathered on Amba Sel's broad crown, time was needed to regroup. The Portuguese had to bring up fresh arms from the depot they had established at Debre Damo on their march south, and had to decide who should take over da Gama's command. It seems Galawdewos made the cultural blunder of supporting the candidature of Ayres Dias, who, as a mulatto and certainly not a *fidalgo*, most of the surviving Portuguese would never have accepted as their leader. However, precisely because of his outsider status he had consorted more closely with the Ethiopians than had other Portuguese, and had taken the trouble to learn their language. The upshot of the abrasive leadership crisis was a decision not to select anyone as captain. Instead, as de Castanhoso expressed it: 'We desired none save the banner of Sancta Misericordia [Holy Compassion] to lead us, for it was not to be anticipated that we should follow another, having lost what we had lost.'[22]

Galawdewos proved a more gifted soldier than had his father. During late 1542 he won some minor victories over Grañ's local commanders with the aid of the Portuguese arquebusiers still at his disposal. These successes, coupled with his inspiring leadership, began to attract more and more Ethiopians to his cause. By February 1543 he believed that his army had grown as large as it ever would, and that the time has come to confront Grañ directly. For his part the *imam*, overconfident and comfortable in his camp at Lake Tana with his wife and children, thoroughly underestimated the threat Galawdewos posed. He did little to prepare to fight him in a campaign that would prove short, sharp and, for him, a very unwelcome surprise.

On Shrove Tuesday, 6 February 1543, Galawdewos and his Portuguese allies began their march northwestwards towards Lake Tana, 200 miles away. Galawdewos had some 8,000 foot, armed with their bows, bucklers and spears, and 500 horse. Many men of the small Portuguese contingent of 120 or so still had open wounds, but all were determined on revenge. About sixty of them were mounted on horses given them by the *negus*. This time Galawdewos left his mother, Sabla Wengal, behind in relative safety at Amba Sel.

In mid-February, the allies came upon Grañ at Weyna Dega in the hills close to the eastern shore of Lake Tana and pitched their camp in sight of him. Grañ was astonished by their audacity, and was especially amazed that the Portuguese should attempt to beard him after their catastrophic defeat at Wofla. For a couple of days the two armies skirmished with each other. The Ethiopians enjoyed such a string of successes under the inspired leadership of one of their generals called Azmach Keflo that Grañ arranged to have him treacherously shot down during a parley. The death of such a favourite captain was bad for Ethiopian morale, while the menacing noise of repeated salutes fired by Grañ's superior artillery echoing among the hills further frayed Ethiopian nerves. Realising that many of his men, hovering uncertainly on the hilltops, were about to melt away, Galawdewos decided to offer battle on the morning of 22 February 1543.

After general confession, the allies advanced, with the Portuguese in the centre of the vanguard with the banner of Sancta Misericordia raised on high, flanked on either side by 250 Ethiopian horse and 3,500 foot armed with buckler, sword, spear, bow and sling. The *negus* led the rearguard, which consisted of the remaining half of the Ethiopian cavalry and infantry. Grañ's dispositions were a mirror copy of Galawdewos', and his men were similarly armed. As always, he positioned himself in the van of his army. He and his 200 matchlockmen were in the centre with 600 of his excellent cavalry in their steel cuirasses and 7,000 infantry on their flanks. A second 'battle' followed behind with numbers of cavalry and infantry equal to those in the leading one.

Grañ's army was double the size of that of the allies, and superior in training. He skilfully exploited his greater numbers to fling out his troops to envelope Galawdewos' flanks and hold them fast in their grip. Meanwhile, his artillery, matchlockmen, archers and slingers pounded Galawdewos' ensnared line with every kind of lethal projectile. But this time the Ethiopians, led by their charismatic young *negus*, held on grimly as arrows and stones clattered down on their shields and as far deadlier cannon and musket balls drilled holes through their ranks.

As for the little band of Portuguese in the van, their quarrel was a very personal one with the *imam* himself. Many of them were mounted, and this allowed them, with support from Ethiopian cavalry, to force their way through the press of enemies. They made straight at Grañ, where he sat conspicuously on his white horse in the midst of his matchlockmen, a splendidly dressed Turkish horseman on either side of him. João Galego fought his way close enough to fire a ball straight through Grañ's chest before the *imam*'s companions cut him down. Grañ fell over his saddlebow and was led dying from the field. Some 300 years later they were still showing the tree Grañ is supposed to have struck in pain and fury with his sabre, realising that death had finally come for him.

As had happened at the first battle of Antalo, once Grañ's men saw him wounded they lost heart, and soon his whole army was breaking apart in flight. Only forty of his matchlockmen escaped, but they and some 300 horsemen of the guard protecting Grañ's doughty widow, Bati Del Wanbara, managed to carry her away with them to the coast, along with the *imam*'s entire treasure. Their son, Mehmed, fell captive into the allies' hands. He was brought grovelling to Galawdewos, who exercised diplomatic clemency and kept him alive for future prisoner exchanges. Otherwise, the victors gave quarter to none save the women and children they found in Grañ's camp. Many of these women were Christians who had been kept in bondage or concubinage by the Muslims, and they were greeted with tears of joy by their rescuers, many of whom were family members.

With a merry din of muskets and captured artillery Galawdewos' celebrating warriors brought Grañ's bleeding head to the *negus*, who had it set upon a spear. He first sent the gruesome trophy to his mother, Sabla Wengal, who had suffered such loss and hardship at the *imam*'s hands, and then had it shown about all the country to prove that Grañ was truly dead. And Grañ's death did indeed show just how essential his personal leadership had been for his *jihad*, for once he was no more his army dispersed and his Muslim sultanate rapidly collapsed.

The End of the Portuguese Presence in Ethiopia

Thanks to his decisive victory at Weyna Dega, Galawdewos could set about reclaiming his kingdom. However, the future was less rosy for the Portuguese arquebusiers without whom he could never have won the battle. Quite simply, they were marooned. Their compatriots would never risk running the gauntlet of the Ottoman fleet to take them off at Massawa. A very few did manage to find passage on chance passing ships, but most had no option but to settle down in Ethiopia, marry local women and gradually merge into the population. Thirteen years after the battle, ninety-three were reported still to be alive, and to be living like Ethiopians.

Galawdewos had the truly daunting task of rebuilding the political and cultural framework of Christian Ethiopia. Despite the fact that he was deeply orthodox and was determined to rehabilitate the Church, that central pillar of the Solomonic kingdom, Islam remained entrenched on the plateau. Moreover, tensions between the *negus* and his ambitious nobility remained as great as ever. Worse yet, large areas of the highlands had been devastated and dislocated by decades of war and abandoned by their longstanding frontier garrisons. That left the defenceless and displaced peasantry vulnerable to armed encroachment by the peoples of the plains below. Even before Grañ's defeat and death, the Cushite-speaking Oromo (or Galla) of the semidesert to the south of the plateau, who believed in the sky god Waqa and were neither Christian nor Muslim, were making deep inroads into the highlands. By the end of the sixteenth century the Oromo gained control over much of the south-central Ethiopian highlands, and the Ethiopian population there was absorbed into Oromo society, adopting its culture and ethnicity.

Faced with such intractable problems, within a few years Galawdewos began to think it would be an excellent idea to renew an alliance with the Portuguese, who had been so instrumental in rescuing his kingdom from Grañ. The Portuguese knew that, realistically, they were no longer in any position to intervene militarily in the Horn of Africa or Red Sea. On the other hand, by this juncture the Roman Catholic Counter-Reformation was in full, triumphalist flood in Portugal, and Galawdewos' diplomatic approach presented an opportunity to further its proselytising agenda. The Portuguese therefore intimated that their condition for an alliance was the reconciliation of the Ethiopian and Latin Churches under the authority of Rome. Galawdewos, under increasing pressure from the Oromo and a temporarily revitalised Adal,* warily accepted these terms. In 1555 Jesuit missionaries† duly entered Ethiopia. However, their religious militancy and doctrinal rigidity soon proved a disruptive embarrassment. In 1556 Galawdewos refused point-blank to convert and in the end did not secure Portuguese military assistance.

Nevertheless, Galawdewos retained his admiration for Portuguese military technology and training, as did his successors. After all, it was clearly disciplined Portuguese firepower that had won Ethiopia back from Grañ. Successive rulers made efforts to equip the Ethiopian forces with matchlocks, and by the 1630s they had about 1,500 of them. But without proper training or discipline matchlocks were little help in withstanding the mounted Oromo spearmen, and the proud *chavas* of the *negus'* army with their aristocratic code of honour continued to dominate military practice. They proved unable to defend Ethiopia from the enemies threatening it on every side, and Ethiopian

---

* In 1559 a new leader of Adal, Nur Ibn Mudi, would raid the Ethiopian heartland and kill Galawdewos in battle. The Oromo ambushed him on his way back to Adal and hacked his army to pieces.

† The Society of Jesus was founded by St Ignatius of Loyola and received papal approval in 1540. It was a missionary order, dedicated to the 'propagation and defence of the faith'.

kings consequently began to avoid the pitched battles of the past and to rely instead on walled defences built on the flat-topped *ambas*.

Their deteriorating situation revived the lure of a Portuguese alliance. Negus Susneyos (r.1607–1632) attempted to renew ties and gain access to Portuguese weaponry and technology by being received into the Latin Church by Jesuits missionaries still active in Ethiopia. All he achieved was to provoke popular revolts by his subjects, who remained determinedly attached to the traditions and doctrine of the Ethiopian Church and bitterly resentful of the Jesuits. In 1634 his son Fasiladas (r.1632–1667) expelled all Jesuits and executed their Ethiopian converts. When in 1638 Fasiladas discovered a few Jesuits still ministering secretly to their tiny congregations, he had them hanged.

With that, all contact between Portugal and Ethiopia ceased utterly, leaving the realm of Prester John more isolated from Europe than it had been for centuries. In Ethiopia the self-sacrificing, crusading role the Portuguese had played in rescuing it from Muslim rule would be remembered – if at all – as the stuff of legend. As for the Portuguese, nothing whatsoever remained of de Albuquerque's high ambitions for control of the Red Sea and the Horn of Africa.

CHAPTER FOUR

God Drove Them from Fort Jesus

Ali Bey Seizes Mombasa

Its triangular sails filled with the monsoon winds blowing steadily from the northeast in the early months of 1585, a solitary oared galley, built low in the water, slipped down the northern Swahili coast. By the late sixteenth century the only galleys in these waters were pirate vessels. They lurked among the off-shore islands and bent their oars in short, violent bursts of speed to seize unwary merchant craft. This particular galley was something more than a mere pirate ship, however, despite the unsavoury appearance of its crew, fifty scrapings from the Red Sea ports. Its commander was Amir Ali Bey, and he sailed with the official blessing of the Ottoman Vizier of Arabia, Amir Asenasi. While his official mission was to reconnoitre the coast for future Ottoman operations against the Portuguese, he was also 'licensed' to harry them as he went. This made Ali Bey a privateer rather than a lawless pirate, and meant he could invoke the resounding Ottoman name to secure the assistance of the Swahili towns against their infidel overlord. Fortunately for him it did not prevent him from simultaneously making himself as rich as he could from plundering the Portuguese.

Ali Bey could confidently expect the Swahili to support him because the Christian interlopers had thoroughly alienated the people of the coast. 'Proud or violent as a Portuguese'[1] went the bitter Swahili saying. Not that there were many of them. This part of the coast was less commercially significant than Moçambique to the far south, with its lucrative trade in gold and ivory, and only a thin scattering of several hundred Portuguese had settled from Pate Island in the north to Pemba Island in the south. However, those few who had were only too typical of former Portuguese *soldados* (young, unmarried men

who had sailed out to the Indies as soldiers) and other drifters throughout
the *Estado da Índia*. Too insignificant socially to enjoy the lucrative grants and
offices that always went to *fidalgos*, the *soldados* made do as informal settlers
along the loosely controlled margins of the *Estado da Índia*. On the northern
Swahili coast they operated as private traders in co-operation with Gujarati
and Arab merchants, kept native wives or mistresses along with sundry slaves,
and surrounded themselves with dependents and hangers-on.

Many were settled in their unfortified *feitoria* in Malindi, where they were
welcome because the sultan was the oldest and most dependable ally the
Portuguese had on the north coast. Nevertheless, their largest concentration
was in Mombasa, which they preferred as a market for ivory, coir and other
goods. Residing there was a risk, because they knew the townspeople would
never forgive the brutal Portuguese sackings of their town in 1505 and again
in 1528. To add to their nagging unease, the Portuguese were aware that they
were profoundly unpopular for attempting to convert the Muslim Swahili to
Christianity. The offended Swahili would hiss at them as they went by: 'Go
away Manoel [their name for the Portuguese], you have made us hate you, go,
and carry your cross with you.'[2]

It was not only the Swahili of the coast whom the Portuguese settlers had
to fear. A few miles inland from the narrow coastal strip with its trading ports
and palm plantations lay a belt of cosily fertile hills and valleys. The Mijikenda
were settled there, a Cushite-speaking farming folk whom the Oromo (or
Galla) – the very same people who even then were aggressively spilling across
the Ethiopian highlands – had driven south from the Horn of Africa during
the course of the sixteenth century. The Mijikenda lived in large villages
fortified against further attacks by the Oromo and other pastoralist peoples
who roamed the plains of the *nyika*. (The *nyika* is what the people of the coast
called the frightening, unexplored wilderness that stretched endlessly into the
bowels of Africa on the far side of the low barrier of familiar hills.) Trade goods
usually passed peaceably enough between the coast and the Mijikenda. Even
so, the Swahili and Portuguese merchants were very wary of the Mijikenda,
who fought with bows and poisoned arrows and who were not at all averse to
raiding the coastal strip or to cutting off essential supplies to the towns if they
wished to make a point. Many Swahili towns consequently paid them a form
of tribute to keep them sweet and trade moving. With more unpredictable

consequences towns might also strike military alliances with the Mijikenda to aid them in their frequent petty wars against their neighbouring city states.

The Portuguese were aware that all these simmering threats, resentments and uncertainties jeopardised their continued presence on the northern Swahili coast. However, by the end of the sixteenth century the *Estado da Índia* was dangerously overextended and facing hard choices over priorities. It had more than forty isolated forts and *feitorias* to defend, and these were dotted irregularly at strategic points along the coasts of Africa and Asia all the way from Sofala at the southern extremity of the Swahili coast to Nagasaki in Japan.

In this essentially maritime empire naval supremacy was the key to their security. By the late sixteenth century the fully rigged, decked Portuguese sailing warships of up to 1,000 tons were built strong enough to carry as many as fifty cast-metal guns firing fourteen-pound iron shot. These cannon delivered the devastating broadsides that blew the lightly built, less heavily gunned vessels of the Indian Ocean out of the water. Ironically, ease of initial conquest deluded the Portuguese into believing that they had the naval resources to control the vast ocean distances. In reality, there were not nearly enough Portuguese warships for them to be everywhere danger threatened. Unavoidably, Portuguese maritime power was at its most effective in the seas closest to their main bases: Goa (the only one with shipyards) and Diu, both on the west coast of India; Melaka in Indonesia; Hormuz at the entrance to the Persian Gulf; and Moçambique Island on the southern Swahili coast.

Otherwise, in order that distant *feitorias* were not left defenceless until a naval task force could be mounted to rescue them from attack, the Portuguese were obliged to shoulder the crippling expense of constructing massive, permanent fortresses to protect their key harbours. In the remoter regions of their far-flung empire, however, they did so only if the cost seemed justified. The Swahili north coast was not such a place. Therefore, instead of asserting their presence there through a great fortress and its garrison, the Portuguese decided – despite all the obvious dangers menacing it – that for the time being it was enough to control the Swahili north coast indirectly through client rulers such as the Sultan of Malindi. At its best, this solution was ineffectual. The client sultans evaded Portuguese customs houses and trading regulations with impunity, because the distant viceroys in Goa were willing to turn a blind eye if they would but remain loyal to the Portuguese.

Even that was asking too much of most of them. When Amir Ali Bey sailed into their harbours in his little galley, proclaiming that he was sent by the Ottoman sultan himself to free them from the Portuguese, all the cities of the northern coast – with the exception of loyal Malindi – welcomed him with open arms. The Swahili gleefully swept the scattering of Portuguese away and made their formal submission to Ali Bey as the sultan's representative. With nothing to hinder him, Ali Bey went on a merry privateering spree and captured twenty Portuguese prizes. He finally sailed back to the Red Sea in 1586 laden to the gunwales with booty. In his disappearing wake the Swahili belatedly realised that Ali Bey had deluded them. Ottoman rule was not going to be extended to their towns as he had led them to believe it would be, and with his departure they now lay at the mercy of the humiliated and vengeful Portuguese.

The Portuguese were not long in coming. Loyal Malindi alerted Goa of Ali Bey's depredations, and the viceroy despatched a fleet of eighteen sail to reassert Portuguese control of the north coast. Believing in the efficacy of making one dreadful example to cow the rest, in January 1587 the Portuguese sacked and destroyed the town of Faza on the north shore of Pate Island. They ruthlessly butchered its unfortunate population and sent the head of its executed sultan to Goa as a grisly trophy. Horrified by Faza's fate, the other Swahili cities sullenly submitted and the Portuguese set up compliant new rulers whom they believed they could trust.

The problem for the Portuguese was that they had no means of maintaining the authority of their puppet rulers once their punitive task force had sailed back to Goa. For no sooner was it out of sight than the bitterly resentful Swahili secretly sent word to Ali Bey, urging him to return. Ali Bey duly sallied out again in 1588. This time he came with a much larger force of four galleys and a pinnace,* and carried with him letters of official Ottoman sanction. The coastal towns immediately rose up, turned on the Portuguese settlers and deposed the puppet rulers imposed on them. Fuelled by the recent Portuguese atrocities in Faza, in many towns the revolt took a very nasty turn. In Pemba, for example, the Swahili systematically massacred all of the Portuguese settlers. Predictably, Malindi stood fast and repulsed Ali Bey; but the people of

---

* A pinnace is a small, light sailing craft used as a tender for war vessels.

Mombasa, who were particularly hostile to the Portuguese, at length invited the swaggering corsair to set up his headquarters in their town and establish a permanent Ottoman base.

The Zimba Terror

No sooner had Ali Bey settled down to build a fort at the entrance to the harbour at Mombasa to protect his new base when, in early March 1589, an army of terrifyingly ferocious African warriors unexpectedly appeared on the mainland opposite the island on which the town was built. These were the Zimba.

Their identity has long intrigued and puzzled historians, but it seems the Zimba can be traced far to the south of Mombasa, to the lands between Lake Malawi and the Zambezi river. As we shall see,* in the late sixteenth century the Portuguese were attempting to establish a monopoly of the ivory trade in the Zambezi river valley. This was an intolerable challenge to the Lundu *mambo* (ruler) in the valley of the Shire river that ran into the Zambezi from the north. He ruled over one of three major federations of Maravi chiefdoms settled around the southern shores of Lake Malawi (all of which loosely acknowledged the *karonga*, a single paramount king).† The Portuguese knew all the Maravi chiefdoms to be 'very warlike', and to be thoroughly feared by their African neighbours.[3] Certainly, Lundu kingship was all about exacting tribute through the deployment of the *mambo*'s compact and implacable bands of warriors armed with swords and spears, and redistributing it to loyal vassals. Tribute could include grain and cattle as well as iron tools and weapons (the *mambo*'s subjects were famous ironsmiths), but the major item was ivory. Lundu hunters trapped the great herds of elephants in deep pits and then the *mambo*, to his considerable profit, traded the ivory tusks down the Zambezi to the coast.

It was to stop the Portuguese from interfering with his vital ivory trade that in 1589 the *mambo* unleashed his bands of warriors against the Portuguese

---

* See Chapter 5.

† Maravi (or Malawi) meant 'flames'. This name distinguished the aristocracy – who had originated far away to the northwest in the Luba kingdom of central Africa – from the commoners they had subjugated in the fifteenth century. Fire was so sacred to the *karonga* that he lived in seclusion, tending a sacred flame that was fed with the mats used by girls during initiation ceremonies. Its black smoke was believed to turn into clouds, and then into rain.

trading posts along the Zambezi and on the coast. Their African victims knew these Lundu warriors as the 'Zimba', a generic term applied to marauders. The name of the Zimbas' leading general has come down in oral tradition as Tundu, and there is still the cult of a violent spirit called Chitunda in the Shire valley.

It is possible the Zimba warrior bands included slaves who had escaped from the Portuguese in the Zambezi valley, as well as refugees from devastating drought in central Africa. But whoever made up the bands, they all subscribed to the ferocious Zimba way of war. This involved extreme terror tactics against their enemies that included eating the men they killed in war along with their war captives when they were no longer fit for work, as well as (it should be added) their own sick and badly wounded. Father João dos Santos, a Dominican friar sent from Lisbon as a missionary to the Swahili coast in 1586, described his first-hand experience of the Zimba in his book, *Ethiopia Oriental*, published in 1609:

> All . . . as a rule are tall, well-proportioned, and very robust. The arms
> they carry are battle-axes, arrows, assegais [spears], and large shields with
> which they entirely cover themselves. These shields are made of light wood
> covered with the skins of the wild animals which they kill and eat. They are
> in the habit of eating the men they kill in war, and drinking out of their
> skulls, showing themselves in this boastful and ferocious.[4]

One band of Zimba advanced south against the Portuguese in the Zambezi valley, resoundingly defeated them and drove them into their forts at Sena and Tete.* Another band rampaged north along the coast, in dos Santos' words: 'destroying and plundering all they found, and devouring every living thing not only men, women and children, but cattle, dogs, cats, rats, snakes and lizards'.[5] To save themselves – or to participate in the plundering – men joined the Zimba as they moved up the coast, swelling their ranks until they numbered many thousands. The Swahili towns had regularly been threatened before by Africans from the hinterland, but never so catastrophically as now.

Kilwa on its off-shore island was no longer quite the noble city that had excited Portuguese admiration and cupidity nearly 100 years before. The

---

* See Chapter 5.

Portuguese sack of 1505 and the loss of her Sofala gold trade to the interlopers had already reduced the port to an impoverished ghost of its former self. Nonetheless, its fine buildings remained, and they still sheltered several thousand inhabitants who were overwhelmed by dread when the fearsome Zimba host appeared on the mainland opposite.

Yet with capitulation no option, the people of Kilwa had to defend themselves as best they could. For several nerve-racking months they managed to fend off the Zimba, because the marauders could not find a way to cross the sea channel between the island and the mainland. Then, so tradition has it, at the low ebb of the spring tide a traitor led the Zimba over a ford they had not known existed. In the early hours of the morning they fell upon the inhabitants of the town, sunk deep in exhausted sleep, and slaughtered most of them before they could put up any organised resistance. The Zimba then comprehensively looted Kilwa, and over the following days systematically ate any prisoners they had taken alive. According to the sensationalist Portuguese chronicles, among the victims were a considerable number of women, 'many of whom were very beautiful and delicate'[6] – and so, presumably, good to eat.

This savage sack dealt the death blow to the beautiful port that once had been the greatest town of all along the Swahili coast. As dos Santos (who left the coast in 1597) lamented: 'Even at the present time the ruins of the vast and sumptuous mosques and dwelling-houses give proof of its former grandeur.'[7]

Shocked word of these horrors, which easily topped Ali Bey's more conventional depredations, flew across the ocean to Goa. The Governor of the *Estado da Índia* despatched his brother, Tomé da Sousa Couthino, as admiral in command of a large fleet of twenty sail to retrieve the situation. The Portuguese fleet dropped anchor outside Mombasa on 5 March 1589. To their consternation, those on board discovered that only a few days before the Zimba, fresh from ravaging their way up the coast from Kilwa, had encamped on the mainland across from the walled town, now held by Ali Bey and his Ottoman forces.

The Zimba were the wiser from their success at Kilwa. It was their intention to cross over the narrow straits at the Makupa ford on the northwestern side of the island at low tide when the water was only waist high. To deter them, Ali Bey had stationed two of his galleys at the ford and the remaining two and the pinnace close to the walls of the town at the entrance to the harbour.

For several days their cannon fire had been sufficient to deter the Zimba from attempting the crossing, but Ali Bey knew there was not sufficient gunpowder to keep up the bombardment indefinitely.

Now, to add to his difficulties, da Sousa Couthino's fleet surged into the channel on the eastern side of the island that led to the harbour – its proud flags flying, drums rolling and trumpets shrilling. The great Portuguese ships were heavily armed and swiftly silenced fire from Ali Bey's fort at the entrance to the harbour. They also completely outgunned Ali Bey's outnumbered galleys and captured them all, along with their rich cargoes of precious metals, amber, ivory and fine cloth, as well as the slaves chained to the oars. Having made short work of Ali Bey's flotilla, da Sousa Couthino landed his troops on the island beneath a flag bearing the figure of Christ on the cross. Twice before, the Portuguese had comprehensively sacked Mombasa. Meeting no resistance now from the despairing townspeople and the demoralised survivors of Ali Bey's sunken ships, they sacked Mombasa for a third time. They then returned to their ships, staggering under the weight of their plunder.

Meanwhile, the Zimba on the mainland looked on in astonishment as the Portuguese blew the Ottoman galleys to pieces. Duly impressed by this display of overwhelming power, their leader, who might have been the selfsame Tundu who has come down in memory, sent an emissary to da Sousa Couthino on board his ship in the harbour. The Zimba herald announced that his chief recognised the Portuguese as 'gods of the sea', even as he was still 'god of the land'. Once this diplomatic statement had sunk in, he then had a request to make of the Portuguese admiral. Would he permit the Zimba chief 'to enter the island and kill and eat every living thing he should find in it'?[8] As far as da Sousa Couthino was concerned, the Portuguese had already plundered what they could, the rebellious Mombasans deserved no pity and they were hated Muslims to boot. What point would there be in taking up arms to keep the Zimba off the island? So he agreed to the hideous Zimba terms.

On 15 March the Zimba duly waded unhindered across at the Makupa ford and eagerly flung themselves on the people of the island. There was a despairing, wailing stampede to the harbour, where the Portuguese ships rode at anchor. Increasingly appalled by the nightmarish scene his pact with the Zimba had unleashed before his unwilling eyes, and moved by the piteous screams for help, the admiral had a change of heart. He sent in his boats and under a rain of Zimba arrows they succeeded in bringing off hundreds of Swahili, along with Ali Bey, who rode his horse into the sea, as well as thirty of his leading men. Those who did not make it to the ships fled into the bush and palm groves, where the Zimba systematically rounded them up and devoured them at their leisure.

The sickened da Sousa Couthino left the Zimba to their ghastly pleasures and sailed on to Lamu, whose ruler, Sultan Bwana Bashira, had given his whole-hearted support to Ali Bey. This was a mortal miscalculation that could not be undone. The Portuguese publicly beheaded the sultan in the presence of the trembling rulers of the neighbouring towns of Pate, Faza and Siu. With exemplary justice done, the coast duly pacified, Ali Bey in chains and his Ottoman patrons foiled, da Sousa Couthino complacently sailed back to Goa with his hold full of the booty of Mombasa. It did not seem to concern him that the Zimba were still on the loose.

Indeed, the Zimba were not yet done. Having sucked the last bones in Mombasa clean, they struck up the coast to Malindi. Atypically for a Swahili town, it lay vulnerably along a bay on the mainland instead of on an off-shore island. Its only protection was a low wall on its landward side. Malindi's sultan had proved inflexibly loyal to the Portuguese, but in this moment of the town's mortal peril their practical assistance was limited to a motley force of thirty soldiers and resident merchants under the command of Matheus Mendez de Vasconcelos.

Fired up by all their previous successes, the moment the Zimba reached Malindi they began furiously assaulting its inadequate ramparts. Although Portuguese matchlock fire cut many down, the Zimba were at the very point of overwhelming the defenders and taking the town when Malindi was saved by an extraordinary *deus ex machina*: the arrival of several thousand Segeju, who were the allies of the Sultan of Malindi.

These Segeju were pastoralists who subsisted mainly on the blood and milk of their great herds of cattle. They were migrating slowly southwards down the coast from the Horn of Africa, prodded along by the selfsame aggressive Oromo who had uprooted the Mijikenda. Dos Santos described them as a warlike people who anointed themselves with clay and oil and who still wore skins. According to him, until the Segeju achieved manhood by killing a man in war – and displaying his foreskin as a trophy – they did up their hair with pounds of clay, which they polished until it resembled a helmet.

Be that as it may, the Segeju attacked the disconcerted Zimba from the rear with such energy and military skill that they promptly put them to flight. Breaking up into smaller bands, the defeated Zimba tried to make it back to their homes in the Shire valley. On the way they had to pass through regions where they had committed awful atrocities on their bone-strewn path to Malindi. Their surviving victims did not hesitate to take their revenge on them now that they were fugitives. Tradition has it that only about 100 of the Zimba, along with their indefatigable captain, ever reached their own country again.*

The Portuguese Fortify the Swahili Coast

The dreadful coincidence of Ali Bey's seizure of Mombasa and the catastrophic incursion of the Zimba, which left stretches of the northern Swahili coast partially depopulated and some of its major trading ports in ruins, might very easily have spelled the end of the Portuguese presence in that region. Instead, it was a wake-up call for the viceroy in Goa, Matias de Albuquerque. Clearly, it was no longer enough to rely on the loyalty of the Sultan of Malindi to secure the coast, and the viceroy now exerted himself to bring the north coast more closely under the umbrella of the *Estado da Índia*.

Administratively, the *Estado da Índia* was divided into captaincies. Each captain served for three years as military commander and chief administrative officer for the distant viceroy, and had his headquarters in a massive fortress.†
There was already a Captaincy of Moçambique, but now there would be a new one north of Cape Delgado.‡ Its capital was fixed at Mombasa, which despite its recent sack was still potentially the most important port on the north coast. The Zimba had practically eliminated its previous inhabitants, but it

---

* More prosaically, some historians contend that the leaders of the Zimba succeeded in establishing chiefdoms in the areas they had conquered, which endured into the colonial period.

† Captaincies were distributed as grants (*mercês*) by the Portuguese crown, but in practice they could be bought, sold or even inherited. They were sought after less for the salary they brought than for the opportunities they provided for private gain. The Captaincy of Moçambique was known to be especially lucrative and was highly coveted.

‡ Cape Delgado is just south of the present Tanzania–Moçambique border.

was gradually being repopulated by Swahili from the nearby islands and by the Kilindini people from the coastal strip.

Moçambique Island was already protected by the daunting hulk of the Fortaleza de São Sebastião, completed in 1558, and it was essential to build a similar fortress in Mombasa, one strong enough to withstand future attacks by the Ottomans or the likes of the Zimba. Many Portuguese forts in the *Estado da Índia* had started out as simple, makeshift palisades of stakes erected behind ditches. However, in Europe highly sophisticated defensive structures were evolving in response to the gunpowder revolution. It was primarily to deter Indian Ocean enemies armed with cannon that the Portuguese soon decided to reconstruct the key forts in their empire along the same lines.

What spurred along the revolution in military architecture were the typically tall, brittle, stone curtain walls of mediaeval fortifications. They were designed to prevent attackers from scaling them, but could neither resist cannon balls nor provide a stable platform for their own defensive artillery. From the mid-fifteenth century military engineers in Italy pioneered a design solution to these linked problems that came to be known as the *trace italienne* (Italian trace). 'Modern' fortresses that conformed to the *trace italienne* were constructed as low as possible to avoid presenting a target to artillery. They were thickly built of materials such as rubble, earth or brick that absorbed cannon balls and were often faced in stone.

The fortress itself consisted of a number of angular bastions – usually shaped like diamonds or arrowheads – connected by straight curtain walls of the same height. This design gave the whole structure its characteristic, 'star-shaped' form. The bastions offered broad gun platforms that projected from the walls to provide supporting flanking fire to sweep the enemy as they tried to penetrate the outer defences.

The purpose of outer defences was always to stall assailants for as long as possible in the exposed killing field. When a fortress was built on the seashore, as were those the Portuguese erected in the *Estado da Índia*, the sea itself served as a major obstacle on the seaward sides. On the landward sides a broad ditch, filled either with water or obstacles, served the same purpose. An exposed, sloping *glacis* (embankment), usually littered with traps and obstacles, led up to the ditch. In the Indies, the Portuguese eschewed the increasingly complex attempts back in Europe to ensure ever greater depth of defence by erecting

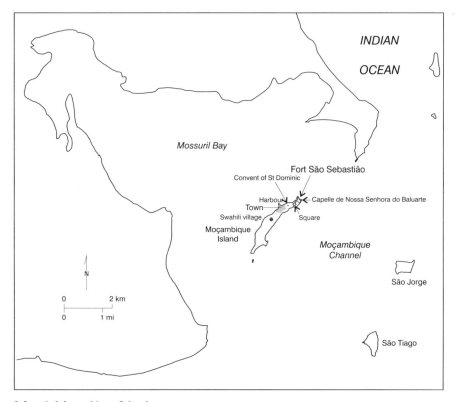

MAP 6 *Moçambique Island*

baroque systems of outworks beyond the ditch and *glacis* – the whole ornate panoply of crownworks, hornworks and ravelins that provided elaborate mathematical challenges for armchair engineers and geometricians.

Once erected, bastioned fortresses were labour-efficient because relatively small garrisons were required to defend them. On the other hand, laying siege to such fortresses required large numbers of troops and considerable patience. Besiegers had to construct a chain of entrenchments and redoubts surrounding the fortress to cut it off from supplies or reinforcements. Trenches – zigzagged to prevent the defenders firing directly down them – could then be advanced close enough to the walls to permit massed heavy siege artillery to bombard a selected length from close range. Once the artillery opened a breach, the besiegers could attempt to storm and capture the fortress if it did not hurriedly surrender. Alternatively, the attackers could sink a mine under

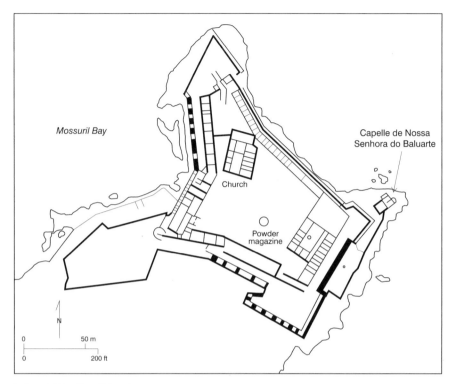

Mossuril Bay

Capelle de Nossa
Senhora do Baluarte

Church

Powder
magazine

N

| 0 | 50 m |
| 0 | 200 ft |

MAP 7 *Fort São Sebastião*

the fortifications, pack it with gunpowder and explode it to make the desired breach. Defenders might send in tunnels of their own to interdict the enemy miners in horrible, subterranean, hand-to hand fighting, or they might sink their own counter-mine beneath the enemy and blow them up.

Even if a breach were made, commanders were reluctant to embark on a direct assault because of the inevitably high casualties involved. The preference was always to blockade the fortress as effectively as possible and starve out the defenders. When, as with the Indian Ocean enemies of the Portuguese, there was a dearth of siege artillery capable of making a breach, there was no alternative for the besiegers but to wait for hunger and spiralling disease among the cooped-up defenders to take their deadly toll.

The fortress of São Sebastião, which Dom João de Castro commenced in 1546 on the northern tip of Moçambique Island at the entrance to the harbour (and which replaced the makeshift affair first thrown up in 1507), was

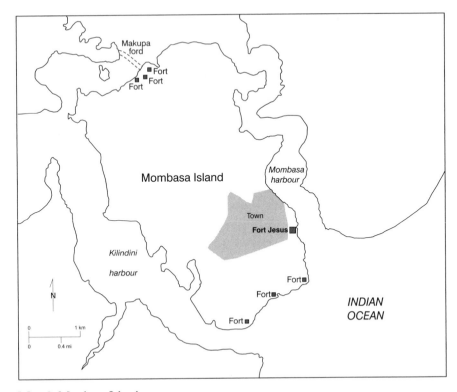

MAP 8 *Mombasa Island*

a typical enough 'star fort', although it lacked the desired symmetry of design. By the time it was finished in 1558 it was an immense, trapezoidal structure with four massive bastions.* To command the sea and land approaches, the two westerly bastions stretched much further out than the easterly ones, so that from the air the fort puts one disconcertingly in mind of a vast, headless, spatchcock turkey with enormous legs and stubby wings. Typically, inside the fortress walls barracks surrounded a wide parade ground. There were also a strongly built gunpowder magazine, a church and storerooms for rice and millet. The island was without ground water, so rainwater was conducted to a vaulted underground cistern from the fort's roofs and walls.

From its inception, the new fort at Mombasa was to be an outstandingly up-to-date example of the *trace italienne*. Its design was entrusted to the Italian

---

* With walls thirty-nine feet high and with a circuit of 2,460 feet, in the sixteenth century the fortress of São Sebastião was the largest inhabited structure south of the Sahara.

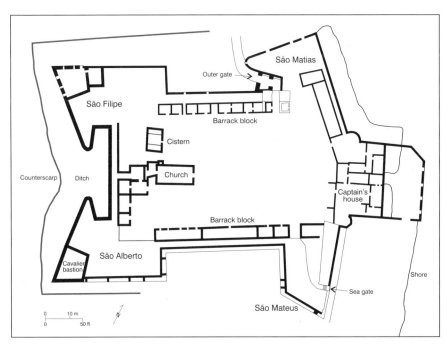

MAP 9 *Fort Jesus*

military architect João Batista Cairato, since 1583 the chief architect for the *Estado da Índia* and in charge of all its fortifications. He was a master of the art, already responsible for supervising the stupendous fortifications on the island of Malta for the Knights of the Order of St John of Jerusalem, as well as others for the King of Spain in his Italian duchy of Milan. Cairato traced the plan of the fortification, which would be named the Fortaleza de Jesus de Mombaça, across two acres of ground a mile from the old Swahili town on the southeastern side of the island. It was to be erected on a coral ridge, too hard to be undermined, which commanded the narrow channel to the harbour between the island and the bluff on the mainland to the east of it. About 100 yards to its south lay a sandy beach, where boats could land supplies during a siege while under the protection of the fort's guns.

The site was dedicated on 11 April 1593. Experienced masons came from the Portuguese possessions in India to cut the blocks of coral rag, which faced the walls of red earth and rubble. Labourers from Malindi, Portugal's loyal ally, put the blocks in place. Its design was deliberately anthropomorphic and referred to the human form – God's supreme creation – which was associated in Renaissance architectural theory with geometrical perfection. However, if from the air Fort São Sebastião resembles nothing so much as a spatchcock turkey, from above Fort Jesus looks like a turtle with a rectangular shell, short flippers and partially retracted head.

The fort's open central courtyard, longer than it was broad (the turtle's shell), was surrounded by massive walls. Typically, the captain's house, barracks, a church and a powder magazine were built around its perimeter. Water from the roof ran into a cistern that was to prove too small in an emergency. A triangular bastion (or flipper) at each of its four corners rose to a man's height above the connecting curtain walls, and a rectangular bastion (the head of the turtle) commanded the entrance to the harbour. A wide, dry ditch surrounded the fort on its landward sides. The fort's walls, built forty-five feet high, digressed from the low, European pattern, because it was recognised that assailants in the Indies were more likely to attempt to scale them because they lacked the artillery to make a breach.

Fort Jesus was essentially completed by 1596, but improvements and additions continued to be made into the 1640s. In the 1630s three little rectangular, loopholed forts were built on the northwestern side of the island to command the shallow Makupa ford, where the Zimba had crossed over from the mainland in 1589.

Because of its excellent design that allowed for deadly defensive crossfire between its bastions, the fortress did not require a large establishment to defend it. Pedro Barretto de Rezende described it in 1634 as carrying sixteen pieces of artillery with a garrison of seventy-five men. A further twenty-five men served in two small ships that patrolled the coast and another twenty-five manned three Makupa forts 'on the side by the mainland at a place where one can cross dry foot'.[9]

The Dutch Besiege Fort São Sebastião

The Portuguese built their great fortresses at Moçambique and Mombasa to deter Indian Ocean and African enemies, but a far deadlier foe from Europe was preparing to challenge them for control of the *Estado da Índia*.

Once King Felipe II of Spain had enforced his claim to the Portuguese throne in 1580,* Portugal and its empire became embroiled in Spain's interminable wars against the Protestant Dutch.† In 1595 a Dutch exploratory expedition of four ships under Cornelis de Houtman burst open the door to the *Estado da Índia* when it rounded the Cape of Good Hope and crossed the Indian Ocean to Banten (Bantam), the Javanese pepper port controlled by the Portuguese. Half the Dutch crews died in battle and of disease before de Houtman's expedition limped back to the Netherlands the following year, but packed in the ships' holds were spices worth a fortune. The Dutch knew that, according to the prevailing economic doctrine of mercantilism, economic power was the key to winning their war against the Spanish. Already the Dutch navy was denying essential European home markets to the Spanish, but if they could expel them and their Portuguese subjects from their lucrative trading posts, colonies and foreign markets, then the Spanish monarchy would no longer be able to sustain its far-flung military machine.

The Dutch and their Protestant English allies could only project the power necessary to challenge Spain across the world because, unlike their financially conservative enemy with his insurmountable load of debts he could barely service, they had pioneered the means of sustaining the crippling cost of war. Their productive market economies and innovative deficit financing made it possible for their governments to raise low-interest loans from flourishing traders and merchants with money to invest. What made it even more difficult for the financially unenterprising Spanish to compete was the sophisticated relationship between the Dutch and English states and chartered, joint-stock companies. In essence, the two Protestant powers subcontracted their aggressive expansion into the Spanish empire to investors who were willing to venture their capital in enterprises of great risk but of even greater potential profit. Thus the capital market paid for armed force on the seas and managed the commercial enterprise overseas.

The English were first in this field, when Queen Elizabeth I granted a royal charter on 31 December 1600 to the East India Company, based in London, to trade in the East Indies. The East India Company was initially weaker and

---

* See Chapter 1.

† The United Provinces of the Netherlands' struggle for independence from Spanish rule lasted from 1568 to 1648 and is known as the Eighty Years' War.

more cautious than its Dutch equivalent, but it would prove a useful ally in India and the Persian Gulf in ruining Portuguese trade.*

The East India Company's big relation, which would prove the nemesis of the *Estado da Índia*, was granted its charter on 20 March 1602 by the States-General of the Netherlands. The Dutch East India Company (DEIC), as it is generally known, or the *Vereenigde Oost-Indische Compagnie* (literally 'United East Indian Company', or VOC), was a joint-stock company with its headquarters in Amsterdam. Its charter, besides granting it the Dutch monopoly to trade in Asia, endowed it with quasi-governmental powers. The VOC was authorised to wage war, negotiate treaties, coin money and establish colonies. Its advantageous trading privileges, when combined with the energetic economic acumen of its directors, propelled the VOC into conducting itself as a major maritime power in its own right, and made its shareholders very rich.

The aggressive and determined intrusion into the Indian Ocean of the VOC – and to a lesser extent of the East India Company – was of enormous concern to the Portuguese. They had previously faced no serious challenge to their trade monopoly in those waters from European competitors. Now, as they rapidly had to concede, they had no means of keeping them out. The Portuguese had failed to maintain their initial technological edge in naval warfare, and found themselves outclassed by the large Dutch and English ships, many of them more than 400 tons and bristling with heavy guns. Moreover, the cost of building ships was crippling, and the Portuguese simply had not the resources to keep up with the number of vessels their rivals were capable of laying down. Between 1602 and 1619 the VOC sent 246 ships to Asia compared to only seventy-nine Portuguese vessels – only just over half of which ever made it back to Lisbon. Nor did the VOC content itself with merely disrupting Portuguese trade in the Indies. As the newly dominant sea power in the region, it set about systematically capturing the Portuguese forts and *feitorias* so as to drive them out of the Indian Ocean altogether.

Long, narrow Moçambique Island, with Fort São Sebastião hunched at its northern tip, was the main Portuguese stronghold and harbour on the Swahili coast. The island itself was very dry so that water, provisions and firewood had

---

* The EIC ruled over much of India from 1757 until 1858, when the British crown assumed the direct administration of the sub-continent. The EIC's extensive trade monopolies were dissolved in 1874.

to be ferried across from the nearby mainland, where profitable palm groves, citrus trees and fruit orchards flourished. As described by the Dominican friar João dos Santos, a fine square as wide as 'a good musket shot' adjoined the fort whose garrison was stationed at the gates during the day and on the bastions and curtain walls at night. Facing the fort across the square was the convent of St Dominic, 'newly built and very beautiful'. Beyond the convent lay the town where the 2,000 or so Portuguese and other Christians lived. At its centre were the remains of an old fortress and the cathedral built into it. The dwellings of the chief officials were close by, as were the town cistern, prison and hospital. Two gunshots distant, at the lower end of the island, was the wretched village of the Swahili who served the Portuguese. Dos Santos reflected that these labourers showed remarkable loyalty to the Portuguese despite living in squalor: 'either through fear or because they are always dependent upon them'.[10]

Such was the strategic and commercial significance of Moçambique that the Dutch early identified it as a major objective. Consequently, when in 1604 twelve VOC vessels sailed into the Indian Ocean to wrest the eastern trade away from Portugal, their admiral, Steven van der Hagen, could not simply pass by the island. To the consternation of the Portuguese soldiers keeping watch from the eastward-facing bastions of Fort São Sebastião, on 17 June the Dutch sails appeared over the horizon and bore straight down on the island. Alerted, the panicky Portuguese civilians fled into the fort. The garrison, which consisted of only sixty soldiers as opposed to the 100 laid down in the regulations – an indication of how overstretched Portugal was in the *Estado da Índia* – resolved to resist the Dutch as they made for the harbour on the western side of the island. In successfully gaining it, the Dutch displayed their superior seamanship and nerve by sailing down the treacherous channel, which was only 500 yards wide, and by braving the fire from the walls of the fort that loomed close above them. Fortunately for the islanders, van der Hagen decided he did not have the time to attempt to reduce the powerful fortress. So after taking on supplies he sailed off on 25 August for India, his hold filled with ivory from a Portuguese trading vessel he had captured in the harbour.

The Dutch raid alerted the Portuguese to Moçambique's vulnerability. Determined to hold it at all costs, King Filipe II of Portugal (who was also Felipe III of Spain) ordered that São Sebastião's garrison be increased and the fort better prepared to withstand a long siege. Unhappily, it was an indication of Portugal's exhaustion that nothing had yet been done to meet these orders when, on 20 March 1607, a tattered galleon from India anchored in Moçambique harbour with the alarming news that a Dutch fleet was close behind it.

Dom Estevão de Ataíde was the Captain of Moçambique, and he did what he could over the next few days to prepare his defences. He was despondently aware that many of his wooden gun carriages were rotten, making the cannons mounted on them unserviceable, that most of his men's pikes were equally useless, because their wooden hafts were also decayed, and that he was dangerously short of gunpowder. De Ataíde was fortunately able to double the number of his fighting men when the inhabitants of the town took refuge in the fort with all their goods, valuables and furniture. Thirty men of the town joined the garrison and – one presumes rather less enthusiastically – another thirty who were on their way to the Zambezi trading forts and found themselves caught up in the emergency. About 120 women and children also came into the fort and worked hard to block up the gates with stones and sandbags. To reduce pressure of food supplies in the fort, de Ataíde moved as many slaves and Swahili to the mainland as he could.

On 29 March 1607 nine Dutch ships with about 1,000 men on board under Admiral Paulus van Caerden anchored in the lee of São Jorge, a little island that lay about three miles to the east of the fort and the harbour entrance. The admiral immediately raised the flag of battle to indicate his hostile intent. Still, van Caerden hesitated for two days while he assessed the area of operations, and the delay allowed the Portuguese, who had been thrown into a surging panic by his fleet's anticipated but nevertheless daunting arrival, to recover their nerve and make their final preparations.

The Dutch finally made their move at high tide on Sunday 31 March. With standards flying, drums beating, and trumpets and fifes sounding, two files of Dutch ships, each in line of battle, audaciously crossed the bar of the port very close in under the guns of the fort. In taking this risky course van Caerden had calculated correctly. The defenders found they were not able to depress their cannons sufficiently (those, that is, whose decayed gun carriages could take the strain) to cause the Dutch ships much damage except to their topmost sails and rigging. True, one of the ships did run on to a reef. However, with admirable sang-froid and skill the Dutch lowered some boats and managed to pull her off and tow her back into the channel.

Having burst through to the landward side of the island, the Dutch sailed past the harbour and anchored in a bay well out of range of the fort's guns. Some 500 musketeers then waded ashore. With considerable aplomb and in good order, they marched straight through the town with their band provocatively playing until they reached the Dominican convent, directly opposite the fort across the broad, open square. There the Dutch fortified themselves and sited the guns they had brought up from the ships.

The besiegers quickly realised that their guns at the convent were too far from the fort to have any effect on its stout walls. Therefore, in accordance with the prescribed practices of siegecraft, they pushed trenches forward across the square to a closer position. There, on 6 April, they constructed three batteries with bags and casks filled with earth, and mounted nine pieces of heavy artillery in them. Soon they were battering the fort's walls with eighty 25-pound balls a day, and one great cannon was discharging 52-pound balls, which did considerable damage. Next, from these batteries the Dutch pushed forward four deep trenches closer towards the fort's main gate. There they built a sandbagged platform of earth and timber, on which they mounted five pieces of artillery. These guns pounded the São António bastion, which covered the gate, but the women inside the fort worked desperately to repair the damage with sandbags.

Van Caerden himself, resplendent in breastplate and bearing his staff of office – thereby making a conspicuous target – actively encouraged his men in the advance trenches. Not unexpectedly, a musket ball shot from the walls finally found its mark and broke his leg. Carried to the rear, the indefatigable van Caerden continued to direct the siege. Dutifully following the manual of siegecraft, the Dutch then constructed timber mantlets (bullet-proof screens). Under their cover they reached the fort's wall with the intention of undermining it. However, the determined defenders hurled rocks down on them with such effect that after three days they abandoned this particular ploy.

To escape Portuguese fire from the walls, the Dutch did as much of their digging, hammering and manoeuvring as they could under cover of darkness, but the defenders had an answer for that too. They fastened pots of burning tar and pitch to long poles, which they hung over the walls to illuminate the ground below. The garrison also regularly sallied out in small parties at night and successfully cut up the Dutch when isolated in forward positions. Throughout these operations de Ataíde proved an inspiring commander, being (in dos Santos' words): 'foremost in watching and in fighting, thereby greatly encouraging his soldiers'.[11]

The Dutch were growing greatly discouraged by the failure of all their up-to-date and professional efforts. On top of that, encamped on that hot, waterless and malarial little isle,* up to thirty of them a day were coming down with fever and dysentery. Moreover, van Caerden, his painful broken leg in a splint, was becoming anxious that a Portuguese fleet might attempt to relieve the fort. Just over a month after making his dramatic landing he decided he had had enough. By 6 May all the Dutch guns were back on board and his fleet was ready to sail.

The frustrated Dutch admiral was not quite finished with the Portuguese, however. He sent a message to the fort that if the Portuguese desired to save their churches and houses on the island from being burned, along with their palm groves and farms on the mainland, then they must pay him a hefty ransom. De Ataíde disdainfully refused to treat. Accordingly, on 13 May the Dutch (true to their Protestant prejudices – for this too was a holy war against the 'Bishop of Rome') broke and otherwise destroyed all the Catholic images and altars on the island, looted the houses and then set fire to them along with the Dominican convent. Then, as threatened, they laid to waste the farms on the mainland. They also burned two unfortunate Portuguese ships from India, laden with valuable merchandise, which had unsuspectingly entered the harbour.

At last, in the early, foggy hours of 16 May, the Dutch weighed anchor and ran the gauntlet of fire from the fortress as they sailed out over the bar. This time they took heavier punishment from the fort's guns, and had to abandon one of their ships that ran aground on a reef. After anchoring off São Jorge Island for three days to effect repairs, they finally sailed away towards the Comoros Islands. There was renewed alarm when the refreshed Dutch fleet appeared over the horizon again on 4 August, but this time it hovered cautiously out of range for a fortnight before finally making sail.

---

* The Dutch had to collect their water from the mainland and run the gauntlet of the hostile inhabitants.

The determined Portuguese defence of Fort São Sebastião had been a near-run thing, and King Filipe once again sent out frantic instructions for strengthening its defences. Predictably, before anything was done the Dutch decided to have one more go. On the afternoon of 28 July 1608, thirteen Dutch vessels carrying 377 guns and 1,840 men under the command of Admiral Pieter Verhoeven appeared off São Jorge. At this now-familiar if still-alarming sight the people of Moçambique rushed into the fortress. The enterprising de Ataíde was still in command, and he allocated thirty men to each bastion.

While four light Dutch pinnaces diverted the Portuguese defenders by forcing the harbour under the guns of the fort and towing off two great ships heavily laden with goods, Verhoeven brought his nine larger vessels to the far end of the island. He landed his troops there, and they immediately marched the length of the isle to the music of their band, menacingly firing their muskets as they went. As in 1607 they made straight for the Dominican convent, now in ruins, and started to drive trenches towards the fort. The defenders, despite the unlucky explosion of barrels of gunpowder that killed nineteen of them, had not lost their verve. In a sortie on 29 July they killed a number of the Dutch who were incapably drunk from drinking looted wine and arrack.

The besiegers landed their siege guns on 31 July and mounted them in forward batteries. The siege proceeded much as the previous one. The guns fired 1,250 balls and broke down some of the curtain wall between the landward bastions. Working furiously, the defenders plugged the breach with rocks, earth, sandbags and bales of cloth. On 8 August twenty-five of the defenders armed with swords and lances sallied out unexpectedly at midday. To wild cheers from the walls they routed the Dutch in their forward trenches before proudly retiring with captured drums, muskets, flags and other trophies. The Dutch then tried, and failed, to drive a mine under the walls. With that, Verhoeven had had enough, and on 15 August the Dutch guns went silent.

That day several Catholics from the Dutch ranks deserted and the Portuguese hauled their co-religionists up the walls of the fort. For Verhoeven, insult was now added to injury, and he vehemently demanded that the renegades be handed back to him. If they were not, he swore he would shoot the thirty Portuguese inhabitants of the island who had fallen into his hands when they failed to make it to the sanctuary of the fort. De Ataíde resolutely refused to negotiate. However, Verhoeven was not bluffing. To the dismay of the defenders watching from the ramparts, on 17 August the Portuguese captives were marched on to the broad square in front of the fort. Verhoeven selected six unfortunate men and had them lined up with their hands tied behind their backs. When de Ataíde still would not parley, the Dutch execution squad shot down the six victims.

That same day the Dutch ships intercepted a stray Portuguese galleon that had become separated from the annual, India-bound armada. After receiving three Dutch broadsides the galleon struck its colours. Now, with even more Portuguese prisoners in his hands, Verhoeven extravagantly threatened to hang them all if de Ataíde did not hand over the deserters. The captain stood fast. Faced with the distasteful and dishonourable reality of having to kill so many defenceless prisoners, Verhoeven found he could not bring himself to follow though. Thwarted and vindictive, he instead ordered his men to set fire to the partially rebuilt town and to cut down all the trees on the island. He then re-embarked his troops and sailed off, leaving devastation behind him. As for the prisoners, he kept hold of the officers and dumped the rest on São Tiago, the southernmost of the two little islands off Moçambique.

The sieges of Fort São Sebastião in 1607 and 1608 may have been quite small beer so far as sieges go, but their significance was enormous. They were the first serious armed encounters between European colonial powers to be fought in Africa, and the consequences were far-reaching. If the Dutch had captured Moçambique Island, it is doubtful whether the Portuguese would ever have been able to assemble a force large enough to retake the modern fortress of São Sebastião. If Moçambique had been lost, it would have been impossible to continue with Portuguese expansion in the Zambezi valley.* On the other hand, if the Dutch had succeeded in seizing Moçambique Island, they would not have been compelled to establish an alternative refreshment station on the way to the Indies. They might then never have settled at the Cape of Good Hope, and the history of South Africa would have taken a very different course.

---

* See Chapter 5.

Yusuf ibn al-Hassan and the Portuguese Siege of Fort Jesus

Further north up the Swahili coast in the Captaincy of Mombasa, the town of Mombasa, sheltering under the lee of Fort Jesus, began to recover from the horrors of the Zimba sack of 1589. It remained the preferred market and place to live for the 900 or so Portuguese thinly settled along the coast from Pate to Zanzibar, their numbers regularly thinned by the ravages of malaria. By 1606 a street of seventy Portuguese houses, dominated by the monastery of the Augustinian monks (who had settled there in 1597 and whose order specialised in the unrewarding field of converting Muslims), had sprung up between the gates of Fort Jesus and the original Swahili town. The street stopped short before reaching the outskirts of the old town, because a wall and a thicket – as well as ground left deliberately vacant – ensured that the Christian and Muslim settlements did not co-mingle. This physical 'apartheid' only mirrored the abiding and undisguised distrust and dislike with which the two communities regarded each other all along the coast.

Lethally for the arrogant, if heavily outnumbered, Christian community, the Swahili angrily resented the blatant corruption and sharp dealings of Portuguese officials and traders, and abhorred the increasingly energetic attempts of Christian missionaries to convert them. As a consequence, insurrection boiled just below the surface of the outwardly thriving Swahili towns of the Captaincy of Mombasa.

The Portuguese were not unaware of their vulnerability and had no option but to court the collaboration of local rulers to keep a lid on revolt. Since Vasco da Gama had first set foot on the coast, no allies had proved more loyal than the sultans of Malindi. Recognising this, the Portuguese decided to raise up the ruling sultan, al-Hassan bin Ahmad, and make him the keystone to their control of the north coast. The last ruler of Mombasa had perished in the sack of 1589, so in 1606 the Portuguese transplanted al-Hassan bin Ahmad to Mombasa to reign as king over that town as well as over Pemba (which was being punished for its enthusiastic support of Ali Bey) and his native Malindi.

Unhappily for him, the new Sultan of Mombasa was subordinate to the Portuguese captains appointed to Fort Jesus. Predictably, as *fidalgos* intent on lining their own pockets as swiftly as possible, they disputed the sultan's share of revenues and tribute and arrogantly treated him with insulting disdain. Cut-throat Swahili dynastic politics also played their deadly part. Sultan al-Hassan bin Ahmad quarrelled openly in 1614 with Captain Sima de Melo Pereira, who was being egged on in turn by the sultan's ambitious uncle, Mwami Nasser. Fearing arrest, the sultan ran away to the mainland. Unfortunately for him, the Mijikenda people among whom he took refuge were at that moment the allies of the Portuguese. To please the white men, they killed the unfortunate sultan and delivered his body to the gloating de Melo Pereira. He in turn pickled the 'traitor's' decapitated head and triumphantly despatched it as a trophy to the astonished viceroy in Goa.

That left the Portuguese in search of a reliable replacement for the disgraced sultan. They lit on Yusuf ibn al-Hassan, his seven-year-old son and heir, and sent him to faraway Goa to receive a Christian education in an Augustinian priory. The plan was to place this carefully trained Christian prince on the throne of Mombasa once he was fully grown. Meanwhile, they rewarded his treacherous great-uncle, Mwami Nasser, by appointing him to act as regent.

In Goa, Yusuf duly converted to Christianity as Dom Jerónimo Chingulia* and took a Eurasian Portuguese wife. As planned, he adopted a thoroughly Portuguese way of life and even served with the Portuguese fleet in the Persian Gulf. Thoroughly pleased with the progress of their puppet, the Portuguese restored him to the throne of Mombasa in 1626.

Nothing worked out as planned. The Swahili of Mombasa did not take to their quisling sultan. As a biased, local history asserted: 'When he obtained power, he governed in a most tyrannical manner; he compelled the people to eat pork, and was wicked and an infidel.'[12] For their part, the Portuguese of Mombasa deeply mistrusted him as a Christian convert. Very soon, like his father before him, the young sultan was at loggerheads with the current and insufferable Captain of Mombasa, Dom Pedro Leitão de Gamboa. When Sultan Jerónimo learned that de Gamboa was secretly planning to arrest him and send him to the Inquisition in Goa on the charge of being a renegade Catholic who was observing Muslim ceremonies, he decided he might as well be hanged for a sheep as for a lamb. He abjured Christianity, resumed the name of Yusuf, and moved swiftly to pre-empt de Gamboa's plans.

---

* In Swahili *kingulia* means to belch.

On the Feast of Our Lady of the Assumption, 15 August 1631, Yusuf assembled 300 picked followers and entered the fort as though on a ceremonial visit to mark the holiday. While sitting in stilted conversation with de Gamboa in his formal reception room, he suddenly drew his jewelled, ornamental dagger and cut the captain's throat before he could react or even shout out. Yusuf's followers then fell upon de Gamboa's stunned guards and the unwary garrison elsewhere in the fort and hacked them all to death.

Manuel de Faría y Sousa, a well-informed contemporary who gained his information from eyewitnesses, recounted that when Yusuf tried to persuade de Gamboa's horrified widow to espouse Islam with the promise he would make her his queen, 'she turned on him like a tigress'. Yusuf had no better luck with her pitifully trembling daughter, despite her awful fear of death. According to the pious de Faría, an enraged Yusuf beheaded both mother and daughter. A priest who had been saying mass for them when Yusuf's men broke into the room joined them in their exemplary martyrdom.

With Fort Jesus secured, Yusuf and his men burst out and stormed into the Portuguese part of town where the unwary Portuguese and Christian converts were all merrily gathered for the festival. Those who could, fled to the Augustinian monastery of São Antonio with as many of their valuables as they could snatch up, leaving Yusuf's men free to set about ransacking and burning their houses. For seven days while supplies lasted the refugees in the monastery desperately resisted all attempts to drive them out. Yusuf finally promised them their lives if they left the building without arms. But it was a ruse. De Faría indignantly recorded that: 'as they emerged defenceless [Yusuf] had them mown down with arrows. The women and children who remained within were dragged outside to suffer the same fate.'[13] It also seems that, instead of being shot, some were instead thrown into the harbour to drown. About 150 people died in the massacre, including all the Portuguese except for an Augustinian prior and four laymen who escaped in a canoe to Pate. A gunner apostatised and saved his life. As many as 400 of their servants and converts were sold as slaves to Arabian merchants.

In command of Mombasa, Yusuf called on the neighbouring Swahili towns to join the revolt. Their response was timidly cautious, because memories of Portuguese retribution after the revolt of 1589 were still painfully fresh. While half-hearted negotiations limped along, word of the fall of Mombasa reached

Goa on 9 October 1631. The viceroy, the Count of Linhares, understood that it was essential to retake the town to maintain Portuguese prestige on the Swahili coast and to prevent the revolt from spilling over into the Moçambique captaincy. Besides, threatened all over the Indian Ocean by the Dutch and English, it was more important than ever for their reputation and trade that the Portuguese hang on to East Africa.

Certainly, the *Estado da Índia* was in very poor shape. The English East India Company, which had its base at Surat in northwestern India, had struck an unholy alliance in 1622 with Shah Abbas of Persia to drive the Portuguese out of the waters of the Persian Gulf. The great, redstone fort on the little island of Hormuz, from which the Portuguese had commanded the entrance to the Persian Gulf, duly fell to these unlikely allies. Then in 1631 the King of Kandy in Ceylon (Sri Lanka) had risen in revolt and annihilated a Portuguese army; meanwhile, Portuguese *feitorias* in western India were under mounting threat from the Mogul emperors at Delhi. Dutch and English ships swept the Indian Ocean with impunity.

Even so, despite all these disasters and menaces, de Linhares managed to rake up some twenty-five vessels, both big and small, from right across the *Estado da Índia*. They were to carry 800 soldiers and six siege guns under the command of Dom Francisco de Moura, who had served in both India and Brazil, and were to retake Mombasa.

The expedition appeared before Mombasa on 8 January 1632. Yusuf was holding the fort with 200 men and had an equal number in the old town. He also had with him more than 500 Mijikenda allies who had decided to throw over the Portuguese and join the Swahili.

After some dithering, de Moura landed on 28 January with 400 men. They came on shore in a sheltered cove in the Kilindini harbour on the western side of the island, which was prudently out of sight of the fort. They immediately threw up a redoubt to defend their landing place, and then began to push through the thick bush towards the fort. Reaching relatively open ground below the daunting fortifications, they began to entrench their position and erect defensive barricades from the trunks of felled palm trees. But Yusuf's men were not prepared to look on idly while the Portuguese constructed their advance posts. They sallied out of the land gate tucked into the protective flank of the northeastern São Matias bastion and fell upon the unprepared

Portuguese with considerable determination. De Moura himself nearly died in the furiously contested, hand-to-hand affray in which firearms played little part. He 'defended valiantly with a sword and shield, receiving seven most dangerous arrows with poisoned points'[14] shot by the Mijikenda. Yusuf's men prevailed, and the Portuguese fell back in disarray to their landing place. They left many dead behind them, including two *fidalgos*.

The Portuguese never regained the initiative. Once he had recovered from his wounds (devoted attendants had had to suck the poison out), de Moura made several more ineffectual attempts to capture the fortress. However, it was increasingly obvious that his demoralised troops had no stomach left for the siege. Ironically, the Portuguese were foiled by their own excellent fort building and found that their artillery was not of sufficient calibre to make any impact on the massive walls. Casualties from disease mounted, and the Mijikenda cut off essential supplies from the mainland. As if all that were not bad enough, the drenching monsoon rains were about to begin. Besides making the lives of the sodden besiegers miserable, they would also put pay to the effectiveness of gunpowder weapons. With absolutely no prospect of taking Fort Jesus, de Moura aborted the half-cocked siege on 19 March 1632 and sailed back to Goa, his tail between his legs.

The viceroy, pressed as he was on every side, was in no position to assemble another fleet to resume the siege. But Pedro Roiz de Botelho, a grizzled military veteran of forty years' experience who had been granted the now apparently notional post of Captain of Mombasa in succession to the assassinated de Gamboa, was determined to seize what was his. In 1633, while he was wintering in Zanzibar in command of a few small coastguard vessels, he learned that Yusuf, unnecessarily fearful that the Portuguese would return in even greater strength, had evacuated Fort Jesus several months before and had sailed away on 16 May 1633 with several hundred followers.

Acting on this belated intelligence, on 5 August Roiz de Botelho sidled into the harbour at Mombasa with only seventy-five men. He found the fort abandoned, partially dismantled and all the artillery gone. The Mijikenda had gone back to their mainland hills and the sullen Swahili on the island put up no resistance to the Portuguese. In Goa the news of Roiz de Botelho's bloodless recovery of Mombasa was received with both surprise and relief. A small flotilla duly sailed with eighty soldiers to garrison Fort Jesus, along with twelve pieces of artillery. Once there, the men put the damaged fort to rights. But Mombasa itself never regained its previous prosperity; nor did Portuguese traders ever settle there in the same numbers as before.

As for Yusuf, for five years he kept up his struggle against the Portuguese, annoying them considerably by raiding all along the coast and by stirring up petty revolts. He fraternised with the captains of Dutch and English vessels he encountered and tried to persuade them to attack Mombasa. The Portuguese routinely dismissed Yusuf as a 'pirate', but they had to take his escapades seriously, because they mistrusted the uncertain and easily subverted loyalty of the Swahili in the Captaincy of Mombasa.

To forestall a general uprising, in November 1636 the Portuguese struck harshly at Pate, which they identified as the epicentre of disaffection. With exemplary thoroughness they burned the town down along with all its shipping in the harbour, and carried out mass executions against the local elite. Pate's terrible fate instantly brought all the other towns of the Lamu archipelago to heel, and thereafter the gates of all the towns along the Swahili coast were closed to Yusuf. Pursued by Portuguese ships, he was forced ever further north up the coast. Undeterred, he tried to interest the Ottomans in his cause. He was still actively planning to strike back at the loathed Portuguese when in 1638 (if conflicting accounts can be pieced together) Arab pirates boarded his craft near the entrance to the Red Sea. He was wounded in the scuffle and died at Jedda.

The Omani Challenge

When the Portuguese were finally ousted from the Captaincy of Mombasa it was not by their longstanding rivals along the Swahili coast – the Ottomans or Dutch – or even by another local revolt. Instead – and who would have anticipated it? – it was Arabs from the Gulf of Oman who conquered the northern Swahili coast in the late seventeenth century, and would rule it until the coming of the British two centuries later.

Date palms made the fortune of the Omanis. The mountains of Oman in the southeast of the Arabian peninsula capture a little of the monsoon rains, enough to nourish huge plantations of these trees, whose fruit feeds camels as well as people. Dates keep and travel well, and the Omanis traded them all over the Indian Ocean from their ports, of which the main one was Muscat. These seafaring Omanis were Ibadis. That meant that in matters of faith they belonged neither to the Sunni nor Shia main branches of Islam, but to a different group, the Kharijites. This Arabic term means 'those who leave', and in the seventh century the Kharijites were the first Islamic group to break away from the wider community of faith. They did so on the theological grounds that the caliph (successor of the Prophet) should be chosen on the basis of merit, rather than on account of his descent or power as a ruler. Ibadis adhered to this principle, and only elected an *imam* to command their community when a suitable candidate appeared.

In the second quarter of the seventeenth century various members of the Ya'ariba dynasty of Oman garnered enough religious prestige to be regarded as *imams*. As Ibadis, theirs was a demanding and militant form of Islam requiring absolute piety. Their example encouraged Muslims throughout the region to stand up to the infidel Portuguese who in 1507 had taken control of their ports and continued to dominate the seaways off the Arabian peninsula.

The port of Muscat was the key to Portuguese power in the Gulf of Oman, and they were determined to hold it. In 1587–1588 they had built the nigh-impregnable, twin fortresses of al-Jalali and al-Mirani to guard the narrow entrance to the harbour. For a time it seemed that the East India Company would challenge their presence there, but the Anglo-Portuguese truce of 1635 ended their hostilities in maritime Asia. There would be no repetition of the English involvement that led to the humiliating loss of Hormuz in 1622 to Persia.

Meanwhile, back in Europe, the successful Portuguese revolt of 1640 finally threw off Spanish Habsburg rule and the native House of Bragança took the throne. This technically removed the justification for the Dutch assault on the Portuguese empire, but they pressed on regardless. In 1641 the VOC captured Melaka, the main Portuguese base in southeastern Asia. This was a crushing blow to Portuguese fortunes and morale, and badly affected its ability to struggle on across the wide expanses of the Indian Ocean. Consequently, while thrice in the 1640s the Portuguese were able to repel strenuous Omani attempts to capture the Muscat fortresses, there was a limit to their battered endurance. Their exhaustion was exposed in their singularly feeble and poorly conducted defence of the Muscat fortresses in 1650, which finally fell to the

Omanis led by the dynamic and ambitious Ya'ariba *imam*, Sultan I bin Saif (r.1649–1688).

The *imam* followed up his victory by immediately developing a powerful, modern navy. His fleet had as its core the Portuguese vessels he had captured, but he could also depend on the naval expertise of the people of Muscat, who knew how to design and build these Western ships. The Omani fleet benefited also from European mariners who took service with it, and from the assistance of the Dutch and English, who, seeing the Omanis as useful allies against the Portuguese, seconded them navigators, gunners and arms suppliers. Soon the Omani navy with its well-gunned, up-to-date warships was the largest and most formidable fleet in the western Indian Ocean. This was particularly unfortunate for the Portuguese, who were their ancient and hated enemies.

Omani merchants had been settling all along the Swahili coast since the seventh century, although the Swahili as Shafis (a sub-branch of the Sunnis) kept them at a slight distance because they were Ibadis. But both groups found common ground in their resentment of Portuguese regulations and taxes, which hampered their trade, and looked to the *imam* of Oman to help them throw off the rule of the hated foreign infidel. Certainly, it made sense ideologically, geographically and commercially for the Omanis to follow up their own liberation from the Portuguese by sweeping them from the Swahili coast and supplanting them as overlords.

Only two years after they captured Muscat, the Omanis struck hard against the Captaincy of Mombasa. In 1652 Imam Sultan's fleet raided both Pate and Zanzibar and, with enthusiastic local support, horrifically wiped out the local Portuguese communities. Francisco de Seixas de Cabreira, the Captain of Mombasa, only dared respond once the Omanis were safely out of the way. He sacked Zanzibar thoroughly in retribution, and for the time being this seemed sufficient to cow the Swahili towns and force them back into the Portuguese system.

However, this was as bad a time as it ever could be for the *Estado da Índia*. Every resource was desperately needed to contain the Dutch. Between 1654 and 1658 they seized the last remaining Portuguese strongholds on Sri Lanka and followed up by systematically reducing their forts along the Malabar coast of southwestern India. They even blockaded Goa. It was at that crucial moment for the Portuguese that the Sultan of Pate invited the Omanis back. They responded, and in December 1660 an Omani flotilla cruised provocatively along the northern Swahili coast.

Vessels and fighting men from no less than nine Swahili towns flocked to join the Omani flotilla, and on 12 February 1661 it sailed into the harbour at Mombasa right under the nose of the fort. The Omanis along with their fierce Baluchi* mercenaries (on whom they heavily relied for infantry in this period) and their Swahili allies disembarked the following day. Portuguese musketeers attempted ineffectually to prevent their landing. A running fight developed through the town until, thoroughly worsted, the Portuguese infantry took refuge in Fort Jesus, which was under the determined command of Joseph Botelho da Silva. The Omanis then comprehensively sacked the houses of the Portuguese part of town, and went on to use their doors and furniture, as well as palm trunks, to build two solid redoubts in artillery range of the walls of the fort. Once again the great walls and bastions of the fort proved too solid for the light Omani cannons. Recognising that they could never take Fort Jesus without proper siege artillery, the Omanis raised the siege on 24 March and sailed away with three Portuguese prizes they had captured in the harbour.

Omani operations against the Portuguese were not confined to the Swahili coast, and their fleets repeatedly attacked the *Estado da Índia*'s bases on the northwestern Indian coast. In 1661–1662 the Omanis raided the *feitoria* at Bombay and even sacked the great base of Diu in 1668, repeating this feat in 1676. Yet, despite these humiliations, the Portuguese situation in their now drastically curtailed Indian Ocean empire was actually stabilising. The reason for this was escalating conflict between the Dutch and English for control of the seas and international trade. The first of the Anglo-Dutch Wars was fought in 1652–1654, and before the next broke out in 1665 the English – who had already concluded a truce with the Portuguese in 1635 – undertook to defend Portugal's few remaining enclaves in Asia against the Dutch. To neutralise this combination, in 1663 the Dutch concluded a peace of their own with the Portuguese, and so spared the heavily mutilated *Estado da Índia* any more amputations. Thereafter, in the Indies the Portuguese would fight no more colonial wars against fellow Europeans. This was just as well, considering

* The Baluchi are an Iranian people who live in what is now southeastern Iran and southwestern Pakistan.

how depleted their resources were. But they still had to contend with the aggressive Omanis, who continued to pursue their ambitions along the entire Swahili coast.

Having benefited from good intelligence gathering, in 1670 a fleet of more than twenty Omani vessels raided Moçambique Island precisely when the captain was away with most of the garrison campaigning in the Zambezi valley. As a result, the Omanis landed without opposition and once again sacked the unfortunate town (rebuilt since the Dutch siege of 1608), burning houses and churches. They then laid siege to the fortress of São Sebastião and pushed forward their trenches to undermine one of the walls. However, the defenders succeeded in exploding a counter-mine that foiled all their endeavours. Like Fort Jesus, São Sebastião was too tough a nut to crack without the siege artillery the Omanis lacked. Disheartened, the Omanis gave up the siege and withdrew with their booty.

Thereafter, the Omanis made no further armed incursions south of Cape Delgado, leaving the Portuguese unmolested to pursue their interests as best they could up the Zambezi valley.* North of the cape, the Portuguese were determined to maintain their hold over the Captaincy of Mombasa, which had assumed much more importance to them now that most of the rest of the *Estado da Índia* had been lost. It was not easy. The Omanis did their best to stir up revolt along the coast. Towns such as Pate were in a chronic state of rebellion despite the draconian retribution the Portuguese regularly meted out, executing its reigning sultan in 1678 and again in 1687. Loyal collaborators were essential for help against such malcontents. However, their close relationship with the Portuguese could be their undoing. The dependable Prince of Faza found his position had become untenable by the 1690s, and he and other loyalist Swahili from Malindi and Kilifi were forced to migrate to Mombasa and settle under direct Portuguese protection.

The Omani Siege of Fort Jesus

In 1696 Imam Saif I bin Sultan of Oman judged the situation was favourable for another major assault on Mombasa. He sailed early in the year with a fleet

---

* See Chapter 5.

of seven vessels carrying 3,000 men. Yet not even an *imam* can command the weather. When his fleet sighted Mombasa on 11 March, unfavourable winds kept it from forcing the harbour before the defenders were alerted, and for two days prevented it from landing troops even on the island.

This delay allowed the defenders to prepare. Only about seventy Portuguese soldiers were garrisoning Fort Jesus under the command of Captain João Rodrigues Leão, and they had with them numbers of women and children. Officially, only Christians were allowed into the fort, but Leão understood that more defenders were essential. He welcomed in about 1,500 armed Swahili, all of them refugees settled in Mombasa under the command of the Prince of Faza. When the eighteen-year-old prince later died recklessly in action, his cousin Bwana Daud succeeded him, despite the fact that his brother was fighting on the Omani side and that they were holding his mother hostage in Pate. Leão also permitted several thousand Swahili non-combatants from the town to take refuge in the broad, deep ditch directly under the protecting walls of the fortress. Fortunately for the defenders, Queen Fatima of Zanzibar remained loyal and sent in supplies by boat whenever they could evade the Omani blockade. Leão also tried to secure the support of the Mijikenda on the mainland, because he looked to them for supplies, but they hung back, refusing to commit to either side.

The *imam* left the systematic conduct of the siege to Emir Sahad ibn Sahdi al-Beluci (a Baluchi mercenary), who had under him about 1,000 men on the island at any one time. They drew in their siege lines around the fort and built artillery redoubts at strategic points, including the mainland opposite Fort Jesus, both to fire on the defenders and to protect themselves from a relieving force. But, as in the siege of 1661, their artillery was not powerful enough to make any impact on the fort's stout walls.

The energetic Leão succumbed to disease on 23 October1696. He was succeeded as commander of the fort by António Mogo de Melo, who lacked his leadership qualities and found it hard to inspire a demoralised garrison suffering from lack of supplies and mounting disease. Yet the besieging Omanis were also dying of smallpox and other diseases. As in any siege, the combatants – and the wretched civilians caught in the ditch between them – presented a disheartening spectacle of suffering, discomfort, deepening deprivation and leaden boredom enlivened by brief flashes of fear and frantic excitement during bombardments or sorties.

The viceroy in Goa, the Count of Vila Verde, feared that if Mombasa fell Moçambique was sure to follow. Yet even though the *Estado da Índia* no longer had to contend with the Dutch threat, its condition was so debilitated that the viceroy simply did not know how he could raise the forces to relieve Fort Jesus. He eventually scraped up two frigates (small warships built for speed and manoeuvrability with between thirty or forty guns on the upper deck) and a pair of two-masted merchant vessels of shallow draught, known as galliots. Some 400 unenthusiastic men were on board, under a commander known to be second-rate – the Indian-born *fidalgo* Luís de Melo de Sampaio.

It was vital that Melo de Sampaio's force reach Mombasa before the Omanis were able to bring in reinforcements to replace the men they had lost to disease. Unfortunately, he completely mismanaged the voyage from Goa. Poor navigation brought the squadron to the Horn of Africa rather than Mombasa. It then had to tack down the coast for a fortnight until, on Christmas day 1696, Fort Jesus finally hove into view. By then the Omanis had succeeded in landing reinforcements, including more Baluchi mercenaries and 400 African slaves, and had established new batteries to tighten the siege even further. Indeed, the fort was on the point of falling, because disease and starvation had reduced the defenders to a mere handful. Even so, Melo de Sampaio's arrival off Mombasa gave the Omanis pause and the garrison brief hope. However, not surprisingly considering his questionable military record, he proved too craven to try and enter the harbour despite the impassioned entreaties of the garrison. In the end, Melo de Sampaio succeeded in landing only about ninety soldiers to reinforce the depleted garrison. Having done his very inadequate best, he then sailed away for Zanzibar on 25 January 1697.

Most unfortunately, the soldiers he had landed brought the plague. Soon it had struck down almost everyone within the walls of the fort. Yet the siege ground on, to the despair of all involved. Finally, on 20 July 1697 the Omanis decided they must attempt to storm the still unbreached walls. They raised five tall, makeshift ladders and began to swarm on to the parapet. The pitiful handful of defenders, who consisted only of the commander, Mogo de Melo, an Augustinian friar, two soldiers and twenty-two Swahili, assisted by fifty women sheltering in the fort, managed to push the ladders off, along with their screaming human freight. They also fired grapeshot at the attackers from two swivel guns mounted on the nearest bastion, and hurled grenades at them. About eighty Omani died in the failed assault.

Within a week Mogo de Melo had succumbed to the wounds he had received in the affray, and by the end of August all the remaining Portuguese had followed him to the grave. It was left to the brave and tenacious Bwana Daud, the Prince of Faza, to hold the fort with the twenty-odd surviving loyal Swahili and the several dozen women still alive. By Bwana Daud's own reckoning, by September 1697 the number of defenders who had perished in the siege amounted to 2,500 men and 500 women.

The timid Melo de Sampaio and his flotilla were still lurking among the islands off the Swahili coast, and in September 1697 he made another typically cautious and reluctant attempt to relieve the garrison. As he gingerly approached Mombasa, his frigate, which was carrying reinforcements and supplies, and was shielding several smaller craft, took heavy punishment from the Omani redoubts along the south shore of the island. The men on board suffered dozens of casualties. Even so, the frigate managed to lower a landing craft, but, harassed by fire from the shore, it ran aground directly under a redoubt. With their muskets waterlogged, the helpless crew of twenty surrendered. The Omanis mercilessly killed all of them on the spot except for one man who flung himself into the sea and swam to safety.

On 20 October the frigate itself with Melo de Sampaio on board ran aground the shoal at the entrance to the harbour opposite Fort Jesus. Despite their desperate efforts, its crew of 150 were unable to refloat it. They had no choice but to make it to the shore and seek refuge in Fort Jesus, assisted by a timely sortie by the tiny but gallant garrison. With no means of getting away, they found themselves willy-nilly the exceedingly reluctant new garrison of the fort. Cursing his misfortune, the unenterprising Melo de Sampaio rapidly succumbed to disease and died on 19 November. His command passed to the captain of the wrecked frigate, José Pereira de Brito. In deference to Bwana Daud's fidelity and courage in holding Fort Jesus, he declined to supplant him as governor of the fort, but took instead the title of Commander and Governor of the Portuguese.

Unlike the ineffective Melo de Sampaio, Pereira de Brito was full of courage and initiative. He was a sailor of humble origin who had worked his

way up to officer rank through professional competence and bravery. In daring
sorties he drove the Omanis from several of their redoubts in ferocious hand-
to-hand fighting. Yet all his efforts were in vain. Omani reinforcements landed
in November, and in early December two powerfully armed frigates sailed
into the harbour to support them. The Portuguese continued to make sorties,
but with ever-deceasing success. By the end of 1697 the Omanis had tightly
encircled the fort with no less than eight well-fortified redoubts.

Meanwhile, despairing efforts were being made in Goa to put together
another relief expedition. Eventually, three frigates and four smaller ships
under Francisco Pereira da Silva set sail for Mombasa. When they hove to under
the walls of Fort Jesus on 30 December 1697, they landed some reinforcements
while the garrison made a fierce sally to assist. Unfortunately for the desperate
garrison, Pereira da Silva was signally unimpressed by Fort Jesus' chances of
weathering the siege. The gallant Pereira de Brito and Bwana Daud entreated
him to continue the struggle and dislodge the Omani besiegers, or at least to
enter the Kilindini channel on the opposite side of the island and destroy the
Omani vessels huddled there. But the unadventurous Pereira da Silva clearly
did not wish to share the equally timid Melo de Sampaio's fate. He would do no
more than land a hundred or so soldiers under Leandro Barbosa Soutomaior,
whom he appointed the new Captain of Mombasa.

The loyal Bwana Daud took deep umbrage at being superseded and almost
immediately quarrelled openly with the undoubtedly brave, but brutal and
arrogant Soutomaior. As a matter of honour the Prince of Faza withdrew
from the fort with his surviving followers, along with Pereira de Brito and
other disgruntled Portuguese stalwarts, and took the 400 women still left alive
in the moat along with them. Most of them took ship with Pereira da Silva
when his flotilla sailed away on 19 January 1698 for Zanzibar, leaving Captain
Soutomaior to his unenviable fate.

The situation in Fort Jesus continued to deteriorate. The Omanis persuaded
the Mijikenda on the mainland to cut off supplies to the garrison, where the
inhabitants were soon dying at the rate of five a day from malnutrition and
disease. Their situation was clearly desperate, and the zealous new viceroy,
António Luís Gonçalves de Câmara Couthino, was determined to help them
at all costs. He pledged his personal credit to outfit a considerable flotilla of
four frigates and a galliot with 1,200 men aboard including the doughty Prince

of Faza. It sailed from Goa on 20 November 1698 under the command of the same pusillanimous Pereira da Silva who had sloped off from Mombasa earlier that year.

Meanwhile, in the tightly invested Fort Jesus, the plague continued to exact its ghastly toll. By mid-December 1698 only the tough Captain Soutomaior, eight Portuguese soldiers, three Indians, two African women and an African boy remained alive. The besiegers could not be certain that the garrison had been so catastrophically reduced, but they strongly suspected it must be so and decided to attempt once more to scale the walls.

On the night of 12 December the Omanis climbed up the rampart walls near the sea gate, which was let into the São Mateus bastion. The pathetically reduced garrison couldn't hold even that stretch of wall, let alone the whole great fort. They had no option but to fall back along the southern curtain wall and concentrate in the 'cavalier bastion', a raised gun position on top of the landward-facing São Alberto bastion. There, surrounded and their situation hopeless, they made their last, grim stand. All night they held out. At around seven o'clock the following morning, as the sun began to play on the limitless blue ocean upon which no rescuing Portuguese sail appeared, Captain Soutomaior made one, final flamboyant gesture. He charged out of the cavalier bastion firing his blunderbuss at the Omanis, who riddled him with bullets, ran him through with their swords and finally cut off his head.

With their captain dead, the survivors surrendered. Six Portuguese prisoners were later taken in chains to Muscat, but, so it is said, not before a seventh had revenged himself on his vanquishers. He lured a large party of Omanis into the powder magazine over the main gate, assuring them that he knew where gold was hidden. Once he had them inside, he lit a spark and blew himself up along with his greedy and credulous captors.

Eight days later, on 20 December, Pereira da Silva's flotilla arrived off Mombasa. Through their telescopes the Portuguese sighted the red flag of Oman flying from Fort Jesus and (doubtless to the relief of many, not least Pereira da Silva) realised they had come too late. After a desperate defence that had endured for two years and nine months the fortress had finally fallen. The Portuguese flotilla immediately stood off and sailed back to Goa, despite the indignant protests of their two most reliable Swahili allies, the Prince of Faza and the Queen of Zanzibar. These two understood perfectly that

Pereira da Silva had effectively ceded the Captaincy of Mombasa to the Imam of Oman.

In their failed defence of Fort Jesus the Portuguese estimated that their sacrifices directly and indirectly (many had perished at sea on the relief expeditions) amounted to 800 Portuguese, 2,500 Swahili auxiliaries and 3,000 Swahili non-combatants. Moreover, a frigate with forty brass guns, a galliot of twenty guns, another eleven middle-sized ships and twenty smaller vessels had all been lost. On both sides the great majority of deaths had been of disease. The Omani casualties are unknown, but would certainly have been far fewer than those suffered by the garrison inhabitants cooped up in their fortress.

Certainly, most of the suffering and loss had been on the Portuguese side. Yet Fort Jesus might have been saved if there had been more commanders such as the Prince of Faza and Pereira de Brito with a touch of initiative and dash, or admirals less cautiously wary of entering either of the two channels to Mombasa's harbour. Nor can one ignore what can only be categorised as incidents of gross incompetence and pusillanimity. Yet one has to acknowledge that the Portuguese difficulty in even raising relief expeditions strong enough to succour Mombasa was an indication of the terminal exhaustion of the *Estado da Índia*. After the fall of Fort Jesus two further expeditions were planned to retake Mombasa, one in 1698 and another in 1701, but neither actually reached the port. In any case, as future events would show, it was one thing to retake Fort Jesus, and quite another to hold on to it.

The Short-Lived Portuguese Recapture of Fort Jesus

Firmly ensconced in Mombasa, the Omanis took possession of the nearby Swahili towns as well. As the Omani historian Sálîl-ibn-Raznîk laconically put it, Imam Saif I bin Sultan 'attacked the Christians, and drove out some of them from their settlements, capturing from them Mombâsah [Mombasa], the green isle [Pemba], Kilwa and other places'.[15] Yet far from being liberators, the Omanis proved every bit as grasping as their Portuguese predecessors. Soon the Swahili towns they governed were plotting and manoeuvring to rid themselves of their new overlords and their thinly stretched garrisons. Between 1724 and 1728 the Banu Ghafir dynasty briefly seized power in Oman from the ruling Ya'ariba dynasty, and this period of civil conflict seemed an opportune moment for the Swahili to strike. The irony must have been obvious to all when the Sultan of Pate, Abubakar Bwana Tamu Mkuu, whose predecessors had repeatedly called on the Omanis to free the Swahili from the Portuguese, urgently sought the Christians' assistance against his Muslim overlord.

The viceroy, João de Saldanha da Gama (potent name!), took the bait. A squadron of six sail under Luís de Melo de Sampaio (ill-omened namesake of the admiral who died in Fort Jesus in 1697) sailed from Goa for Mombasa. On board was the indefatigable Prince of Faza. The tiny Omani garrison in Fort Jesus took one frightened look at the Portuguese ships and allied vessels from Pate and surrendered on 16 March 1728 without a struggle. The whole north coast followed suit and made formal submission to Portugal. Melo de Sampaio then sailed away, leaving a small garrison on Fort Jesus.

It did not take the townspeople long to regret they had ever welcomed the Portuguese back, because they had clearly not changed their profiteering and arrogant ways a jot. Even the Prince of Faza was alienated. Therefore, the Swahili turned back to Imam Saif II bin Sultan of the restored Ya'ariba dynasty of Oman as the lesser of two evils. As an anonymous Swahili history of Mombasa put it: 'The people of the town were made to submit to all kinds of exactions, and were even condemned to death for having gone to Oman to seek the Imam's aid . . . He fought and conquered them [the Portuguese], for God gave him help; and he drove them from the fort.'[16]

In retaking Mombasa the Omanis had the townsmen to thank. Knowing that an Omani fleet was on its way, on Palm Sunday in April 1729 they rose up, attacked the outlying Portuguese posts and drove their garrisons out of the town into Fort Jesus. Aided by the volatile Mijikenda from the mainland, they cut off supplies to the fort and settled down to starve out the Portuguese. The Sultan of Pate prudently withdrew his support from the Portuguese, who were now in desperate straits. When the Omani ships sailed into the harbour, the Portuguese hastened to make terms and surrendered on 29 November 1729. The Omani had not needed to fire a shot, which was just as well as they apparently had no cannon and but few firearms. The majority of the unwarlike soldiers of the garrison converted to Islam and remained in Mombasa to live as traders. Thirty others, with their commander, Captain Alvaro Caetano de

Melo e Castro, were given two small ships on which they ignominiously sailed away to Moçambique.

In Goa, the indignant viceroy, Saldanha da Gama, made one last effort to recover Mombasa. He put together a fleet of five ships and entrusted them once again to Luís de Melo de Sampaio. The admiral cautiously reconnoitred Fort Jesus from a safe distance on 2 February 1730, did not like what he saw and sailed away. Perhaps spinelessness in a commander does not always go unpunished, for on his return voyage to Goa a cyclone struck his fleet on the night of 18 May. Two of the warships were lost with all hands, including the gutless Melo de Sampaio.

Thus, in the violent ocean deep, the Portuguese Captaincy of Mombasa finally sank from sight. In succeeding years the Portuguese were too intent on preserving their last footholds in India from the growing power of the Maratha confederacy ever to contemplate reasserting their presence north of Cape Delgado. After 200 years of exerting a fitful and oppressive hegemony over the northern Swahili coast, another sea power and a Muslim one at that, had supplanted them.*

---

* Only with the succession of Sayyid Said II bin Sultan (r.1804–1856) of the less pious and more commercially minded al-Said dynasty did the Omanis succeed in exerting tight control over their Swahili empire. In 1839 Said moved the seat of government from Muscat to Zanzibar and made it his permanent residence. From there he controlled the coast from Cape Delgado to just north of Lamu. Fort Jesus was used as a barracks for his and his successors' soldiers. When Zanzibar became a British protectorate in 1895, Fort Jesus was turned into a prison. With the end of colonial rule it was restored and opened as a museum in 1960.

CHAPTER FIVE

The Elusive Gold of Mutapa

In Search of the Riches of Mutapa

In April 1569 three fine Portuguese carracks sailed down the river Tagus from Lisbon, devoutly firing salutes at the churches as they passed. A cannon on the flagship burst, and a flying splinter of metal sliced through the richly ornamented cap sported by the *fidalgo* Francisco Barreto as he strolled the high aftercastle in the company of his flamboyant officers. A one-time Governor of the *Estado da Índia* and the General of the Galleys of Portugal, Barreto was the newly appointed captain-general of the Monomotapa expedition and Captain of Moçambique. A great, open-handed lord accustomed to the grandeur of Goa, he suspected that the enterprise he was leading to the wilds of East Africa might be deficient in the glamour of the Indies. It was nevertheless calculated to add to his considerable reputation – although he may now have construed the smoking hole in his bonnet as a bad omen for its success.

From their first arrival on the southern Swahili coast, the Portuguese had entertained high hopes for what soon became the Captaincy of Moçambique. Gold and ivory reached its ports from the interior in tantalising quantities, and the Portuguese were determined to cut out the Swahili traders and secure the sources of these precious items for themselves. This meant penetrating the inhospitable, fever-stricken valley of the Zambezi river to reach the vast inland plateau where the gold was mined and the elephants were hunted.

The Portuguese experienced many vicissitudes in this quest and found themselves being drawn into wars with powerful African societies. For all their superior gunpowder technology and the victories this often brought, they were ultimately unable to transform their short-term military successes in the interior of the Captaincy of Moçambique into the wide-spreading land empire they sought to establish. That would have to wait until the late nineteenth century and the age of machine-tooled rifles and Maxim guns.

When the Portuguese sacked Kilwa and Sofala in 1505,* the ousted Swahili traders took themselves north to various strategic points along the Zambezi. There they established new *feiras* (fairs, or markets) and trade routes up to the plateau and the distant Mutapa kingdom that controlled gold production. Once they had bartered their goods such as Indian cloth for gold and ivory, they carried these precious commodities back to Swahili towns further up the coast from Kilwa. From there their small craft evaded the Portuguese naval patrols and shipped gold and ivory to Arabia or India, thus foiling Portuguese attempts to channel the gold trade through Sofala as a crown monopoly. For the time being the Portuguese, lacking both knowledge of the interior and sufficient military clout, had no option but to let the troublesome Swahili traders be. But their intention was always to take their place in the Zambezi valley and to secure the gold trade at source, in the mysterious kingdom of Mutapa.

The Portuguese early realised it would be no easy matter to advance into the interior. Several exploratory expeditions that made it up the Zambezi to the plateau between 1512 and 1515 reported all the daunting difficulties along the way, and confirmed that military force would be required to secure the gold fields from the rulers of Mutapa and their tributaries.

Plucky Portuguese explorers found that far inland from the trading town of Sofala on the sweltering, sandy Swahili shoreline, and 3,000 feet up from the densely bushed, fever-ridden coastal lowlands, there lay a great plateau. To the northeast it is bounded by the great Zambezi river, which follows a major volcanic fault down to the Indian Ocean. The heavily silted river flows through narrow gorges, over rapids and sandbars. It is subject to flash floods during the summer rains that fall between November and April, when it can swell out to nearly five miles across. But during the desperately dry winter months it dwindles to straggling streams and residual pools.

For 400 miles between the dangerous rapids at Cahora Bassa and the sea, the lower Zambezi flows through a wide, uncomfortably humid valley rife with malaria, sleeping sickness and trypanosomiasis, which are death to humans,

---

* See Chapter 2.

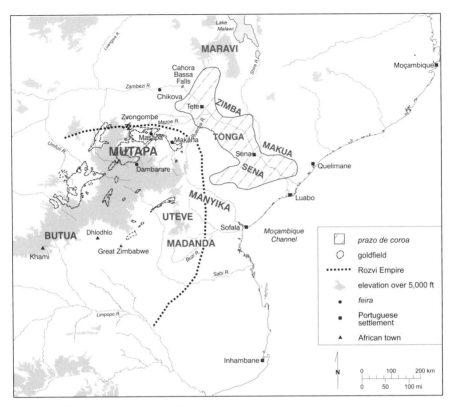

MAP 10 *The Zambezi valley and Mutapa*

cattle and horses.* The low rainfall supports only scrubby bushveld, drought-resistant mopane trees with their distinctive, butterfly-shaped leaves and huge baobab trees that rear up in their bizarrely anthropomorphic attitudes. The valley's dire climate with its frequent droughts allows only for basic, subsistence agriculture to supplement hunting and fishing. What indifferent crops the people in their scattered village communities do succeed in raising on the riverbanks or islands are regularly ruined by floods and the depredations of hippopotamuses.

When it reaches the coast, the now languid river spreads out and meanders through the mudflats and mangroves of a vast delta that has some of the highest, continuous rainfall in all of southern Africa. The Portuguese quickly

---

* Malaria is mosquito-borne, and sleeping sickness and trypanosomiasis are both carried by tsetse flies. The Portuguese had no idea that these diseases were caused by the bite of these insects.

grasped that their smaller seagoing vessels of up to 100 tons were able to enter the main channels of the delta to discharge their cargo into very light, long vessels called *almadias*. These craft could navigate the notoriously fickle, treacherous Zambezi as far upstream as the towering granite barrier at Cahora Bassa. So, for all its disadvantages, the Portuguese identified the river as the best available route inland to the great plateau and the riches they believed it contained.

The plateau itself the Portuguese scouting parties found to be an attractive and abundant land of summer rainfall, and they saw at once its potential as a place to settle permanently. Many rivers traverse this airy plateau. They rise in wide, shallow valleys and then cut down through the edges of the plateau in ever deeper, more rugged gorges as they drain into the Zambezi and other major rivers. Savannah woodland, with thorn trees dotted over the wide, grassy spaces, covers much of the plateau, although the woods are thicker in the valley bottoms while the grassy higher regions are almost treeless plains. The cool, refreshing highlands that run from north to south along the eastern edge of the plateau are covered with mountain trees and plants.

The early Portuguese explorers reported that the people who lived there behind wooden palisades in their round, thatched huts of wattle and daub with a central supporting pole spoke Shona or Kalanga, its close linguistic relative in the family of Bantu languages. Women sowed, weeded and hoed the fields to grow the millet from which they made their basic diet of porridge (which they enhanced with a relish of vegetables and fruit from their gardens) and from which they also brewed their beer. Indian maize and rice, staples today, did not reach the plateau until the eighteenth century. The primary duty of men was to herd their livestock, although they also hunted everything deemed edible from monkeys to crocodiles and fished with traps of woven reeds to supplement their monotonous diet. For a society that counted its wealth primarily in cattle and women, good grazing and reliable sources of water decided where people established their villages.

As for the Mutapa kingdom that held sway on the plateau, the Portuguese understood little of its origins although they observed its practices and culture. It has been left to much more recent archaeologists, anthropologists and historians to gain more of an understanding.

The Mutapa Kingdom

It is now generally accepted that the Mutapa kingdom evolved from the Late Iron Age Zimbabwe kingdom that had flourished from the 1200s to the 1450s as southern Africa's first really extensive state. Zimbabwe, as it expanded, incorporated other, smaller Shona-speaking statelets on the plateau, and by bringing gold, ivory and cattle (all the main sources of wealth) under the firm control of its rulers made it possible as never before to regulate the enriching, long-distance trade with the Swahili coast.

From the mid 1200s through the 1300s the Zimbabweans built a great capital city on the southern plateau, known today as Great Zimbabwe. Between 15,000 and 18,000 people are believed to have lived there during the capital's heyday in the mid-fourteenth century. It was strategically situated at the upper watershed of the Sabi river to command the trade that passed down the river from the gold fields of the western plateau to Sofala and Kilwa on the coast. At Great Zimbabwe's ceremonial core were enormous enclosures for court and state ritual, their massive, towering walls constructed of stonework without the aid of mortar. Hundreds of round huts made of thatched wattle and daub crowded closely around the royal precinct. The great ceremonial centre proved awe-inspiring to the empire's tributary states, whose rulers built their own, smaller 'Zimbabwes' across the plateau and down to the edge of the lowlands.

Zimbabwe was stumbling by the beginning of the fifteenth century. It is thought that it was losing sole command of the vital gold trade to competitors, and that trade routes and populations were moving north to the Zambezi valley and to the very periphery of its zone of control. Be that as it may, the empire broke up in the 1420s, and Great Zimbabwe was abandoned by the 1450s, only a few decades before the Portuguese arrived on the Swahili coast. The extensive ruins of the centre's stone structures still stand today. In the sixteenth century the Dominican friar Father João dos Santos was amazed by their scale and sophistication, and could not bring himself to believe that they could have been the handiwork of the ancestors of the Africans he saw around him. Rather, he conjectured they had been built by the biblical Queen of Sheba, and that the plateau was the fabled land of Ophir from which gold was sent down to King Solomon's fleets.[1] Thus an enticing legend was born that remained current well into the twentieth century.

Two smaller empires arose to take Zimbabwe's place. One was the kingdom of Butua on the southwestern plateau with its reigning Torwa dynasty. Its capital, Khami, was built on the plan of Great Zimbabwe (although reduced in scale) and kept alive its masonry tradition with its elaborate drystone walling in herringbone and chevron patterns. Gold continued to be mined and exported, but Butua's wealth was based much more on the Torwa kings' control and redistribution of the vast cattle herds that grazed the grassy plains.

The Kalanga-speaking Mutapa kingdom was the second of the Zimbabwean successor states, and was forged on the northern plateau in a series of military campaigns waged between the 1440s and 1480s. Its ruler was known as the *mwenemutapa* (lord of the conquered land). The Portuguese called him the Monomotapa, and applied that term to his kingdom as well. Mutapa was centred in the fertile Mazoe valley, a region rich also in alluvial gold, and the peasants were expected to wash it for the *mwenemutapa* and lesser chiefs as tribute. The Mutapa kingdom also claimed sovereignty over the copper-mining regions of the northwestern plateau as well as over the ivory-producing areas along the southern banks of the Zambezi, where enormous herds of elephants roamed. Hunters secured their tusks by hamstringing the unfortunate beasts with axes or caught them in pits before stabbing them to death. Africans in the mid-sixteenth century insisted to the Portuguese chronicler João de Barros that 'four to five thousand elephants die every year' for the ivory that found its way mainly to India.[2]

Yet, despite its appearance of wealth and might, the power and cohesion of the Mutapa kingdom were, in fact, somewhat illusionary. Mutapa was really more of a loose paramountcy than a centralised kingdom. Its core on the northern plateau measured only 145 by 95 miles, and was surrounded by partially loyal subordinate chiefdoms over which the *mwenemutapa* exercised only tenuous authority. The most unreliable vassals were the major kingdoms down the eastern side of the plateau and on the coastal plain below. The *mwenemutapa* depended on their erratic and often grudging tribute in lion and leopard skins, ostrich feathers, cattle and gold that supplemented the labour of the peasantry in his fields and their rent paid in kind.

By the early 1500s Mutapa was in decline. When the Portuguese first came into contact with the subordinate kingdoms at the eastern foot of the plateau – according to dos Santos, these were Uteve, stretching as far east as the outskirts of Sofala, Madanda to its south along the Sabi river, and Manyika to its north with its extensive gold mines[3] – they had already effectively hived away from Mutapa's control. They continued nevertheless to perform their ritual and tributary obligations to the *mwenemutapa*, although this did not deter them from going regularly to war with him. The Tonga and Sena chiefdoms along the lower reaches of the Zambezi were persistently resisting his overlordship and foiling Mutapa's spasmodic attempts to command the lucrative trade routes down the river to the sea. For the Portuguese, these divisions, conflicts and weaknesses in Mutapa would give them ample opportunities to meddle in its affairs to their own advantage.

At first, though, without the resources to send in the necessary military expedition to take firm control of the lands they had their eyes upon, the Portuguese settled for a creeping, informal advance up the Zambezi towards the interior plateau. By the 1520s they were setting up among the Africans of the coastal plain and the Zambezi valley, and were installing themselves alongside the Swahili merchants at their inland *feiras* and taking service with local African rulers as interpreters and advisers.

These tough pioneers were what the Portuguese termed *sertanejos* (backwoodsmen) – private adventurers and traders, former soldiers, *degredados* (deported criminals), sailors who had jumped ship, drifters, a few Dominicans in their white habits and black capes and some Jesuits in their stark, black habits. Along with this motley bunch were their African converts, sundry dependents and hangers-on, wives, mistresses, orphan girls, prostitutes and slaves. The trading opportunities also soon lured in *canarins* (Christian Indians from Goa).

By the late sixteenth century these 'Portuguese' living along the Zambezi are best described using the Swahili term as *wazungu* (*mzungu* in the singular). It means 'a person of foreign descent', and was first used on the coast to mean a Portuguese. However, the term was increasingly understood to describe someone of mixed Afro-Portuguese or Afro-Indian descent. Indeed, the *wazungu* of Zambezia came within a generation or two physically to resemble the Africans among whom they lived, although they retained their Portuguese names, their Catholicism and nominal loyalty to the crown. They were usually fluent in Portuguese but conversed easily in Tonga or other local languages, and increasingly identified with local customs and lifestyle. They swiftly developed into true 'transfrontiersmen' with a foot in both Portuguese and African culture.

The Portuguese took a more formal step in their long-term strategy to command the Zambezi trades routes when in 1531 they sent a small armed expedition up the Zambezi valley to fortify and garrison two settlements. Sena was 160 miles from the mouth of the Zambezi and Tete another 160 miles further upstream, where the temperature rises to a suffocating fifty degrees Celsius (122 degrees Fahrenheit) in summer. The forts at these outposts began as typical palisades of stakes surrounded by a ditch. As the fortunes of Sena and Tete rose and declined over the coming years, so the sophistication of their forts fluctuated too. They were in their heyday in the late sixteenth century, when Father dos Santos described them as being 'of stone and mortar furnished with several pieces of large and small artillery'. Within each fort was the residence of the captain, the *feitoria* (factory) and church. The friar counted 800 'Christians' at Sena, and several hundred fewer at Tete. Of these 'Christians', he identified only forty or fifty at each place as Portuguese (probably first-generation *wazungu*), and the remainder as 'Indians [*canarins*] and native Kaffirs'.[4]

By the time their small garrisons were settling down at Sena and Tete, the Portuguese understood that to wrest the trade with Mutapa from the Swahili middlemen they had to establish direct contact with the Kalanga-speaking kingdom on the plateau and gain the *mwenemutapa*'s friendship and co-operation. The Portuguese consequently began to send missions to his court to learn about his kingdom and to find out how they could establish closer trade links.

When in the mid-sixteenth century the Portuguese finally came into direct contact with the *mwenemutapa*, unlike his recent forebears he was no longer living in thatched, wattle-and-daub dwellings still surrounded by Zimbabwe-style stone walls. Rather, his palace at Zvongombe was described in the mid-1600s by Antonio de Bocarro (the official chronicler of the *Estado da Índia*) as being 'composed of many houses surrounded by a great wooden fence, within which there are three dwellings, one for his own person, one for the queen, and another for his servants who wait on him within doors'. As de Bocarro went on to explain, his many wives were 'his relations or sisters, and others are the daughters of the kings and lords who are his vassals. The principal one . . . is always one of the king's sisters.'[5]

The *mwenemutapa* was served by young men of the aristocracy and attended by his great nobles. When he walked among his subjects, carrying a spear of black wood with the point made of solid gold, he was preceded by an attendant beating his thigh with his hand to let the people know their king was following. His subjects approached the *mwenemutapa* on their bellies, and before they could speak to him or any of his wives they had first to offer a gift according to their station, such as cloth (which the Portuguese always presented to him) or livestock. Dos Santos recalled that when suppliants were so poor that they had nothing of real value to offer they brought the king 'a sack of earth in acknowledgement of their vassalage, or a bundle of straw to thatch his houses'.[6]

All this courtly ceremony partially disguised the fact that the *mwenemutapa*'s functions were primarily ritual ones and that he had delegated his authority to his relations, subordinate chiefs, officials and wives. As ruler, his most important role was to propitiate the powerful shades of his royal ancestors on behalf of the nation, begging them especially for rain and asking their advice on all matters of policy. He did so through respectful, ritual consultation with the *mhondoro* (powerful spirit mediums) through whom the ancestors spoke at their shrines. He diligently observed the cult of the royal graves, never failing to visit them before any major military expedition so that the ancestors would bestow their blessing.

Dos Santos described the *mwenemutapa* and all his vassals wearing 'a white shell on the forehead, hanging from the hair as an ornament', which was the special insignia of men of Mutapa that distinguished them from those in other kingdoms. Men wore their hair as long as possible and arranged it in elaborates styles. In the sixteenth century multiple hornlike tufts were the most fashionable, the hair of each horn being 'made to stand up as straight as an arrow by being twisted around a thin piece of wood' and smeared with vegetable gum to make it firm.[7]

By the sixteenth century the growing of cotton and weaving of cotton cloth were established on the plateau, and supplemented the older practice of weaving fibres of bark into fabric. Most of the Mutapa elite wore the standard dress of the wealthy Swahili. This consisted of cotton or imported silk cloth girt around the waist and hanging down to the ankle, and usually another cloth draped over the shoulder as a cloak. The really wealthy wore their clothes so long that they trailed on the ground and frayed away in a display of conspicuous consumption. But older customs in dress persisted, and animal skins continued to be worn, mainly by the poor who could not afford the desirable cloth garments and had to make do with monkey and other cheap skins attached like an apron in front. The elite draped themselves for prestige in valuable and attractive skins like those of wild cats or leopards. According to Barbosa, an early sixteenth-century commentator, they wore them 'trailing along the ground like tails, to show quality and gallantry, making leaps and gestures that make those tails go from one side to the other'.[8]

Women wore similar clothes from waist to calf, the less well-off having to be content with imported Indian cottons, often dyed in stripes, while the richest were dressed in imported silks, damasks, satins and cloth of gold, often embroidered or decorated with ribbons. Indeed, the insatiable desire for fine cloth was the foundation of commerce on the plateau. Heavy copper bangles covered women's calves, but they also craved the coloured beads brought in by the Swahili traders. Fashion in beads changed with bewildering rapidity, and traders had to be deft so as not to be landed with stock in the wrong colour.

While at the *mwenemutapa*'s court the Portuguese took care to observe his army carefully in anticipation of inevitably going to war with it. It was the observation by Damião de Goes (a noblemen and chief chronicler of Portugal until he fell foul of the Inquisition in 1571) that: 'whether in time of peace or war he [the *mwenemutapa*] always maintains a large standing army, of which the commander-in-chief is called Zono [*sono*, or war leader], to keep the land in a state of quietness and to prevent the lords and kings who are subject to him from rising in rebellion.'[9] Certainly, there was a strong link between the *mwenemutapa* and his army because his wealth and survival depended on it.

Recalcitrant district chiefs (many of whom were the *mwenemutapa*'s own relatives) signalled their rebellion by refusing to proceed to his court to accept his ritual gift of fire with which they annually rekindled their own sacred hearths, or by staying away from the harvest festival at his capital, Zvongombe, during which the unity of the state was reaffirmed. That is when the *mwenemutapa* would despatch his army to bring them to heel; but it was also potentially dangerous for him to do so because it was difficult for him to control his *sono* and the troops under his command when they were operating at a great distance. Yet the *mwenemutapa* needed his army not only to keep overmighty subjects in check, but also to extract tribute in grain, livestock or gold from them and the peasantry, and to ensure that the foreign traders, whether Swahili, Islamicised Africans or Christians, paid their dues on their commercial transactions.

The *mwenemutapa* also required his warriors for the massive royal hunts that were organised like regular military operations. Thousands of warriors were mobilised to drive the game – lions, elephants, buffalo and anything else – into a large, open space where they surrounded the cornered animals. They then set their dogs on them and killed the desperate beasts with arrows and thrusts from their spears.

Because they were a Late Iron Age people, the Kalanga understood well how to smelt and hammer iron into arrowheads, spear blades, hoes, hatchet blades and, as dos Santos noted, 'a kind of half sword which they call *lupangas*'.[10] With the Kalanga, as with the Portuguese, bearing arms was a matter of honour. Dos Santos reflected that as to 'the Kaffirs going about with bows and arrows, it is as common with them as with the Portuguese it is to wear a sword in the girdle and no Kaffir ever leaves home without these arms'.[11]

The army was made up of levies of men who would have had some training in fighting when they were youths, but who otherwise would be going about their normal business, herding livestock, hunting, helping with the crop at harvest time or mining gold. It is difficult to know how big a Mutapa army ever was, because the Portuguese routinely grossly exaggerated the numbers of enemies they were facing. Maybe at the height of Mutapa's power the kingdom could field an army of up to 30,000 men, but as its power decayed so too did its ability to mobilise the peasantry for war. Generally, and quite understandably, it can be said that Mutapa was always more successful in raising its part-time warriors to defend their own land from attack than for distant campaigns of aggression.

The *mwenemutapa* did maintain a small force of a few hundred men on a permanent footing, but this was a royal guard, a warrior elite related to him by blood or marriage. There is some debate about this, but it seems they accompanied him everywhere loudly reciting his praises to the sound of drums and bells. Besides protecting his person, they also acted as his executioners.

Emphasising how the customs of Mutapa were 'very similar, and almost exactly the same' as those of Uteve where he worked as a missionary, dos Santos described how the fearsome executioners in the entourage of the ruler of Uteve went about their work. They instantly killed those the king pointed out to them by first striking them on the head with 'a wooden club about three quarters of a yard long', exactly as if 'killing a pig', and then cutting off the head with 'a very bright iron hatchet'.[12]

When going on campaign, an army from Mutapa (and also from Uteve and other tributary states) would be led out by its chief *sono*. These *sonos* would be clad in distinctive, valuable animal skins, and wore their *lupangas* (short swords) in gold-ornamented, wooden sheaths hung by belts of dyed cloth from the waist. The army marched under battle standards of basketwork covered with cloth, which were in the shape of leopards, lions, elephants or bulls. These were the totems, or emblems, that identified warriors of the same clan lineage. The warriors started out carrying their own food from home, and if they were lucky the *mwenemutapa* would send cattle to their camp to supplement their dwindling supplies. Otherwise, they had to live off the land, and this always limited the duration of operations. In the desiccated Zambezi valley a large force could not stay in the same spot for more than three days without starving.

The army was organised into groups of varying size depending on their *sono*'s rank. He conveyed his orders through signals from horns and drums, and the distinctive note of each *sono*'s drum could easily be distinguished by his men. It is true, as de Bocarro commented, that the Kalanga habitually fought hand to hand in the open field because they had 'no weapons of defence, fortress, or walled cities'.[13] Yet an army from Mutapa did not deploy by immediately spreading out to outflank and envelope the enemy in the fashion of neighbouring peoples such as the Tonga of the Zambezi valley. Rather, Mutapa *sonos* preferred to employ defensive tactics. When the *sono* gave the agreed signal on drum and horn, his men took up a formation like three sides of a square (or a U) with their baggage in the middle and the fourth, rear side open. Then each warrior, who was carrying a large, wooden, man-high shield three palms wide, planted the spike at its base into the ground to make a barricade. From behind the security of their shield walls the opposing armies showered each other with flights of arrows and spears hurled most dextrously. If they thought they had the upper hand, warriors from one side might sally out into the open in attacking waves and try to break through the enemy's formation in hand-to-hand fighting with clubs and *lupangas*. If their assault failed, they retreated to the safety of their own shield wall.

What about the use of firearms? Matchlocks had been in the hands of the Kalanga and other local people since about 1515. The Uteve kingdom, a reluctant tributary of Mutapa, early opened relations with the Portuguese and secured matchlocks to overawe their African enemies. The volatile Zambezi valley with its conflicting interests also saw a great initial interest in the new weapons and a growing trade in them. The *mwenemutapa* was equally impressed and appreciated how they had helped the growth of Uteve's ability to resist him. Clearly, the Portuguese, who knew best how to use firearms, were both a threat and possible auxiliaries against rival rulers and insubordinate regional chiefs. So, warily, the *mwenemutapa* began to court the interlopers when they visited him on the plateau as potential allies, and also to try and secure some firearms from them. Yet, as it would turn out, matchlocks would fall far short of being a decisive weapon in the coming wars. Not only were they not imported in large enough numbers until the eighteenth century to make much of a difference, but they were also never such superior weapons that they could save an incompetent commander from the difficult terrain, inhospitable climate and a determined enemy.

Lust for Gold

In 1540 the Portuguese succeeded in regularising their trading relations with Mutapa. Although Mwenemutapa Neshangwe Munembire (r.c. 1530–1550) did not sever his commercial relations with the Swahili merchants already operating in his kingdom, he decided to allow the Portuguese to trade freely in return for paying tribute and a hefty tax on their transactions. He also agreed to the presence of a permanent trade and diplomatic mission at his court headed by a Portuguese officer called the Captain of the Gates. As the insignia of his office he carried a black spear with a golden point, just like the *mwenemutapa*, and a gold bracelet. The *mwenemutapa*, nevertheless, left the Portuguese in no doubt about their inferior, suppliant status in his realm, and he insisted that they conform to the demeaning rituals of his court that marked them as his subjects.

Even so, by the end of the sixteenth century these arrangements made it possible for the Portuguese to establish *feiras* throughout the gold-bearing regions of the plateau, including Mutapa, Uteve and Manyika. Archaeological excavations at the sites of three of the most important *feiras* – Luanze, Ongoe and Dambarare (the chief one) – have shown that they were of similar construction to the more rudimentary Portuguese forts in the Zambezi valley. They consisted of walled enclosures made of mud or sun-dried bricks with wooden palisades that were allowed to take root. Outside each stockade there was a ditch with corner bastions that could take cannon. Within was the house of the captain of the *feira*, which also served as a storehouse, and sometimes a chapel. The Portuguese traders lived scattered among the local communities and not inside the *feiras*, so when danger threatened they had to scramble to get inside the stockades in time.

What the Portuguese wanted most from Mutapa was its gold. The *mwenemutapa* fully grasped this, and to exercise his control over its production and exchange tried to keep the Portuguese away from the areas where it was mined. These were extensive, for gold was widely present in the granite-based plateau dominated by Mutapa and on in its eastern slopes ruled by Manyika, the *mwenemutapa*'s fitful tributary. The men, women and children of the villages in the gold-bearing regions exploited the deposits together in group enterprises under the direction of their headmen.

For centuries before the coming of the Portuguese these people, whether under the rule of Zimbabwe or Mutapa, had been exchanging the gold they mined for beads, cloth and other items at *feiras* established far inland by Swahili traders based at Kilwa. The Portuguese ingenuously believed that the moment they cut out the Swahili middlemen and reached this land of gold that they would be able, as dos Santos wryly expressed it in the last years of the sixteenth century, simply 'to fill sacks with it and carry off as much as they chose'. The reality was very different. The friar, who was familiar with the whole laborious process, commented that once the Portuguese actually 'saw the difficulty and labour of the Kaffirs, and with what risk and peril of their lives they extracted it [the gold] from the bowels of the earth and from stones, they found their hopes frustrated'.[14]

Compared to panning for nuggets and flakes of gold in the rivers, mining the subterranean gold reefs was arduous, dangerous work, and required sophisticated techniques. It was first necessary to crack open the rock faces by heating them with fire (for which much firewood was required) and then rapidly cooling them with water. Next, deep vertical shafts, or stopes, were dug down through the rock using special tools such as hoes, picks, hammerstones and iron gads to reach the veins of ore. These veins were then followed along horizontally dug tunnels until the ore pinched out or went below the water table. When that happened, or water burst into the shafts drowning those working there or a stope simply caved in (leaving an ominous crater at the surface), a new mine had to be opened. If all went well, the miners passed the excavated jumble of earth, rocks and ore to the surface in baskets and bowls. Then, in a tedious milling process the gold-bearing quartz was separated, roasted, crushed and gold washed out. Dos Santos described the glittering, desirable fruits of all this labour:

> This gold is found in many different shapes, that is in dust-like sand [which was packed into hollow reeds or quills for exchange], in grains like large and small beads, in fragments, some of which are so solid that they seem to have been melted down, others in branches with many shoots, and others . . . [that] remain hollow within like a honeycomb.[15]

By the mid-sixteenth century it seemed to the Portuguese that they were developing a harmonious relationship with Mutapa that might well lead to their desired control of the gold. Then suddenly in 1561 everything fell apart. The previous year a zealous Jesuit missionary of noble blood, Father Conçalo da Silveira, had been welcomed at the *mwenemutapa*'s court. It was the Society of Jesus' effective and proven strategy to concentrate on converting the elite to give a lead to the rest of society, and da Silveira homed in on the young and impressionable Mwenemutapa Negomo Chisamharu (r.1560–1589). His efforts swiftly paid off. In January 1561 Father da Silveira baptised Negomo Chisamharu along with his mother and some 300 royal relatives and councillors.

For a heady moment it seemed to da Silveira that Mutapa was on the verge of becoming the Christian kingdom the Jesuits so fervently desired. It would not be. Kalanga conservatives and the influential *mhondoro* were aghast at the possibility. They launched inflammatory rumours suggesting that da Silveira had come to spy out the land for a planned Portuguese invasion of

Mutapa, and that the water of baptism was an evil charm that would fatally weaken the *mwenemutapa* and those around him. It seems too that the Swahili traders at court alongside the Portuguese energetically fanned these fears to undermine their trading rivals and religious enemies. It was not long before Negomo Chisamharu began to veer smartly around and reverse his opinion of the Jesuits and their motives. Sensing the dangerous shift, da Silveira resolutely prepared himself for approaching martyrdom. In the early hours of 16 March 1561 the *mwenemutapa's* executioners broke into his hut, strangled him and threw his body into the river. Many of his more recent converts shared his lamentable fate.

The irresolute *mwenemutapa* soon began to have second thoughts about what he had done, and his courtiers warned him against inevitable Portuguese retribution. To placate the Portuguese he turned on the Swahili traders who had been egging him on to kill the missionary and his converts, and executed them in turn. As a result relations with the local Portuguese were more or less patched up, but Father da Silveira's death would indeed have dire repercussions.

Far over the seas in distant Portugal, King Sebastião achieved his majority in 1568 at the tender age of fourteen and thereafter ruled without a regent to guide or restrain him. The pugnacious teenager instantly signalled his thirst for war and military glory wherever it could be found.* Morocco would become his primary target, but Mutapa beckoned too.

As a devout Christian monarch Sebastião had been raised to accept that no war he waged could ever be considered legitimate unless Mother Church had first sanctioned his cause as just. In January 1569 a learned concourse of seven lawyers weightily assured the king that with specific reference to the 'the emperors of Monomotapa' war could be made upon them 'lawfully and without sin' because they had failed to eject infidel 'Moors' from their territories, had 'robbed and detained' Portuguese ambassadors and had put a Christian missionary and his converts to death. All these heinous crimes justified Sebastião sending soldiers to Monomotapa to enforce the safe preaching of the gospels by laying waste, taking prisoners or whatever other measure were permissible according to the 'rights of lawful warfare'.[16]

---

* See Chapter 1.

That was well and good, but Sebastião's pious eyes were fixed on Mutapa for excellent material reasons besides. His inspiration was the example of the Spanish *conquistadores* in Mexico and Peru whose silver mines were yielding such sensational returns. Mercantilists advised that if mines located in the *Estado da Índia* and reputed to be as rich as Spain's could be made to yield their bounty, then Portugal's empire would be made truly profitable at last. And by all accounts it was the legendary mines of Mutapa that seemed to hold out the best prospects for this glittering windfall. Thus crusading zeal and the lust for gold became fatally intertwined in the Captaincy of Moçambique.

Failed Portuguese Military Expeditions into the Interior

In March 1569 Sebastião appointed the highly experienced administrator and soldier Francisco Barreto (he whose cap was shredded by an exploding cannon at the beginning of the chapter) captain-general of the expedition to conquer Mutapa and its gold mines. Half the gold he took was to go to the king, another third was to be divided among the members of the expedition and the rest would stay in his pocket. The lure of such rich rewards as well as the military honour to be gained drew thirty *fidalgos* to join the expedition, and eager men stowed away in the three vessels already crammed full with 1,000 soldiers. Yet, despite all the fanfares and the brilliance of the company, the expedition got off to a very slow start. Storms and cracked masts scattered and delayed it, and it was not until May 1570 that two of the three ships were finally anchored in the harbour of the off-shore island of Moçambique.

The energetic and enterprising Captain Vasco Fernandes Homem, a former master of the military Order of São Tiago, was eager to reach the coast and push inland. So too was Barreto's Jesuit confessor and domineering adviser Father Francisco de Monclaros, who was puffed up thanks to the trust he knew the king reposed in him. But Barreto's enthusiasm for the dangerous enterprise ashore had distinctly waned, and he decided that until reinforcements arrived he would take the pleasanter option of cruising up and down the coast to show the flag to the Swahili towns. It was six months before he was back in Moçambique harbour, just as the new viceroy, Dom António de Noronha, sailed in on his way to Goa. Noronha summoned a council of war attended by all the captains, *fidalgos*, officials, Jesuits and Dominicans in the town. At the peppery viceroy's prompting, the shamed Barreto agreed to set out at once for Mutapa, bolstered by reinforcements detached from the viceroy's squadron of five ships.

The question was, by which route should he proceed inland? All the local experts insisted that he should sail to Sofala, and that a lightly equipped column should then go straight inland as fast as it could across the unhealthy lowlands to the kingdom of Manyika on the lower slopes of the plateau. Not only were gold mines believed to be there, but the ruler was at war with the *mwenemutapa*, his titular overlord, and could prove a useful ally. But Father Monclaros and the other Jesuits, burning to exact vengeance for the martyred da Silveira, insisted that to adopt this strategy would be to delay the final conquest of Mutapa. Rather, they urged Barreto to follow the direct route up the Zambezi, even though the old hands unanimously emphasised its notorious unhealthiness. To get their way, the Jesuits nastily warned Barreto that if he did not comply they would withdraw from his expedition and report his craven delays to King Sebastião. Rather than offend the powerful Society of Jesus and their devoted pupil, the king, Barreto gave his unenthusiastic consent. Unfortunately for that great nobleman and his reputation, the consequences of placating the Jesuits would be (as Diogo de Couto, the chronicler of the *Estado da Índia*, later expressed it) his 'ruin and death'.[17]

Barreto's was one of the largest Portuguese military expeditions on land ever to set out in the *Estado da Índia*. On 4 November 1571 1,000 Portuguese soldiers with an overcumbersome train of artillery, horses, provisions, slaves and pack animals (including donkeys and camels) sailed from Moçambique for Luabo on the southernmost branch of the Zambezi delta. There they piled into *almadias* (light riverboats) and sailed up the river to Sena. They reached the outpost on 17 December at the height of the murderously hot summer. The Portuguese set up camp in grass huts under the protection of the mud and palisade fort, São Marçal, close to the village that harboured a handful of *wazungu*. A gunshot away was a separate, larger settlement of Swahili merchants.

Barreto sent emissaries to the local Sena chief to help make contact with the *mwenemutapa*. He then settled down with his soldiers to await their return, time hanging heavy on their hands. The torrid, sweltering months went by. Mosquitoes and tsetse flies feasted on his men and horses, and they began to sicken and die of malaria and horse sickness. Not understanding why they were dying, it was all too easy for the Portuguese with their inbred fear and loathing of *Mouros* to believe that the Swahili in the neighbouring village were poisoning them. They were also enviously aware of the wealth stored in the traders' houses. So fear, credulity, greed and boredom combined in a deadly amalgam.

The Portuguese kidnapped a few Swahili who desperately confirmed the trumped-up poisoning story under unbearable torture, and Barreto felt he had all the evidence he needed. His men savagely fell upon the Swahili village, killing many of its inhabitants out of hand. They were the lucky ones. The Portuguese took seventeen of the leading men in the community hostage, and a few days later Barreto sentenced them all to death. His contemporary, the chronicler de Couto, recorded that: 'Each day they were taken two by two and placed at the mouth of big guns, which blew them to pieces, to strike terror into the others.' One who converted to Christianity the Portuguese hanged (which they considered an act of mercy), but the remainder were put atrociously to death with 'consummate tortures'.[18]

Meanwhile, Mwenemutapa Negomo Chisamharu had received Barreto's emissary with considerable ceremony and friendliness. He sent him back with his assurances that the Portuguese at Sena had his permission to proceed to the gold mines upstream. At the same time, he made it very clear that it would confirm the Portuguese in his favour if they would take time out on the way to punish his vassal the Tonga chief. He lived with his people in the drylands on the south bank of the Zambezi between Sena and Tete, and had been in revolt from Mutapa since the 1550s.

Mounted on one of the few surviving horses, on 19 July 1572 Barreto led his little army out of Sena. It was down to 650 Portuguese divided into four companies, along with a fifth company of sixty *canarins* and eighty locally raised African auxiliaries, whose one advantage was that they were paid so much less than European troops. Their six pieces of artillery and thirty ox-wagons laden with powder, provisions and trade goods made dishearteningly slow progress along the banks of the Zambezi, while an assortment of *almadias* with more baggage kept pace with them on the river.

It was an exhausting month before Barreto's straggling force reached the Tonga country. Intelligence came in that the Tonga were collecting an army to oppose the interlopers. Barreto decided he must locate his foes and meet them in decisive battle. To do so he struck westwards up what was probably the Ruenya river with 200 locally impressed porters carrying essential baggage. The rest of his baggage he left on an island in the Zambezi along with eighty sick. After marching for two days he sent another thirty diseased soldiers back to his island base.

Barreto now had only twenty-three horsemen and 560 matchlockmen under his command, but the latter included 100 musketeers who received double pay. At twenty pounds a musket was a heavier weapon than an arquebus, and its barrel had to be supported on a forked rest when being fired. The musket's range and penetrating power was superior too, but like the arquebus it was still fired by a matchlock, or sometimes by the complicated and expensive wheel lock. The more efficient flintlock would not generally replace the matchlock until the very end of the seventeenth century.

For several more days Barreto's force tramped on, suffering greatly from thirst because the Tonga had filled in all the wells. They quickly consumed all the oxen they had brought with them on the hoof, and were desperately hungry too. Then, on the evening of the tenth day, as they straggled over a rise, they unexpectedly came across their quarry. But the Tonga made for a far more daunting sight then they had reckoned on. Thousands of them (it is impossible to know their real strength and the Portuguese always exaggerated the numbers of their enemies shamelessly) covered the hills and valley before them. The moment the Portuguese came into sight, and much to Barreto's alarm, several formations of Tonga rapidly advanced in open order, uncomfortably reminding de Couto of 'swarms of locusts'.[19]

Barreto fell back to a nearby mountain and drew up his men on its lower slopes to secure them from being taken in the rear. It was a strong position and night was drawing on, so the Tonga decided not to press their attack home. Instead, they halted and made camp only a few miles away from the apprehensive Portuguese, keeping up a steady, nerve-wracking beating of their drums all night long. As dawn broke the drumming suddenly ceased, and Barreto was warned that this meant the Tonga were advancing to give battle.

The Portuguese abruptly shattered the disconcerting silence by beating their call to arms. Barreto led his men forward, his two dozen horsemen feeling ahead for the enemy. They touched the Tonga advance forces in a grassy, reed-covered plain and galloped back to give Barreto the alarm. The experienced commander halted his force and drew it up to receive the enemy in the traditional defensive formation of an infantry square with the baggage in the middle. In fact, it was more a rectangle than a square with two companies in the vanguard, a company on either flank, and the remaining two companies closing up the rear. Barreto placed a swivel gun mounted on a wagon in the rear, a cannon on one flank and a demi-cannon on the other, and the three heavy field pieces loaded with cast-iron balls in the van.

The Tonga approached in a great semicircle in skirmishing order led on by an ancient female spirit-medium who performed a ritual dance. When she was close to the Portuguese she emptied dustlike ritual medicines from a gourd and threw them into the air. (The Portuguese were subsequently told that her powders were supposed to blind them so that they would fall alive into the Tongas' hands.) Seeing how significant she was to the enemy, Barreto coolly ordered his chief gunner to fire the falconet (or light cannon) at her. He did so with such remarkably good aim that his shot laid the old 'sorceress' low. For a moment her unexpected demise stupefied the Tonga, and an elated Barreto took off his handsome gold chain and hung it around his gunner's neck as a reward.

The Tonga rapidly recovered from their shock, however, and (as de Couto expressed it) closed in upon the Portuguese 'in savage disorder, with great cries and shouts, brandishing their swords and darts'. As they came on, their arrows and flung spears wounded some of the Portuguese waiting for them in their tight formation. But Barreto knew that, while the Tonga were still at a distance in their open, 'savage disorder', to open fire on them would have little effect. So he held his men in check until the Tonga were bunched up in the final yards of their charge and formed a solid target. Just as the warriors were about to crash into their ranks, the Portuguese let out a great shout of 'São Tiago!' and fired a deadly volley from handguns and cannons that slammed into the converging Tonga and cut them down as if they were 'a flock of crows'.[20] It took ferocious discipline and considerable experience on the part of seasoned troops to withstand such a blast. But this was the first time the Tonga had ever come under such lethal, concentrated fire, and they turned and fled. The Portuguese charged forward and cut down the panicked fugitives at will, until Barreto had the trumpets sound the recall.

With the Tonga apparently dispersed, Barreto ordered his men (who had returned to their ranks in good order) to advance on the Tonga town, which was nearby. Before they reached it, they came upon a thick wood through which Barreto ordered his pioneers to clear a way. While they were busy at it, the remainder of his troops threw themselves down to rest. Then, at about ten o'clock in the morning, the Portuguese noticed what they took at first to be a rising fog but soon turned out to be a dust cloud thrown up by a great host on the march. The Tonga had regrouped for a second round. Barreto hastily formed up his men and artillery again in battle array, brought the cavalry inside the square, and piled up the tree trunks which the pioneers had felled to fortify his position.

The Tonga came forward as before in a great crescent, and soon its tips touched to enclose the Portuguese position. With menacing cries they all charged the camp in very loose, open order. What followed was a repetition of the battle earlier that morning. The Portuguese held their fire until the Tonga were sufficiently concentrated to make their deadly volley tell. Once again, the field was strewn with the Tonga wounded and dead. When the smoke cleared off, the Portuguese charged forward and chased the disordered Tonga from the field.

Confident the enemy would not return a third time, Barreto moved on the Tonga town, which consisted of thatched huts. His men burned it to the ground but spared the great palisade which surrounded it because they realised it would serve well as a fortification for the camp they were setting up in the smoking debris. They barricaded the entrance to the palisade with felled trees and positioned their artillery pieces to best effect. The place was well supplied with water, and the Portuguese holed up there to recuperate from their wounds and exertions, although numbers continued daily to die of fever.

After a pause of six days the indefatigable Tonga army returned in greater force than ever and attacked the Portuguese behind their palisade. But Barreto's men had fortified their position well. Although the Tonga attacked with grim determination and kept up the assault from dawn until after midday, they eventually fell back thwarted and in disorder. Two of the Portuguese died in the fighting and twenty-five were wounded, including Captain Homem, who was wounded deeply in the right shoulder by an arrow that passed through his sword belt and leather jerkin.

Just as the Portuguese were collapsing to the ground in fatigue after the hours of fighting, a Tonga emissary came jauntily forward with a white flag and requested a parley. Barreto received him with all the éclat he could muster (and it must be said he clearly had been dragging unnecessary furniture about with him). De Couto vividly described the scene:

> The governor . . . awaited his coming seated on a velvet-covered chair, with all the companies drawn up in order with their firelocks and their matches in readiness, the artillery placed in front, and the gunners with their linstocks [match-holders] in their hands. The governor wore a strong coat of mail with sleeves, with a sword ornamented with silver slung crossways, and a page stood near him with a shield of shining steel.[21]

As Barreto intended he should, the Tonga emissary 'trembled from head to foot' in overawed amazement – whether real or feigned – and negotiations were successfully concluded. The Tonga made over cattle and sheep to the hungry Portuguese and threw in a few gold nuggets and elephant tusks. They also agreed to permit the Portuguese to march on unmolested. But the Portuguese could not continue. Their sick and wounded numbered 120, the country was dry and barren and they simply could not face being attacked again. So they fell back on the Zambezi, picked up the party they had left on the island, and boats took them across to the north bank and safety.

Barreto's depleted force finally staggered back into Sena on 26 October 1572. There he found an embassy from the *mwenemutapa* that had been waiting to continue negotiations. Barreto sent back an ambassador with the demand that Negomo Chisamharu expel all the Muslims from his realm, protect Christianity and transfer a large number of gold mines to the Portuguese. But Barreto was not waiting around for a reply. He made over his local command to the wounded Homem, whom he left in charge of the 400 survivors at Sena, and on 4 December 1572 he and Father Monclaros left for Moçambique to find the means to renew the campaign.

Barreto arrived back in Sena on 15 May 1573 with powder and provisions, but 150 of the men he had left in Sena had perished of disease. Holed up in Sena, with his dreams of the gold of Mutapa dissolving like vapour in the fever-stricken air, it was only a few days before the captain-general took ill in his ramshackle hut and died. Far from the scenes of his former glories in Goa and Lisbon, he made an exemplary end, confessing himself at length and taking the sacrament. As befitted a great nobleman (although hardly a fortunate one) his body was taken back to Lisbon and given a sumptuous funeral. All the galleys in the harbour were hung in black in mourning for the deceased General of the Galleys, and members of the court walked in the stately funeral procession.

Homem succeeded to the doomed command of the fever-ravaged Monomotapan enterprise. To his surprise the *mwenemutapa*'s emissaries returned to Sena acceding to all the demands Barreto had made the previous year. But these great concessions came too late. The Portuguese had neither the manpower nor technology to exploit the mines made over to them. Only 180 members of the expeditions still survived and all were down with fever. Disease, drought and the determined resistance of the Tonga people of the valley had shown all too clearly that, while the Portuguese might have enjoyed some spectacular military successes because of their superior weapons technology and combat discipline, they were unable to translate these victories into anything permanent. They simply did not have the resources to exert their authority over the people of the interior.

Homem's council in Sena decided his remaining men must return to Moçambique to convalesce and reinforce. It was also resolved that any new expedition would not again attempt the fatal Zambezi valley. Instead, it would make for Mutapa by way of Manyika (as all the locals had urged Barreto in 1571 before he gave way to the Jesuits) and conquer the latter's fabled mines on the way.

Homem took time to convalesce in Moçambique during 1574, and managed to obtain 412 reinforcements from the annual outward fleet (although fifty-two deserted when they realised they were due for the interior). On 16 November 1574 Homem reached Sofala just as the rainy season was beginning. But fearing his disaffected men would desert if he lingered, he pushed on. For eleven days he marched up the Buzi river valley in drenching rains before coming to a halt in Uteve territory. The locals had tried to hide all their food stores from the invaders, and Homem's men became involved in constant skirmishes as they raided for provisions. It was a sign of their frustration that they killed all their prisoners. Some of his soldiers planned to desert by sailing downstream to the coast, so Homem foiled them by burning all the boats.

With no option but to go forward, the Portuguese reached the Sitabonga fields where the Uteve army tried to stop them. They fought their way through, took many prisoners, including the ruler's three sons, great wife and brother and burned his capital at Simbaoé to the ground. The ruler of Uteve thereupon submitted to Homem and agreed to pay tribute to Sofala. Homem marched on into Manyika territory where he learned that Mutapa was mobilising against him. Not liking the odds, Homem decided the moment had come to retire to Sofala, which he reached on 26 September 1575.

It was while he was in Manyika that Homem realised the gold mines were very far indeed from what the Portuguese had imagined them to be. The workings were small, mining full of risk and panning unproductive. It was, as de Couto put it, 'altogether a poor and miserable business'[22] that yielded very modest returns for backbreaking and dangerous labour. Homem grasped that, to make the mines pay, great capital outlay and a huge workforce would be required – both of which were beyond Portugal's means. The mineral wealth of the interior was proving to be a chimera.

But if the gold was a distinct disappointment, then there was always the possibility of silver deposits on a South American scale. Silver was said to be present in great quantities far up the Zambezi, and that was to be the long-suffering Homem's next mission. By 29 October 1575 he was back in Sena, where 138 recruits joined him, only to perish quickly of malaria. There were now only 230 Portuguese left alive in the whole Zambezi region. Even so, the indefatigable Homem pushed upstream to Tete, where he built a fort of mud and stone. He voyaged on up the Zambezi to Cahora Bassa, left his boats below the rapids, and continued nearly 150 miles to the territory of Chief Sachurro of Chikova, which was supposed to be rich in silver, as were the Boquisa hills north across the river. For forty-two days the Portuguese remained in the area, desultorily prospecting during the day and returning to a fortified camp at night. Ambassadors from Mwenemutapa Negomo Chisamharu reached them there, and magnanimously made over all the silver mines to the Portuguese – if they could find them, and if the local people would let them work the ore.

Homem returned to Moçambique for orders and left his men in their stockade under the command of António Cardoso de Almeida. Chief Sachurro's people, pretending to be friendly, offered to take them to the elusive mines. They led a contingent of Portuguese to a defile in the hills where they unexpectedly set on them in an attempt to kill them all. A handful of survivors escaped the massacre and made it back to the fort. There they and the forty or so soldiers who had been left to guard it withstood a siege over several months. At last, starving and with no relief in sight, they sallied out and died honourably to a man.

Thus the protracted Barreto and Homem expeditions ended in dismal failure. Certainly, Homem was of more stubborn stuff than the half-hearted former Governor of the *Estado da Índia*, but without a major military commitment from Portugal he too could achieve little that was lasting. And with the *Estado da Índia* living on a shoestring and facing more enemies every day and on every front, that was never to be. After Homem's final failure, military expeditions into the interior were infrequent and scaled down. However, Portuguese involvement in the affairs of the Zambezi valley and the plateau was far from over. The Swahili traders had been killed or driven out, and the Portuguese took their place in the economy of the region. Their forts at Sena and Tete with their tiny garrisons continued to serve as advanced bases for future penetration inland. True, the Mutapa and subsidiary kingdoms of the region retained control of their territories and economies, but the Portuguese now played an increasing part in the trading system.

The Struggle to Control the Zambezi Valley

The inability of the official Portuguese forces to play any effective role in the Zambezi region was confirmed between 1589 and 1592. The Lundu *mambo* in the valley of the Shire river that ran into the Zambezi was becoming angered by the Portuguese interruption of his monopoly of the ivory trade, and despatched his warriors, known as the Zimba, against them and their African allies.* In 1589 a band of Zimba conquered the lands of a Makua chief allied to the Portuguese north across the Zambezi from Sena and settled

---

* See Chapter 4.

down in a fortified camp as sophisticated as any Portuguese engineer could devise. The ousted Makua chief elicited the aid of André de Santiago, Captain of Sena, who responded by crossing the river with most of the Portuguese garrison armed with matchlocks and with two cannons in support. When de Santiago realised that the Zimba were secure behind their double palisade of wood, loopholed for firing arrows, strengthened by earthwork ramparts and surrounded by a deep, wide ditch, he knew he was not strong enough to take their camp, regardless of his gunpowder weapons. He therefore fell back to an entrenched camp closer to the Zambezi and requested the aid of Pedro Fernandes de Chaves, Captain of Tete. The captain responded in the approved headstrong, chivalrous fashion of a *fidalgo*. He immediately marched downstream with 200 Portuguese and *wazungu* armed with matchlocks and accompanied by drummers and trumpeters. Some 2,000 auxiliaries provided by allied Tonga chiefs around Tete followed in their wake. These Africans were armed with bows, spears and axes and marched behind their totem-bearers.

Zimba scouts learned that the overconfident matchlockmen were a mile or so in advance of the African auxiliaries, and that, to de Couto's disgust at their slack self-indulgence, 'they were marching without order, being carried in palanquins and hammocks.'[23] Hardly believing their luck the Zimba laid an ambush for them in the thick bush near their fortress and succeeded in catching the matchlockmen completely off guard. They butchered them almost to a man with their battle-axes, arrows and spears, while protecting themselves with their light, small shields. The Tonga auxiliaries, on approaching the field of slaughter, quickly grasped what dire fate had befallen the feckless matchlockmen and made a swift about-turn, retreating in good order to Tete.

Meanwhile, the Sena contingent under de Santiago, whose intelligence gathering was as lax as that of their ill-fated compatriots from Tete, knew nothing of the previous day's disaster. The first they learned of it was early the next morning when the Zimba sallied out of their fortress and bore down on de Santiago's camp near the river, derisively beating the drums they had captured from the Tete matchlockmen. To their unbounded horror, the Sena soldiers beheld the Zimba chief, transgressively dressed in the chasuble of a Dominican friar (who, it seems, had been captured alive in the ambush but had been subsequently shot to death by arrows), prancing ahead of his men. The Zimba warriors behind him carried along the bloodied limbs of the dead Portuguese they had hacked off as trophies, and to drive home the point brandished Captain de Chaves' head on a lance.

There was no question of even trying to hold their entrenched camp. The panicking Sena contingent abandoned it in the greatest confusion and tried to make it back across the river to the fort at Sena. The Zimba cornered them on the banks of the Zambezi and butchered about 130 of them, including the unfortunate Captain de Santiago. The survivors of the debacle held on to Sena, but they had lost control of the valley. The Zimba continued to terrorise the district from their fortified camp and regularly to attack traders on the river.

The Captain of Moçambique, Dom Pedro de Sousa, decided at length that he must dislodge the Zimba to restore trade again to the interior. In 1592 he assembled 200 Portuguese matchlockmen and 500 African auxiliaries and launched an attack on the Zimba stronghold. The Portuguese cannons had no effect on the stout defences. De Sousa then attempted to take the place by direct assault. However, confronted by the combined and deadly effects of the defenders' accurate archery, the boiling fat and water they poured down over the assailants, and the wicked, long iron harpoons they thrust out of the loopholes at them, the Portuguese quickly gave up the attempt. Not able to take the stronghold by assault, the Portuguese settled down to besiege it. After two fruitless, disease-ridden months de Sousa had had enough and raised the siege. The gloating Zimba fell upon the disorderly retreating Portuguese column and captured most of its artillery and baggage.

Unable to dislodge the Zimba by force of arms, the Portuguese authorities realised they had no option but to try and live side by side with them. For their part the Zimba were anxious to settle down on the northern bank of the Zambezi and secure their slice of the lucrative river trade. So the two antagonists eventually came to an agreement and the increasingly domesticated Zimba became a permanent presence in the valley. But this had only been possible because the Portuguese were too weak militarily to evict them.

With the Captain of Moçambique in no position to launch any more significant armed sorties into the interior, and with the garrisons at Sena and Tete reduced to the merest skeletons, other institutions emerged that were able to fill the vacuum left in the Zambezi valley by the evaporating Portuguese military presence.

These were the *prazos de coroa* (leased crown estates), huge landholdings in the Zambezi valley held by *wazungu* and religious foundations. Some were confiscated Swahili estates, and others originated as concessions by local African chiefs or the *mwenemutapa* in return for gifts and military assistance. In this way much of the territory and many of the inhabitants of the Zambezi valley gradually came under the rule of these *prazeiros* (*prazo*-owners), who set up fortified stockades (like the *feiras*) as their bases.

Because the presence of the Portuguese crown was so weak in the hinterland of the Captaincy of Moçambique, it had little choice but to confirm individual *wazungu* in their *prazos* in return for paying quitrent (land tax). Periodic attempts to limit the size of *prazos* and regulate the rules of inheritance generally proved futile. Seventy-two *prazos* were registered by individuals in the Zambezi by 1637, four by the Jesuits, two by the Dominicans and two by African chiefs. By the mid-eighteenth century there would officially be 103 *prazos*. Some *prazos* grew to cover 1,000 square miles or more and were so vast that it took several days to march across them. A *prazeiro* ruled over his estates like an African chief. He only secured respect in his domain if he ruthlessly imposed tribute (which he extracted in labour and kind from his peasantry, who were the descendents of the Africans who had occupied the land when it became a *prazo*), sentenced miscreants to death and went to war with his enemies.

Early in the seventeenth century Antonio de Bocarro made mention of the *prazeiros'* 'slaves, fighting men, who serve as sailors on the *almadias* and guard their masters and the merchandise they carry inland'.[24] These were the *chikunda* (military retainers) the *prazeiros* recruited and armed with spears and firearms to police their estates, exact tribute and labour from their peasantry, protect trade and follow them to war. Over the years the *chikunda* also became increasingly involved in hunting elephants for ivory, a natural extension of their warrior function.

The term '*chikunda*' comes from the Shona verb, *kukunda* (to vanquish). They were usually organised into military units of about a dozen men under a junior officer, and these were then banded together to form regiments. Commentators such as de Bocarro usually referred to the *chikunda* as slaves, and many were indeed bought (young boys commanded the highest price as they could best be trained into the military life) or captured in raids or war. But others were voluntary recruits, fleeing war or famine for security. Their children born on the *prazo* were raised to follow their fathers and become *chikunda*.

The number of *chikunda* in any one *prazeiro*'s service might range from a few dozen to several thousands, and by the early nineteenth century it was estimated that there were about 20,000 of them all told. They lived apart from the peasantry in their military villages, where they developed their own distinctive language, a tongue that was an amalgam of many others. As slaves they had lost their own ancestral spirits, so they sacrificed instead to the spirits of their common ancestors – *chikunda* who had died on the *prazo*.

They fostered a distinctive warrior culture that emphasised daring, bravery and military discipline, which they regularly expressed in violent ceremonial dancing. As warriors living dangerous lives they disdained agriculture as women's work, even though in the Zambezi valley (although not on the plateau) male peasants worked in the fields. This attitude served to set them firmly apart from the contemptible local peasantry they policed and exploited, and who were expected to clap their hands in deference when they encountered one of the *chikunda*. The *chikunda* also differentiated themselves from the peasantry by outward signs such as their facial tattoos on each cheek and the forehead received after initiation, and by their front teeth, filed into ferocious points. Their garments were of imported white calico received from the *prazeiros* and also served to differentiate them from the inferior peasantry in their woven bark and skins.

Nevertheless, despite all their privileges and outward defining marks and dress, the fact remained that the *chikunda* were still to all intents and purposes slaves. They were not free to leave their *prazo*, and were subject themselves to terrible punishments if they dared turned their hands against their masters. For their part, the *prazeiros* lived in constant fear their *chikunda* would rebel, as many did. Others ran away and established free communities in the hinterland from which they sallied out to threaten outlying *prazos*.

Meddling Perilously in the Affairs of the Kingdom of Mutapa

As their military power waxed in the Zambezi valley, *prazeiros* and their *chikunda* could not resist being drawn into the complex and dangerous affairs of the

Mutapa kingdom. On several occasions during his reign Mwenemutapa Gatsi Rusere (r.1589–1623) called on them for military aid against invaders and rebels. In return he ceded more peripheral land in the Zambezi valley for *prazos*, and made over the notional rights to gold and silver mines, which the *prazeiros* were never in a position to exploit. More problematically, he allowed Dominican missionaries into his kingdom to replace the Jesuits martyred in 1561. Soon the Dominicans were becoming actively involved in the politics of Mutapa. So too were the *prazeiro* warlords and the *wazungu* traders at their *ferias* from which they controlled their commercial network across Mutapa and its tributaries. Naturally, this lobbying and meddling had immediate benefits, but rendered the Portuguese community on the plateau very vulnerable to dangerous political shifts.

The first time the *prazeiros* came to the military aid of Gatsi Rusere was in 1597. Two groups of Maravi people from the southern end of Lake Malawi had crossed the Zambezi and invaded the plateau. They and the fearsome Zimba were of the same origin and shared the same military culture.* Appealed to by the *mwenemutapa*, the *prazeiros* and their *chikunda* took part in a joint expedition with the Mutapa army against the more northerly of the two forces. Reportedly fearing the Portuguese firearms, the Maravi fled, devastating the countryside behind them so that the pursuit had to be abandoned. The second Maravi force moved rapidly up the Motambo river to within striking distance of the *mwenemutapa*'s capital at Zvongombe. With his main army still away to the north, Gatsi Rusere decided to temporise. The Maravi were migrating to find a favourable place to settle and run their herds, so he allowed them to remain as his vassals. Unfortunately, they proved ungrateful and dangerous, only too prone to ravaging their neighbours. So at some point in 1599 or 1600 the *mwenemutapa* decided to expel them and called again on the Portuguese.

Seventy-five Portuguese and *prazeiros* and 2,000 *chikunda* assembled under the command of Belchior de Araujo, Captain of Tete. Meanwhile, the forces of Mutapa, numbering many thousands, had ineffectually surrounded the Maravi fortress, held by only 600 men. The fortress was of typical Zimba design with a high palisade, a deep, wide ditch and earthworks. It seems the Portuguese had learned from their disastrous attempt to storm the Zimba

---

* See Chapter 4.

fortress near Sena in 1592, only a few years before. This time, as related by
Antonio de Bocarro, who had succeeded Diogo de Couto as chronicler of the
Estado da Índia:

> . . . they made large wickerwork screens, open at the back and covered at
> the top, which could hold fifty Kaffirs, who carried them before them like a
> wall until they reached the enemy's fort, without the arrows harming those
> who carried them. There were loopholes in the screens, through which our
> Kaffirs discharged their arrows and the Portuguese their guns.[25]

The assault lasted all day, and although the fort did not fall, the Maravi
suffered heavily, especially from the matchlock fire. Deciding their position
was untenable, they broke out that night and fled. It was clear to Gatsi Rusere
that he owed his victory to the *prazeiros* and their *chikunda* and he was suitably
grateful in terms of grants of land.

In 1607 Gatsi Rusere was faced by internal revolt and turned for help to the
prominent adventurer Diogo Simões Madeira, whose trading headquarters
were at Tete. In return for the cession of elusive silver mines on the plateau,
Madeira propped the *mwenemutapa* up on his throne. His forces, made up of his
chikunda and Maravi-cum-Zimba mercenaries, numbered several thousands,
but the elite were the small striking forces of between thirty and seventy
musketeers. Between 1607 and 1609 these musketeers co-operated repeatedly
with Gatsi Rusere's armies to defeat their numerically superior foes in a series
of stiff engagements in which their firepower lent them the winning edge. This
civil war was also the making of Madeira. He became the effective ruler of
great tributary territories under the *mwenemutapa* and completely dominated
the Zambezi trade.*

The hard-fought civil war of 1607–1609, in which firearms had played such
an important role, ushered a new and dangerous element into the conflicts of
the region – as Madeira himself was soon to discover. In 1613 he deployed his
private army of *chikunda* to suppress a revolt in the Zambezi valley near Sena
that was inconveniently disrupting trade. The rebel leader, Chombe, fell back

---

* Madeira's successes eventually inflamed the envy of other Portuguese traders. They impeached him to
the crown authorities, raided his estates, carried off his women and children and stripped him of all his
possessions. Madeira, however, was extremely tough, and he managed to claw his way back to honours
and wealth.

with his men into a typical fortress that consisted of a strong wooden palisade surrounded by a wide ditch. When Madeira's musketeers and *chikunda* attacked it, they discovered to their dismay that Chombe's confident followers were (as de Bocarro put it) 'well provided' with firearms, powder and ammunition, which they had traded with merchants from the coast. Madeira's men finally succeeded in storming Chombe's stockade, but, de Bocarro conceded, they were now nervously aware that the 'Kaffirs who were formally terrified by the discharge of a gun now use them, and most of the powerful Kaffirs in these parts have a better arsenal of guns than there can be in the captain's factory [in Moçambique]'.[26] The Portuguese clearly no longer enjoyed a monopoly in firepower, and this was at a time when the situation on the plateau was becoming daily more volatile and dangerous.

During the early 1600s Kalonga Masula, the senior Maravi chief, who was to die in 1650, established a powerful Maravi empire by conquest. In 1623 his army crossed the Zambezi and invaded Mutapa. The foray proved no more than an extensive raid and the Maravi warriors withdrew, loaded down with booty in gold. The shock of this incursion discredited the *mwenemutapa* and weakened Mutapa. Yet the kingdom had to face even worse disruptions following Gatsi Rusere's death later that year

Gatsi Rusere's successor as *mwenemutapa*, Nyambu Kapararidze, was determined to destroy the influence of the Portuguese on the plateau, take back control of trade from the *feiras* and re-establish royal authority over all Mutapa. In 1628 he exploited the failure of the Portuguese Captain of the Gates to pay the annual tribute for the trading concession as his excuse for tough action. He turned violently on the unprepared *wazungu* community in Mutapa, but most of the traders managed to escape to their fortified *feiras*. From behind their walls they sent out desperate cries for help. Assistance came from Sena and the surrounding *prazos*, where 250 men of the garrison and *prazeiros*, along with thousands of *chikunda*, took the field. In December 1628 and again in May 1629 the *prazeiro* armies defeated Nyambu Kapararidze.[27]

The defeated *mwenemutapa* fled, and the Portuguese marched to his capital at Zvongombe, where the self-interested *prazeiros* began to fall out over who they should place on his throne. The voice of the Dominican friars in Mutapa prevailed in this dispute because it was known they represented the interests of the crown, and the *prazeiros* still accorded it their perfunctory loyalty. As it just so happened, the Dominicans had a tame candidate they had groomed for the job: Mavura Mhande, the deposed *mwenemutapa*'s uncle. So on 24 May 1629 the Portuguese proclaimed him ruler in the place of his deposed nephew, and he in turn declared himself a vassal of King Felipe III of Spain (who was also King Filipe II of Portugal) and agreed to pay him tribute in gold. Later that year he also accepted baptism as Felipe from Father Luís Espírito Santo, the leading Dominican – much to the delight and satisfaction of his namesake, the King of Spain and Portugal.

While Mavura's submission to the Portuguese certainly compromised him in the eyes of many of his subjects, for their part the Dominicans were soon disappointed in their puppet. He possessed neither the will nor authority to control the *prazeiros* and traders wrangling violently to monopolise the blighted trade of the plateau. His subjects soon had enough of him too, and in 1631 the undaunted and vengeful Nyambu Kapararidze led them in a widespread uprising. He was determined this time to drive the hated *wazungu* out of Mutapa, and most of the *feiras* indeed fell to his men. His forces swept on down to the Zambezi valley, where only the forts at Tete and Sena held out. They came finally to a halt only when they reached the walls of Quelimane on the coast at the northern channel of the Zambezi delta. According to the doubtless inflated estimation of contemporary chroniclers, between 300 and 400 *wazungu* perished along with 6,000 of their African adherents.[28] Father Luís Espírito Santo fell alive into Nyambu Kapararidze's hands. Knowing full well that the Dominican was the usurper's puppet-master and had baptised him, Nyambu Kapararidze had Santo tied to a tree and stabbed to death with spears.

Nyambu Kapararidze's revenge was undoubtedly the biggest disaster that had ever overtaken the Portuguese in the Captaincy of Moçambique. They were only saved thanks to the energy and determination of the captain, Diogo de Sousa de Meneses. With 200 Portuguese arquebusiers shipped in from Moçambique Island he relieved Quelimane early in 1632. He then proceeded upstream, ruthlessly restoring the Portuguese presence in the Zambezi valley. From there he marched on to the plateau, his force swollen to 300 Portuguese soldiers and *prazeiros*, along with many thousands of *chikunda*. On the morning of 24 June 1632 he confronted Nyambu Kapararidze's army in battle and crushed it with great slaughter. By all accounts the Portuguese matchlockmen played the decisive role. The victorious de Meneses put Mavura back on his wobbly throne, and he survived as *mwenemutapa* until 1652, when he died of an accidental gunshot wound. De Meneses also re-opened the battered *feiras* and did his best to get trade going again.

Yet none of this could ensure the long-term survival of the *wazungu* in Mutapa. The beleaguered *Estado da Índia* was in no position to establish its authority over the plateau, and would be even less so after 1640 when Portugal regained its independence from Spain. This meant that the *wazungu* and *prazeiros* were now on their own, and that there would be no repetition of de Meneses' dramatic rescue. At the same time their interfering presence destabilised the weakened Mutapa state, and tributaries such as Uteve, Madanda and Manyika ceased paying tribute once and for all. Increasingly, the *mwenemutapas* reigned as the pliable puppets of the Portuguese interlopers. In 1654 they came to the aid of Mwenemutapa Siti Kazurukamusapa (r.1652–1663) and put down a widespread revolt against his rule. On the other hand, when he ceased co-operating with the *prazeiros* they assassinated him in 1663 and replaced him with an apparently more compliant puppet, his brother Kamharapasu Mukombwe (r.1663–1692), whom the Dominicans baptised as Alfonso.

The regular oppression by the *prazeiros* and *wazungu* operating in Mutapa, who insisted that all trade must pass through their *feiras*, eventually provoked widespread resistance among the local peasantry. Many fled to take service with warlords who were building up private armies to secure cattle and grazing lands, fight rivals and resist the Portuguese. The resulting low-level warfare disrupted the mining and distribution of gold on the plateau and by the late seventeenth century led to a marked falling-off in gold production.

One of the new warlords was Dombo, called Changamire after his lineage, who was said to have started life as a herdsman of the *mwenemutapa*. He built up a highly disciplined and well-trained armed following on the northwestern plateau. These warriors came to be known as Rozvi (destroyers). The Rozvi army was never particularly large, numbering only several thousand. The *changamire* (as the Rozvi ruler came to be called after the founder of the kingdom) maintained a small bodyguard on a permanent footing. It was recruited from young, unmarried men with insufficient cattle to pay a bride price, who earned the right to marry through this military service. Otherwise, the rest of the Rozvi forces came from households settled in proximity to the *changamire*'s capital. As part-time soldiers they served only when they were called out for specific campaigns. The *changamire*'s conquered, tribute-paying subjects did not form part of his army, which was intended as a dependable instrument for putting down rebellions.

It may have been a compact force, but the Rozvi army was especially efficient and the most feared in the entire region. It was organised into regiments with smaller subunits under a hierarchy of officers. Warriors were thoroughly trained in the use of typically Kalanga weapons and in military exercises. They wielded bows and arrows, *lupangas*, spears, battle-axes and cudgels and could manoeuvre in organised fashion and deploy in their favoured crescent formation to outflank and envelope their foes.

In the 1680s Dombo led his Rozvi and their great herds to the southwestern plateau where Butua, one of Zimbabwe's successor states after its fall, still flourished. Dombo overthrew it and established his much larger Rozvi kingdom in its place. He made his capital at Dhlondhlo and later shifted it to Khami, the old Butua centre. The Rozvi maintained the Zimbabwe-style drystone architecture that was Butua's heritage. The royal court, according to a nineteenth-century description, consisted of 'three large stone houses, each with many rooms . . . surrounded by walls of ivory tusks'.[29] There the *changamire* ruled in close consultation with the *mhondoro* serving as the mouth, ear and eye of the creator god Mwari, who expressed himself through natural phenomena such as lightning and earthquakes at his chief shrine in the Matopos hills. This spiritual sanction legitimised his rule over the militaristic, predatory Rozvi state.

Secure in his conquest state on the southwestern plateau, Dombo felt ready to challenge Mutapa and the Portuguese for control over the rest of it. In 1684 Rozvi bowmen stood up to Portuguese musketeers in the pitched battle of Mahungwe, in which the *prazeiros* and their *chikunda* were supporting the forces of Mwenemutapa Kamharapasu Mukombwe. A report by the thoroughly aghast Father Antonio da Conceição described how, despite 'the heavy mortality inflicted by the Portuguese firearms',[30] Dombo rallied the Rozvi forces five times so that the battle was still undecided at sunset. The Portuguese encamped on the field in the hope that the Rozvi would choose to retire in the course of the night. Just after midnight camp fires suddenly sprang up all around the Portuguese in their bivouac, leading them to believe that they were being surrounded by the Rozvi who were bringing in reinforcements. It was not so, and the fires were Dombo's deliberate ruse. But it worked. The *chikunda* and their Kalanga allies fled, leaving the Portuguese no choice but to decamp also. The Rozvi moved in and picked up the booty. The debacle at Mahungwe was a heavy blow to Portuguese military prestige, and they nervously began improving the fortifications at all their bases.

When Kamharapasu Mukombwe had seized the throne of Mutapa in 1663 with Portuguese support, he was unable to lay his hands on a dangerous rival. This was his nephew, Nyamaende Mhande, who the Portuguese baptised as Dom Pedro and groomed in exile at Tete as a possible replacement for his uncle, who was proving ever less compliant to their wishes as the years went by. For his part Kamharapasu Mukombwe became convinced that the Portuguese were plotting to foist Dom Pedro on to his throne and resolved to take pre-emptive action. In a truly fatal moment he called on Dombo and his Rozvi army for assistance.

Accordingly, in November 1692 a Rozvi force suddenly rushed upon Dambarare, the most important *feira* in Mutapa, taking it completely by surprise. The local *wazungu* and Dominican friars had no time to reach the *feira*'s sheltering walls. The Rozvi killed them all. With their flayed skins displayed at the head of their army to strike terror into all who might think to support the Portuguese, the Rozvi flooded over the rest of the northern plateau and down into the Zambezi valley as far as Tete. There the pretender, the exiled Dom Pedro, energetically raised support against them. When the *prazeiros* and their *chikunda* rallied to him he pushed the Rozvi back and invaded the plateau. Many Kalanga chiefs in Mutapa decided to join him. Finding himself abandoned, Kamharapasu Mukombwe fled to take refuge with Dombo. He soon died, and the Rozvi proclaimed their puppet, Nyakambira, to succeed as *mwenemutapa* and helped him hang on to his unsteady throne.

In 1693 Dombo went to war again, determined finally to have done with the Portuguese. He destroyed the *feira* of Masapa and all the others still operating on the northern plateau. The surviving *wazungu* traders fled once again, taking refuge in the forts on the Zambezi while the Rozvi raided the valley. Sena and Tete were only saved by Dombo's death in 1696 because during the ensuing succession dispute the Rozvi armies withdrew to the plateau.

There the Mutapa kingdom was a casualty of the Rozvi's growing strength. By the 1730s the Rozvi controlled all of the plateau except for the far northern edge, where a sadly shrunken Mutapa survived as a minor state under the protection of the Portuguese at Tete. The Rozvi refused to permit the Portuguese to set foot on the territories they controlled and the *wazungu* eventually lost all direct access to gold production. Not that it mattered much because under the *changamires*, whose kingdom survived until the 1830s, most of the gold was retained for their court and crafted into jewellery.

Holding on in the Zambezi Valley

With access to the plateau denied them, the Portuguese in the Zambezi valley switched their commercial interests to the north bank of the river and exploited the gold there. In the course of the eighteenth century they even began to re-establish some *feiras* on the edges of the plateau, but only on the sufferance of the local rulers, and with their armed protection. Whichever way they looked at it, the Portuguese had to recognise that they had lost the plateau and its commercial network, and that they were confined henceforth to the Zambezi valley and the coast.

In the Zambezi valley the enfeebled Portuguese crown had no option but to leave the *prazeiros* alone so long as they provided *chikunda* to keep order, maintain the roads and keep up government buildings. The affluent *prazeiros* pursued an ever more opulent lifestyle surrounded by their milling retainers. A prosperous *prazeiro* typically had a spacious country house on his *prazo* and also spent time in his smart town house in Quelimane or Moçambique. Successive generations of *prazo*-owning families repeatedly intermarried, so that by the mid-nineteenth century four or five *wazungu* family groups dominated the whole Zambezi valley. Small as it was, though, this tiny group of *prazeiros* – with the essential aid of their *chikunda* and with the co-operation of the 1,000 or 2,000 *wazungu* and Portuguese officials in the sprinkling of fortresses and little town of the Captaincy of Moçambique – eventually had a singularly baleful impact on the African population.

When the trade in gold failed in the late seventeenth century, ivory took its place and the *prazeiros* and their *chikunda* hunters exploited the Makua and Maravi lands north of the Zambezi. Caravans of 1,000 porters brought the veritable mountains of tusks down to the coast to help replenish the cobwebbed coffers of the *Estado da Índia*. More seaports were required as outlets for this trade, especially since the loss of the Captaincy of Mombasa had forced trade further south. To this end, in 1727 the Portuguese established a permanent settlement at Inhambane south of Sofala, and another at Delagoa Bay in 1781 even further down the coast.

However, not only ivory was exported through the ports of Moçambique. Before the 1750s the Portuguese had regularly exported small numbers of African slaves to Goa and the Middle East, with some going to the VOC's colony at the Cape and to the Americas. Then, in the later eighteenth century, with the French development of their nearby Indian Ocean sugar islands of Mauritius and Reunion, there was a dramatic jump in the call for slaves to work the plantations. Demand increased even further when, from the early nineteenth century, British anti-slavery squadrons began to interdict the Atlantic slave trade from the Portuguese ports on the west coast of Africa.* The great Portuguese colony of Brazil still required numberless slaves for its plantations, and Portuguese East Africa stepped into the breach. With Moçambique Island as the main port of embarkation, followed by Quelimane, between 1526 and 1867 some 346,000 unfortunate slaves were despatched to Brazil.

The *chikunda* played an essential role in raiding for slaves to despatch to the coast. In the early years of the nineteenth century the *prazeiros*, made greedy by the growing demand for slaves, short-sightedly began selling their *chikunda* as well, leading to widespread insurrection. Then in 1835 the Ngoni people descended on the Zambezi valley. They had been displaced by turmoil in southern Africa and, made fearsome by their ruthless, Zulu-style military organisation, had been migrating north leaving a trail of devastation behind them. They overran half of the forty-six *prazos* still operating in the valley before passing on to settle further north.

Following the destructive Ngoni incursion many *prazos* never recovered, and the *chikunda* once attached to them no longer had *prazeiro* masters. Then, by legislation enacted in 1854 and 1856, the Portuguese government emancipated all the slaves on crown and church lands and set the rest of the *chikunda* free.

---

* See Chapter 6.

No longer slaves, the *chikunda* had to make new lives for themselves. Some returned to the soil and others became freelance elephant hunters or porters. Most migrated to the upper reaches of the Zambezi, where, still maintaining their military culture and organisation, they carved out three conquest states for themselves. For the next quarter-century they made full use of their military and hunting skills to ravage a huge area of southcentral Africa, raiding, slaving (despite the abolition of the trade) and prospering.

Following the Congress of Berlin of 1884–1885, which required the colonial powers in Africa to occupy the territories they claimed on the map, Portugal finally closed its grip on the East African hinterland as part of the Scramble for Africa. In the 1890s it began a long campaign with all the advantages of modern weaponry to subjugate the *chikunda* states as well as the last *prazeiros* who were resisting the restrictions and interference of the modern colonial state. However, during the same period the high plateau – so long the target of its ambitions – would finally elude Portugal when it became the British colony of Southern Rhodesia.

CHAPTER SIX

Wars and Miseries

Slave Wars

When the soil-filled waters of the Congo river – that great, pulsing artery of trade from deep within the heart of west-central Africa – surge into the Atlantic they stain the ocean russet for miles about as if with blood. Ninety miles upstream from this sanguinary mouth through which so many African slaves once passed, where the deep river is still navigable before it is blocked by the Ielala Falls, the port town of Matadi straggles along the Congo's left bank. The houses on its outskirts have spilled around a brown rocky outcrop, once an isolated landmark. On its side are engraved a cross, the arms of Portugal and the following terse message: 'Here arrived the ships of the enlightened King João II of Portugal.' Diogo Cão, the first indefatigable explorer of this stretch of the African coast as far south as modern-day Namibia, caused it to be inscribed in late 1485 at the frustrating termination of his second foray up the river. During an earlier voyage in 1483 he had first ventured tentatively a little way into the river's mouth, much astonishing the local people who, when they saw the white sails of his caravel rising above the horizon like enormous spread wings, believed they must be experiencing a visit from the spirit world. Newly made a knight of the king's household in recognition of his efforts, Cão had returned because he believed the Congo would lead him to the fabled realm of Prester John.

Cão was foiled in any further search inland by the Ielala Falls, but he made contact with the people of the mysterious and apparently enormous kingdom of Kongo south of the great river. He and other Portuguese immediately after him tried to draw Kongo into the orbit of Christendom through conversion to Roman Catholicism.

Tragically, all too soon initially courteous and harmonious relations degenerated into a sordid and immensely lucrative Portuguese hunt for slaves to serve their plantations on the Atlantic islands and in South America. By the late sixteenth century the Portuguese had extended their baleful slaving activities to other African kingdoms south of Kongo. From their coastal base of Luanda they became ever more deeply embroiled in the regional power-politics of the interior, instigating or fighting vicious wars with the prime purpose of acquiring slaves directly, rather than having to rely on African intermediaries to supply them, as was the practice elsewhere in West Africa. An economy developed by the seventeenth century in which slaves worked the Portuguese farms along the main rivers in their colony of Angola* to produce the food to feed the slaves penned up in Luanda awaiting export to the New World.

The Portuguese had not introduced slavery to this part of Africa – by the time of their arrival in the area slave trading was already an accepted institution and an established source of wealth. Therefore, when the Portuguese despatched military expeditions into the interior to capture slaves they were acting no differently from other powerful African rulers. What was critically different was not only the stupendously novel scale and aggression of the Portuguese hunt for slaves, which threw whole societies into disarray, but also the export of their captives out of Africa altogether. The consequences were widespread depopulation across west-central Africa. Indeed, it would not be too much to claim that Brazil, the prime Portuguese colony in South America, was built on the gouged-out ruins of Angola.

Historians have long struggled with incomplete records and patchy documentation to estimate the number of slaves embarking from west-central Africa for the Americas. What does seem clear is that the tempo of slaving accelerated steadily, so that the number of slaves exported during the course of the eighteenth century was double that of the sixteenth and seventeenth centuries combined. In all, it seems that during these centuries some two to

---

* Angola in the period covered in this book refers specifically to the Portuguese colony that comprised the ports of Luanda and Benguela and their immediate hinterlands. This was only the core of modern-day Angola, which encompasses vast territories stretching from the Congo river in the north to the Kunene river 1,000 miles to the south, and as far east as the sources of the Zambezi river in central Africa.

three million slaves were stuffed naked into the suffocating holds of the frightful slave ships and transported across the Atlantic. Another million unfortunates followed them during the course of the nineteenth century in slowly decreasing numbers until slavery was finally abolished in the Portuguese colonies in 1888.

The Portuguese could never have succeeded in forcibly enslaving so many million Africans without successfully wielding the required military force. In their firearms they possessed a potentially decisive advantage over African armies initially without them. However, as they were quick to learn, standard European military doctrine of the time was out of place in equatorial Africa – not least because the great bulk of the forces they fielded in Angola always consisted overwhelmingly of African levies and allies who fought in their own preferred style with their accustomed weapons. The Portuguese consequently had little choice but to adapt their tactics and organisation to conform closely to local military culture. Much to the sorrow of those they enslaved, they succeeded in doing so with considerable success.

The Kingdom of Kongo

When the Portuguese first began slaving in west-central Africa it was to secure labour for their newly planted sugar plantations on the islands of São Tomé and Príncipe in the Bight of Biafra. In 1486 the crown licensed the settlers to begin trading in slaves with the African mainland to the east of them. They did so with gusto and soon began to tranship slaves to other sugar islands such as Madeira and, by the late sixteenth century, to the Americas. At first, most of their stock of black ivory came from the kingdom of Kongo.

The population of Kongo when the Portuguese first set foot on its soil was more than half a million. The sway of the *mwenekongo* (its ruler, *awenekongo* in the plural, and meaning 'Governor of the Kongo') extended some 200 miles inland from the mouth of the Congo river to just below the Malebo (formerly Stanley) Pool. His rule stretched another 200 miles south along the coast through the mountainous region of the Dembo highlands towards the Dande river (just north of modern Luanda), which separated Kongo from the powerful kingdom of Ndongo. The Kwango river marked the easternmost limits of his kingdom. The fringes of the dense equatorial rainforest come down to the northern banks of the Congo river, but in Kongo on its southern

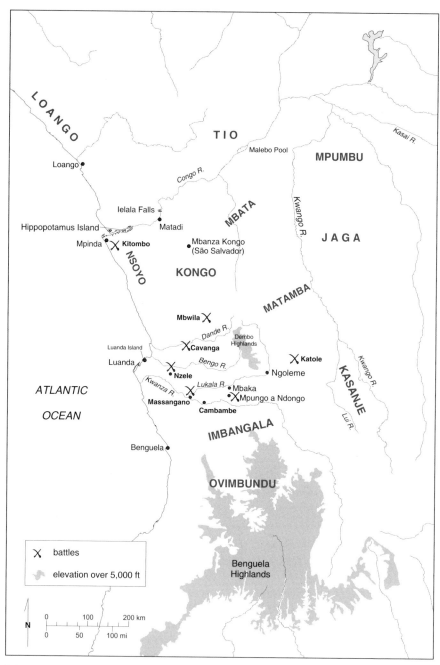

Map 11 *Kongo, Ndongo and the Captaincy of Angola*

side the environment is rather different. A flat, semi-arid, coastal plain covered in dry scrub stretches inland for nearly 100 miles, most of it unwelcoming to agriculture. But in parts many oil palms and mangroves thrive in the short rainy season from February to April. To the east of the coastal strip the land rises through a series of irregular escarpments, terraces, hills and mountains to a wooded, well-watered, fertile plateau of wide, rolling plains, 4,000–6,000 feet high, with a cool, invigorating climate. The rainy seasons there run from October to May with ferocious thunderstorms, particularly in April. From the north of the tableland the Kwango and many other streams flow north to join the Kasai river, one of the largest tributaries of the Congo river. East, beyond these highlands, lies the great central African savannah. Every sort of African animal, both small and great, roamed this landscape, including swelling herds of elephant with their tusks of ivory, always such a desirable commodity for the Portuguese. Human population across this huge region was unevenly distributed, clustered into pockets where conditions were most favourable for agriculture.

According to oral tradition, the Kikongo-speaking people crossed the Congo river during the fourteenth century and settled and intermarried among the Kimbundu-speakers already living on the fertile plateau. Within a century these polygynous Kongo people came to dominate the region through their knowledge of how to work the deposits of high-grade iron ore and copper found in the highlands, which they turned into superior weapons, farming tools and ornaments. Their capital at Mbanza Kongo became the central node of a network of profitable commerce that spread in all directions.

Theirs was a palm-tree culture. From the several species that grew in Kongo the people extracted oil from the pulp of the fruit that looked like green butter and which they used for cooking and as a lotion for their skin; while from the fermented sap they brewed their nourishing if intoxicating palm wine. They used the palm fibres (or raffia) for weaving mats, baskets, storage containers and even their dwellings. Their small, rectangular huts with their single, narrow entrances were made from frames of saplings or palm branches bound together by vines and covered with woven palm-fibre mats or straw. The houses of the elite differed only by being bigger and through their decoration of painted mats. For fear of wild animals and surprise attacks, these dwellings were clustered defensively in small villages low down in the concealing elephant grass and off the main roads. To baffle interlopers the approaches to a village were made into maze-like, complex patterns through live hedges of trees, walls of palm branches and enclosures with narrow entrances. Because villages were built of temporary materials and property belonged not to the individual but to the community, populations were mobile and could shift if beset by drought, bands of soldiers or slaver-hunters.

Clothes too were made from skilfully woven palm fibres, those worn by people of high status being the most intricately figured. For both men and women the basic garment was a cloth secured at the waist by a woven belt and covering the lower part of body down to the feet. The torso was left bare. Men of the ruling class also wore an apron-like decoration in front, made of the skins of wild animals with their heads left dangling. When they were cold, each man had a finely woven, knee-length mantle with fringed tufts to throw over his shoulder. Women of the elite (or, later on, when they became Christians) wore another piece of cloth to cover their breasts as well as a mantle over the shoulders. Nobles used armbands of copper with rich stylised designs to advertise their status. Women stoically ornamented themselves with neck- and ankle-bands of copper that weighed several pounds, as well as with lighter nose- and earrings. Men might wear caps of palm cloth and women loose turbans of the same material.

The Kongo also chose palm fibres to make game traps for wild animals and fishermen's snares for the teeming rivers. It was very difficult to keep cattle because of the trypanosome parasite transmitted by the ubiquitous tsetse fly. In any case, flesh did not make up a major part of the Kongo diet. The basic food was porridge made of cultivated millet or sorghum, although by the seventeenth century ground manioc root (cassava), which the Portuguese introduced from Brazil, began to replace these grains. The addition of legumes and a great variety of spicy sauces pepped up the bland porridge.

When in April 1491 Portuguese emissaries first encountered the *mwenekongo* he was dressed like any other member of the elite, except that a zebra tail hung from his left shoulder as his badge of kingship and token of virility. His capital, Mbanza Kongo, was built on top of a hill in rolling savannah country above the river where it caught the breeze, and was like an overgrown village of typical huts with narrow paths leading in all directions through the tall grass. It was surrounded by an outer palisade pierced by several gates guarded by warriors and trumpeters. At its centre was a large, open square with a spreading tree, from under which the *mwenekongo* dispensed justice. On one side of the square was the inner palisade enclosing the royal palace precinct with the large huts of the nobility snuggling up as close to it as they dared. The palace itself resembled an elaborate village and was approached through a typical maze of screens and entrances. There the *mwenekongo* lived surrounded by his extensive household, many wives and suffocating ceremony.

The *mwenekongo* ruled over a highly organised and stratified society in which there were sharp divisions between the *mwisikongo* (nobles or clan chiefs), free men such as farmers and merchants, and slaves.* Kongo's was a matrilineal culture with the royal line passing through its female members, but the *mwenekongo* was always male, chosen from among the *mwisikongo* of a defined group of aristocratic clans. The *mwenekongo* selected *mwisikongo* as well as members of his own royal family as key officials to administer the provinces and to collect tribute in copper, iron, agricultural produce, salt, fish and slaves. He also owned the *nzimbu* (cowrie) shells divers collected off Luanda Island and controlled their distribution. These shells were the common currency for the entire region and so were a major source of royal wealth.

The *mwenekongo* might rule through the *mwisikongo*, who were his provincial governors, but he had cause to fear them as well. Because their offices were not hereditary and they served at the king's will, they were understandably anxious to increase their own wealth and power while they could, and the perfect way to do so was to attack and conquer Kongo's neighbours in the name of the king. For that purpose they raised and deployed their own provincial armies. If a *mwenekongo* were strong enough to enforce the dismissal of his provincial officials he also by extension retained command over their armies. However, if he lost control over his governors, he also forfeited the loyalty of their armies and faced a real threat to his crown.

Very early in their relationship with Kongo, in 1491, 1509 and again in 1512, the Portuguese provided military support for succeeding *awenekongo* against some of these overmighty provincial governors who were in rebellion, or contesting the royal succession. It seems that the Portuguese initially had

---

* *Babika*, the Kikongo word for slave, also meant war captive, thus revealing how slaves were traditionally acquired.

little faith in the effectiveness of their arquebuses because during these small campaigns they apparently carried only crossbows, pikes and swords. At the same time they became familiar with the way of war in Kongo and learned how to adapt to it.

In contrast to the type of warfare the Portuguese were accustomed to in Morocco, where cavalry was the most potent arm, horses played almost no part at all in west-central African military operations. Horses simply could not long survive parasitic African trypanosomiasis and other tropical diseases. In later years the Portuguese kept the tiniest of cavalry forces going in Angola through constantly and expensively importing remounts from Brazil. It was hardly worth the trouble of doing so (except from habits of knightly prestige) because even in reconnaissance and pursuit – which were the basic tasks of cavalry – *pombos* (the swift foot scouts of the region) outstripped horses in stamina and effectiveness.

With no cavalry to speak of, it was infantry who entirely dominated the battlefield in west-central Africa. In Kongo this infantry was made up of a small core of shield-bearing heavy infantry and a mass of lightly armed troops. In each province the governor was responsible through his subordinates for mustering fighters to accompany the *mwenekongo* to war. The *mwisikongo* who ruled over the villages were expected to serve as the elite corps of heavy infantry. They in turn called on their peasantry to answer the call to arms as light infantry. This system of call-up always creaked badly because peasants were inevitably reluctant to come forward at harvest time, and during the rainy season the winding tracks became nigh impassable. In any case, when an enemy invaded their territory it was always the ordinary people's first response to flee to the mountains or forests for safety, rather than to respond to the call to arms. As a result Kongo was never able to respond quickly to an attack.

The professional heavy infantry were armed with swords, stabbing spears and clubs. They alone carried great shields of buffalo hide that protected them against arrows, and continued to do so even when in later years they were being penetrated by balls fired from the muskets that came increasingly into use. Learning how to use their equipment to greatest effect in hand-to-hand combat required long periods of training combined with vigorous military dancing. Their fighting skills as picked troops were certainly superior to those of the peasant levies armed with bows and arrows. It was true that most

Kongo males had some experience in archery for hunting, and that many used deadly poisoned arrows, but the decisive fighting was always in the hands of the heavy infantry.

Because there were absolutely no pack animals on account of the endemic parasitic diseases, most of the peasantry who responded to the muster ended up carrying supplies on their backs or paddling them in river craft rather than taking part in the fighting. This great *kikumba* (baggage train of carriers) was often larger than the fighting force itself, and was swollen still further by women (wives and daughters of the soldiers) who prepared the food. Yet armies on the march could not dispense with their slowly moving baggage trains because, in a world of scattered, small village communities with their limited stocks of food, they could not live entirely by foraging. This was especially so because an army's laborious progress gave villagers sufficient warning to escape with all the food supplies they could carry. Even so, the progress of an army through the deserted countryside was inevitably destructive of whatever remained and alienated the local population left to starve.

These logistical handicaps – which were shared by the Portuguese – meant armies could not operate too far from base and were always in danger of having to abandon a campaign for lack of food. This was particularly the case when the lengthy blockade of an enemy stronghold became necessary. It also meant that armies were limited in size. In a typical province of Kongo, with about 15,000 adult males, an army would never number much more than perhaps 200 heavy infantry with 2,000–3,000 light troops along with the great gaggle of bearers making up the *kikumba*.

One reason that armies in west-central Africa always seemed larger to the Portuguese than they actually were was because of their open deployment in combat. With no cavalry to run them down it was not necessary to maintain defensively close order as it was in contemporary European warfare, and being spread out gave individual warriors the opportunity to display their martial skills in the toe-to-toe combat they deemed so essential for their personal honour. However, fighting at close quarters was only for the heavy infantry. When the Portuguese first became involved in fighting in Kongo, wars were decided by set-piece battles. Before the massed armies made contact, *pombos* (lightly armed scouts) skirmished between them. Then the light troops loosed an arrow strike into the opposing host (usually no more than a single flight) before falling back to leave the field to the heavy infantry, who had been stationed together in reserve and who only charged forward at the decisive moment. By the early sixteenth century the Kongo were already beginning to use arquebuses (traded from the Portuguese for slaves) as strike weapons, but, although quickly adopted, they were very slow to replace bows and arrows.

The Portuguese always referred to the disorder of such battles, but it was more apparent than real. A Kongo army consisted of distinct tactical units that could be combined to make larger strike forces. Each had its own command structure as well as gaudy standards and flags that identified it. The Kongo also used a complex system of distinctive signals on drums and trumpets of various sizes, which not only allowed soldiers to recognise their own unit's calls over the din of battle, but also made it possible for commanders to drown out the lesser noise made by their subordinates' instruments. Because the members of the *kikumba* were non-combatants and included many women, it was always a problem to know where best to position the *kikumba* during combat. One option was to leave it in the rear and detach troops to guard it, and another was to place it in the midst of the army. The latter was often preferred because, knowing that their womenfolk would be taken as booty by the victors if they fled, its presence gave the soldiers something special to defend.

The clash of heavy infantry usually quickly decided a battle and the losers broke and fled. They did not have much incentive to make a stand because without cavalry to ride them down in flight, and with lightly armed *pombos* unable to maintain too long a pursuit, discretion was the better part of valour. Commanders made little attempt to rally their troops because they knew they could rally them a few days later to renew the campaign. Battles were consequently indecisive in the main with few casualties and only became slaughter grounds if a natural obstacle such as a river in flood blocked the path of flight.

The Conversion of Kongo

Historians have been drawn to study Kongo with singular thoroughness, ensnared by the way in which its elite so readily embraced Christianity and a culture of literacy. However, the fond Portuguese hope that they were creating a Christian kingdom in Africa was largely illusory. The waves of missionaries the crown despatched for more than a century, beginning with the Jesuits in 1545, achieved little outside the biggest towns and attracted only a few Africans to the ministry. Most missionaries rapidly succumbed to disease, loss of vocation and the temptations of keeping concubines and trading in slaves. Only the Capuchin missionaries from 1645 onwards had some degree of success in bringing Christianity to the rural areas.

Yet it is easy to see why Christianity initially found a relatively easy footing in Kongo. The person of the *mwenekongo* was sacred and it was he who was responsible for rain and the fertility of the kingdom. He ruled with the essential backing of the *kitomi* (priests of the ancient spirits of place) who each held sway over a territory defined by the watersheds of important streams. The leading *kitomi* of the area around the capital was normally a dominant member of the king's council. There were also the spirits of the ancestors, those of the *awenekongo* and *mwisikongo* being naturally the most important. In addition, there were also the spirits of the sky and the sea. It seemed to the Kongo that the Portuguese who arrived from over the sea must be sea spirits, especially as their skins were the white of the spirit world, a speculation confirmed by their exotic language and dress. Their belief in a heaven where God dwelt with his angels and saints accorded well with their concept of both sky spirits and the shades of the ancestors.

Thus for most of the Kongo people, especially those in the countryside and outside court circles, Portuguese Roman Catholicism did not so much supplant existing religion as supplement it in the syncretic fashion so common in Africa. Late nineteenth-century Portuguese missionaries were reluctant to recognise this, and typically believed that Christianity had merely 'passed over the country like a heavy rain, which scarcely wetted the surface of the land, and left the subsoil absolutely dry and sterile' – not least because (as they could not fail to recognise) 'by the side of the missionary stood the slave-trader'.[1]

Nevertheless, it is easy to see why the Kongo elite took to Christianity. In it the *awenekongo* perceived the advantages of a state cult over which they might exert full control, and their courtiers gleefully seized the additional offices and perks that came with the new religion. No one in Kongo's government could ignore the fact that the best way to secure the goodwill of the powerful strangers from across the sea, along with the military and commercial advantages that accompanied them, was to adopt their faith and learn their ways.

On 3 May 1491 Mwenekongo Nzinga a Nkuwu accepted baptism and assumed the name of João I in honour of his royal 'brother', the King of Portugal. On his death in 1509 his oldest son and a confirmed Catholic, Mvemba a Nzinga, had to fight for his throne against his traditionalist brother Mpanzu a Nzinga. Besides asserting that Mvemba's new faith endangered the spiritual well-being and continued fertility of the kingdom, his rival also argued that, in Kongo's matrilineal society, Mvemba had no valid claim to the succession because his mother was not a member of the aristocratic *mwisikongo*. The Portuguese rallied to support their convert. Marching shoulder to shoulder with his warriors under the proudly displayed banner of Christ, and miraculously heartened before the battle by a sudden vision in the sky of five flaming swords,* along with a white cross and St James himself at the head of the celestial host (or so Mvemba himself described in a letter of 1509, now lost), the Portuguese played their part alongside Mvemba's heavy infantry in securing victory. With his brother safely captured and beheaded, Mvemba adopted the name of Afonso I and ruled with Portuguese support until his death in 1542. It was he who opened Kongo up to Portugal. In a pioneering cultural exchange he sent some *mwisikongo* to Portugal in return for teachers and missionaries. In 1518 Pope Leo X ordained Dom Henrique, one of his sons, Bishop of Utica *in partibus*, and in 1521 Henrique returned as Africa's first black bishop.

Afonso's grandson Diogo I Nkumbi a Mpudi secured the throne in 1545 after a power struggle lasting three years. During his reign the Portuguese consolidated their influence at court. They settled close to the *mwenekongo*'s palace and were numbered among his advisers, secretaries, chaplains and military commanders. Some even married into the royal family. The Kongo elite were themselves learning to speak, read and write in Portuguese – the very first transcription ever of a Bantu language was the Kikongo catechism, published in 1555 – and began to adopt Portuguese ways that diverged ever more markedly from those of the peasantry. *Mwisikongo* imported rich furniture such as chests, tables, velvet-covered armchairs and rugs for their houses. They and Christians generally increasingly dressed in the Portuguese

---

* The coat-of-arms King Manuel I granted the kings of Kongo included the five flaming swords charged on the shield and making up the crest. The supporters were two decapitated idols with their heads at their feet.

style with capes of scarlet silk, hats, caps, boots and swords. The weaving of palm cloth went into decline as imported materials such as striped and chequered cottons and linens came on to the market. Women of the nobility took to wearing veils topped by caps of black velvet trimmed with jewels, and adorned themselves with gold chains and pearl necklaces instead of the heavy copper bands of the past.

The *mwenekongo* introduced elements of Portuguese court etiquette along with aristocratic titles and armorial bearings for his principal *mwisikongo*, and slotted the elite into a new hierarchy, ranging from royal princes down through dukes, marquesses, counts and barons. Courtiers scrambled for these titles and disputed precedence in state ceremonies replete with European symbols of royalty with all the desperate ferocity of nobles in Portugal.

An account of the coronation in 1622 of Pedro II Nkanga a Mvika provides a snapshot of developed Kongo court ceremonial that deftly combined Christian forms and European style with traditional panoply and pagan symbolism.[2] Pedro's European-style throne of 'crimson velvet, all fringed with silver and gold' was placed on a magnificent imported carpet. Young *mwisikongo* were arrayed on either side holding the royal insignia, which included a large banner sent by King Filipe III of Portugal emblazoned with five flaming swords in commemoration of Afonso I's miraculous victory over his heathen brother in 1509, as well as an array of heraldic devices of Portuguese pattern, and the royal seal. In contrast, behind the throne a second group of *mwisikongo* bore the traditional emblems of the royal family, which comprised designs of feathers stuck down on 'curtains of braided straw' hanging from seven-foot poles. An altar-stone and crucifix stood close to the throne – but so too did the great royal drum that was displayed only at coronations, royal funerals and when the *mwenekongo* went to war. Trimmed with royal leopard skin and with gold and silver embroidery from which the teeth of rebels were strung, it stood on an ornately woven, palm-fibre cloth that kept it, like the *mwenekongo* himself, from touching the ground. It potently symbolised the *mwenekongo*'s occult powers and close relationship with his dread royal ancestors, who guarded the kingdom.

Officially, though, Catholicism was the state religion and the *awenekongo* (even if they never went so far as to repudiate polygamy) promoted it strongly in their capital, Mbanza Kongo. They renamed it São Salvador, and by the end of the sixteenth century had constructed six churches for its 10,000 inhabitants.

Some were built of stone and others of mud and palm matting, but all were filled with crucifixes and images of the saints. Because the *awenekongo* could, therefore, be regarded as Christian monarchs, the kings of Portugal were at first punctilious in treating them as independent brothers-in-arms rather than as vassals to be ordered about.

Their close, equal relationship with Portugal was very gratifying to the *awenekongo*. Nevertheless, it is reasonable to enquire how they afforded the crates of imported luxuries they redistributed to the *mwisikongo* to ensure their loyalty, let alone their ambitious building programmes. The answer lies in the burgeoning slave and ivory trade.

As early as 1509 Afonso I paid the Portuguese in slaves for their military assistance against his rival. Slave ownership may have been common in Kongo long before the Portuguese arrived, but it was the foreigners who rapidly turned what had been a limited, strictly domestic institution into an international trade. The Portuguese and Afro-Portuguese merchants based in São Salvador and the port of Mpinda at the mouth of the Congo firmly controlled the burgeoning slave trade with the assistance of their itinerant African agents in the interior, the *pombeiros*.* The *awenekongo* recognised the threat these traders, especially those involved in slavery, posed to their authority and the well-being of their subjects. On 6 July 1526 Afonso I wrote to 'the most powerful and excellent Prince Dom João, King our Brother', complaining of unrestrained Portuguese slaving that did not stop even at kidnapping *mwisikongo*, and protested that 'so great Sir is the corruptions and licentiousness that our country is being completely depopulated'. He went on to state (in words his secretary underlined) that it was 'our will that in these Kingdoms there should not be any trade of slaves nor outlet for them'.[3]

Yet the unfortunate reality was that the rulers of Kongo were too dependent on the revenues and exotic items the slave trade brought in to try and stop it for long. Portuguese arquebuses were among the expensive imported items the *awenekongo* procured from the profits of the slave trade, and from the middle of the sixteenth century they issued them to the royal bodyguard, who were all slaves.† In many African societies rulers habitually kept slave soldiers in their

---

* *Pombeiros* were named from *Pombo*, the Kikongo name for the people from Malebo Pool on the Congo river, who were early on very active in organising the slave trade.

† It seems that the *awenekongo* did not normally deploy their slave bodyguards in the field until the

service, primarily to protect themselves from rivals and overmighty subjects. However, this was a new development in Kongo, and another indicator of the way in which the Portuguese slaving connection was distorting a traditional society. The distinction began to develop between slaves (such as the royal guards and domestics in *mwisikongo* households) who were not allowed to be sold out of Kongo and became powerful groups in their own right, and those many more unfortunates who could be – and indeed were in astronomical numbers.

The Jaga Incursion

Slavery lay too at the very root of a violent invasion from the east that threatened the prosperity and very existence of Kongo. In 1568 warrior bands, known to the Portuguese as the Jaga and characterised by them as marauding cannibals, crossed the Kwango river from the east and poured into Mbata province, one of the most densely populated and agriculturally rich regions of Kongo. Who these Jaga were has long been debated. In Kikongo their name – Yaka – means 'stranger' or 'brigand'. It seems likely that they were Kikongo- or Tio-speaking groups from the region around the lower Kwango river, who had cultural connections with the Luba people of central Africa – as had the Maravi (or Zimba) who the Portuguese fought in East Africa.* More than likely the rising threat of the Kongo slave trade had been dislocating their communities and encouraging them to forge disciplined, armed bands in defence. Yet the prosperity to be gained from engaging in the slave trade themselves was only too apparent. Consequently, their terrifying incursion into Kongo had more to it than merely the pillaging of a rich neighbour. They were intent on capturing slaves, and as their bands forged west they tried to make direct contact with the Portuguese slavers and traders at the coast. Simply put, it seems they were intending to cut out the Kongo middlemen and to take their place as suppliers of slaves to the Portuguese.

The Jaga chose their moment to attack well, for this was a period of dissension and disarray in Kongo. The *mwenekongo*, Álvaro I Nimi a Lukeni, had come to the throne only that year after the rapid deaths in succession

---

seventeenth century.

* See Chapters 4 and 5.

of his two predecessors in wars against the Tio people of the region of the Malebo Pool in the Congo river. He was, moreover, the first of his dynasty and related to the previous rulers of Kongo only through descent from one of Afonso I's many daughters. Other *mwisikongo* who also possessed claims to the throne were disinclined to accept his authority or to support him, even in a time of national emergency. And even if they were prepared to rally to Álvaro, the lumbering process of military mobilisation in Kongo was ill-suited to cope with an unexpected and determined invasion.

At first there was little armed resistance to the Jaga, and the peasantry did their best to escape to the nearby mountains and forests as the ferocious raiders surged through their villages, burning and taking slaves. Álvaro raised what forces he could at short notice, but the Jaga crushed them in battle. In 1569 he abandoned São Salvador for the Jaga to sack and burn. With his *mwisikongo*, bodyguards, priests and the Portuguese living in his capital he fled to the Congo river. The refugees sailed downstream in the river craft of Kongo, each carved from a single log of a great forest tree and large enough to carry up to 150 people. When they reached the sanctuary of Hippopotamus Island in the river's estuary they disembarked, and there they stayed, cramped and despairing, and suffering appallingly from hunger and the plague that soon broke out among them.

With the Jaga devastating Kongo without hindrance and famine overtaking the land, Álvaro had no recourse left but to appeal to his 'brother', the Portuguese monarch, for aid. The impetuous King Sebastião responded as soon as word reached him. In 1571 he despatched Francisco de Gouveia Sottomaior, *corregedor* (governing magistrate) of São Tomé, to the Kongo mainland at the head of a 600-man expedition. The *mwenekongo* joined them with his surviving followers from Hippopotamus Island and recruited what troops he could to assist. It took more than a year of fighting before the Jaga were finally driven south out of Kongo and São Salvador reoccupied. In gratitude for the Portuguese military aid, without which he would never have been restored to his kingdom, Álvaro acknowledged that he was King Sebastião's vassal and undertook to send him a fifth of the annual collection of *nzimbu* shells as tribute.

Most of the Portuguese expeditionary force remained in Kongo until about 1576, where they assisted in rebuilding the devastated capital and constructed a fortress to protect it against future attacks. They also helped Álvaro keep his restive *mwisikongo* under control. Significantly, they got the slave trade going again, and the *mwenekongo* invested the profits in matchlocks, with which he armed his slave guards while denying them to his provincial governors and *mwisikongo*.

Yet, as the Portuguese were aware, matchlocks still had greater usefulness as prestige weapons than in the field. In the protracted Jaga campaign the Portuguese from São Tomé had found that the power of their matchlock shot was wasted on enemies without protective armour because less powerful weapons would have sufficed. Nor were the Jaga massed closely enough together to make a good target, as would have been the case in Europe. Besides, the Jaga archers maintained a far higher rate of fire than could matchlockmen, as well as outranging them. It is true that at the very first encounters the Jaga had been alarmed by the unfamiliar, fire-spitting matchlocks, but that swiftly wore off when they realised how ineffective they were. Consequently, without the superiority in firepower they had expected to wield, the Portuguese had to accept that on the battlefields of Kongo shock tactics were more important than missile weapons. In other words, the Portuguese learned that they were most effective fighting just as if they were Kongo elite heavy infantry, where their body armour and skill with edged weapons were what counted most. As a young soldier declared nearly a century later when going to fight in the wars south of the Kwanza river: 'I have nothing to fear . . . for I have the weapons of a white man: breast plate, backplate, morione and corselet.'[4]

For the Portuguese, therefore, the campaign against the Jaga was important in instructing them in how to combine their military system with local practices to make it as effective as possible in local conditions. It was a lesson they would soon apply successfully in their new ventures south of Kongo.

The Kingdom of Ndongo and the Captaincy of Angola

From the shore opposite Luanda Island, where the *nzimbu* shells were harvested, the wide coastal plain with its salt pans, mangroves and stands of oil palms and bananas stretches 100 miles inland until it meets a belt of sharply rising mountains covered in luxuriant vegetation through which flow many sandy-bedded streams. This is the escarpment of the high, inland plateau from which a number of rivers drain down to the Atlantic. The most important of these, from north to south, are the Dande, Bengo and Kwanza. All are navigable along their lower reaches, and from earliest times have been avenues for trade deep into the interior. From the highlands to the sea the long valley of the Kwanza river and its tributary the Lukala have always been densely populated on account of the mild climate, generally good rainfall and rich agricultural land.

Yet even the best-watered regions in Africa are subject to recurrent drought. The priests of the Kimbundu-speaking farmers who originally settled in environs of the Kwanza river were responsible for rain and fertility in their shrines, each of which was associated with a defined territory and clan represented by a carved object called a *lunga*. The priests employed their spiritual powers to exercise political power over the people who depended on them for the harvest. According to tradition, their grip on power was successfully challenged by a blacksmith king who came from Kongo and founded the kingdom called Ndongo. In central Africa wise but mythical blacksmith kings are credited as the unifiers of fragmented communities into a single state, and indeed reflect the reality of the southward migrations of Bantu-speaking Iron Age peoples.* In the region of the Kwanza river these workers of iron arrived among the Mbundu people, and gradually overcame them with their iron tools of war and agriculture. Their leading smiths kept the secrets of their powerful technology close, and eventually the prestige of the master smiths overtook that of the priests of the *lunga* shrines. Their power was represented by iron regalia, known as *ngola*. At length their chief, who became the ruler of the kingdom of Ndongo, assumed the title *ngola a kiluanje* (the conquering *ngola*). The Portuguese later transcribed *ngola* as 'Angola' and gave that name to their colony.

The *ngolas* were tributaries of the *awenekongo* until the mid-sixteenth century. Then in 1556 Ngola Inene defeated the forces of Kongo in a battle on the river Dande just south of the Dembo highlands. Ndongo was henceforth

---

* Kikongo and Kimbundu are both of the family of Bantu languages.

an independent kingdom and the Dande formed the boundary between it and Kongo. The rulers of Ndongo then energetically began to expand their kingdom westwards to the ocean from its core between the Kwanza and Lukala rivers, southwards across the increasingly dry, high plateau, and eastwards towards the Kwango river. The Ndongo capital at Ngoleme was on the banks of the Lukala river, and before its destruction by fire in 1564 was described as a settlement of 5,000–6,000 family compounds.

As a state Ndongo was still relatively decentralised. In the mid-sixteenth century the powers of the *ngola* were constrained by a number of *makota* (great nobles; singular *dikota*), who exercised considerable authority in their own domains. Later in the sixteenth century the *ngolas* began greatly to add to their personal power by employing *ijiko* (royal slaves; singular *kijiko*) as state officials at court and as officers in the army. These *ijiko* also supervised the *makota*, reining in their local powers and ensuring the collection of taxes. The *ijiko* were themselves a great source of royal revenue because the *ngolas* planted them in villages around the country and taxed them heavily.

Since the late fifteenth century Portuguese and Afro-Portuguese private traders and renegades from São Tomé had been active at the *ngola*'s court and in his army as mercenaries. Their base was Luanda Island with its secure harbour free of any oversight by the Portuguese crown. Naturally, the crown did become interested in potential income from slaves from Ndongo, as well as from the fabulous silver mine rumoured to be somewhere in the interior. (The Portuguese never gave up the dream of finding silver mines in Africa to rival those of the Americas.) So in 1519 Manuel I despatched an embassy to the court of the *ngola*. Nothing came of this initiative and the lawless entrepreneurs on Luanda Island were left to their own devices for the next forty years.

Following Ndongo's break from Kongo in 1556, the young and eager King Sebastião seized the initiative and despatched a grandson of Bartolomeu Dias called Paulo Dias de Novais to open relations with Ngola Inene Ndongo. But when de Novais finally reached the Ndongo capital in 1559 accompanied by four Jesuits (Sebastião was determined that Ndongo should follow Kongo along the road to Christ), Inene was dead. His successor, Ndambe, viewed the embassy with the greatest suspicion and mulishly detained it at his court for year after year. Finally, with a new *ngola* on the throne, de Novais was permitted in 1565 to make his way back to Portugal. In Lisbon de Novais lobbied for all his worth for military intervention in Ndongo because he had become convinced during his long captivity of the existence of the fabled silver mines. The Jesuits (who had Sebastião's ear) vehemently supported him because they were outraged by the continued detention of their fellows in Ndongo and declared that the kingdom could only be converted to Christianity by the power of the sword.

These urgings at length persuaded Sebastião to act. In 1571 (at the same moment he despatched the expedition from São Tomé to assist Kongo against the Jaga) the king appointed de Novais the Captain and Governor of a new 'conquest' in Ndongo to be called Angola. This was a crucial designation for it meant that as a 'conquest' Ndongo was to be annexed and settled like the Atlantic islands and Brazil, and that its independence and integrity as a kingdom would not be respected as was that of Portugal's ally, Christian Kongo.

To implement this policy, Sebastião granted de Novais a stupendous *donataria* to stretch from the mouth of the Kwanza river to as far inland as he could conquer. A *donataria* was a concession of feudal lordship, which the crown granted to an individual in order to develop a colonial territory. As the *donatário* (proprietor) of Angola, de Novais would have complete freedom to make *sesmarias* (land grants) to his followers or to rent out landholding in all the lands he seized. He would also exercise both criminal and civil jurisdiction and appoint all officials in his captaincy. As Captain and Governor, his was the responsibility to assemble the expeditionary fleet and to direct military operations once it landed. He also undertook to construct three fortresses once he had established his captaincy and to maintain a garrison of 400 soldiers to defend them. Sebastião piously expressed the hope that de Novais would succeed in establishing his captaincy by peaceful means, but was quite reconciled to the prospect of an armed conquest.

It took time for de Novais to mount his expedition, and it was not until February 1575 that he finally landed on Luanda Island, much to the consternation of the forty or so freebooting traders operating there.* De Novais swiftly proceeded to the mainland, where on 25 January 1576 he founded the port of São Paulo da Assumpção de Loanda – now universally known as

---

* Luanda Island was part of the Kongo kingdom, but Álvaro I permitted the Portuguese presence in recognition for their recent help against the Jaga.

Luanda – near the mouth of the Bengo river. This was the essential base from which he could develop the Portuguese settlement and meddle directly with the affairs of Ndongo and the other kingdoms of the interior.

In Luanda de Novais immediately erected the buildings typical to any Portuguese settlement: a fortress, church, hospital, jail and municipal chambers. To look ahead, by the mid-seventeenth century a commercial sector stretched along the bay handling trade with the wider world. It was there, in the lower town with its notoriously high death rate from disease, that more recent immigrants lived. Above them, in the upper town, the Fortaleza de São Miguel (begun in 1634 to replace the earlier, less sophisticated fort) loomed over the adjacent governor's palace, cathedral, Jesuit college and the fine, airy houses of the rich and established Afro-Portuguese families. Their blood-stained fortunes depended on keeping the slaves flowing in ever-escalating numbers across the Atlantic to the insatiable plantations of the New World.

Indeed, it cannot be emphasised sufficiently that from the very outset the slave trade was the lifeblood of the Captaincy of Angola, and that until the eighteenth century even the governor was a prominent slave exporter. In the fifteenth century, when the trade was in the hands of the rag-tag merchants on Luanda Island, single-decked caravels of 100 tons were capable of carrying off 150 slaves; by the end of the eighteenth century the slave ships docking in the port of Luanda could hold four times that number. The slaves were brought down to the coast from the interior by *pombeiros* luxuriously domiciled in Luanda. Almost all of these backwoodsmen were Afro-Portuguese and some were even trusted slaves. They would spend months in the interior collecting their human stock before driving it down to the barracoons of Luanda and other, lesser ports that grew up later. Almost a quarter of these miserable captives would die on the interminable trek down to the coast. Once herded into the disease-ridden barracoons they were baptised and branded. They then might endure dismal months waiting for a slave ship to transport them. Crown factors supervised their sale and embarkation, for it must never be forgotten that the Portuguese state was a major beneficiary of the trade.

De Novais always kept firmly in mind that the Captaincy of Angola was also to be a spiritual conquest. The Jesuits consequently held a privileged position and with the governor's encouragement set out proselytising among the local people, erecting crosses and building churches. Nor did de Novais neglect the Jesuits when he distributed *sesmarias* to settler families on the coastal plains along the lower reaches of the Kwanza, Bengo and Dande rivers. The main purpose of these estates was to grow sufficient food to feed the slaves languishing in the barracoons of Luanda. For this, a dependable workforce was required. To secure it, the Portuguese exerted force on the Mbundu *sobas* (local chiefs) to become the vassals of the settlers. This meant they were obliged to provide labourers when required, or to pay tribute in the form of slaves. Whatever lip service the Portuguese might have paid to seeking peaceful relations with the Mbundu, the truth is that from the very outset their slave economy demanded the forcible subjugation of the indigenous population.

The Portuguese–Ndongo Wars

Even though he was quite reconciled to the use of force, de Novais was also fully aware that he needed time to secure his base around Luanda. He therefore proceeded cautiously at first in his relations with the powerful kingdom of Ndongo. His first step was to send emissaries bearing gifts and soft words to Ngola Kiluanje, but the Ndongo king was understandably extremely wary of Portuguese intentions, not least their Christian zeal. He had allies in the long-established Portuguese free traders on Luanda Island, who resented the imposition of crown control over their activities. They grumblingly relocated to the *ngola's* court and in 1579 succeeded in persuading Kiluanje's successor, Njinga, that he must take stern action against de Novais' Portuguese before it was too late.

The *ngola* struck suddenly. He put to death about thirty Portuguese traders operating at his court under de Novais' auspices, along with their Christian slaves, and confiscated their goods. Njinga then advanced towards the coast and besieged de Novais in his little fort at Nzele, about fifty miles inland from Luanda. Sixty Portuguese and about 200 African auxiliaries held out successfully against an Mbundu army that had insufficient logistical support to remain long in the field. In the wake of this success de Novais swore never again to negotiate with the *ngola*, but to seize whatever territories he required for his colony.

So began an interminable series of wars. During their course the military culture of Ndongo underwent some changes, but perhaps not as many as

1 *A late-sixteenth-century depiction of the busy quayside at Lisbon on the Tagus river. Note the carracks with their open gun ports and the tenders bringing goods ashore.*

2 *A seventeenth-century European artist's view of Marrakesh in southern Morocco, with its formidable city walls and the square-towered minaret of the Koutoubia mosque dominating the surrounding buildings.*

3 *Moroccan civilians, as depicted by a seventeenth-century European artist.*

4 *A Western representation of the siege of Tunis in 1535 by the forces of the Holy Roman Emperor Carlos V, with North African light cavalry in the foreground.*

5 *A janissary (member of the elite corps of Ottoman slave soldiers) holding an arquebus, such as he would have used in north African or Arabian campaigns during the sixteenth century.*

6 AND 7 *Matchlockmen from an early seventeenth-century Dutch drill book, illustrating the twenty-eight positions required for handling the arquebus (below left) and the thirty-two required for the musket (below right). Note the forked rest for the musket and the paper cartridges (in common use by the seventeenth century) hanging from the soldier's bandolier. Each cartridge held a ball and a measured charge of powder.*

8 An illustration from an early seventeenth-century manual, showing a series of drill movements for musketeers.

9 Early seventeenth-century cuirassier armour, weapons and saddlery.

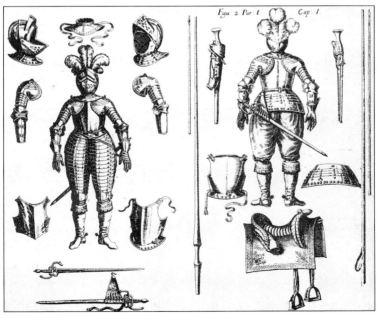

10 *English cavalry, pikemen, arquebusiers and trumpeters of the 1580s on the march. King Sebastião's Portuguese army in Morocco would have been similar in appearance.*

11 *Lance meets pike.*

12 *The method of erecting a camp depicted in a military manual of 1571. Note the artillery park to the right, the wagons in the foreground drawn up in defensive formation, the improvised shelters, the rows of tents and stands of arms.*

13 *An imaginary representation, published in 1540, of Prester John of the Indies, the mythical Christian king beyond the Nile, whom Portuguese explorers were hoping to locate. He is portrayed as a Portuguese monarch of the time.*

14 *A lurid depiction of fearsome Zimba warriors, as imagined by a seventeenth-century European artist.*

15 *An early nineteenth-century view from the harbour of the Portuguese government house on the island of Moçambique.*

16 *Illustration from a manual of 1637, on arms drill for musket, depicting a musketeer with a musket over his shoulder and a sword at his side. He carries a forked rest and wears a bandolier with cartridges and the smouldering match looped through it.*

5

17 *An early sixteenth-century north African galley. Similar craft were active in the Red Sea and Indian Ocean.*

18 *A mid-nineteenth-century view of Fort Jesus from across Mombasa harbour with the town coming down to the water on the right.*

19 *Seventeenth-century Dutch galleons off the Isle of Goeree (Gorée) in west Africa, similar to those that attacked Fort São Sebastião on Moçambique Island earlier in the century.*

20 *Early nineteenth-century view of the mountain of Debre Damo in Ethiopia. In the late 1530s Negus Lebna Dengal and his queen, Sabla Wengal, took refuge from Grañ in the monastery on the mountaintop. In 1541 she joined Cristóvão da Gama's expeditionary force from this stronghold.*

21 *A mid-nineteenth-century European traveller's depiction of armed men of Shoa in southern Ethiopia, with spears and round bucklers.*

22 *A northern Shona hunter with his bow and arrows, photographed in the 1920s, still wearing the hairstyle described by the sixteenth-century Portuguese.*

23 *Ethiopian warriors, as depicted by a nineteenth-century European artist. Note the man on the left with a musket, and the horseman with his big toe in a stirrup ring.*

24 *Kongo noblemen of the kingdom of Loango, described as wearing 'cat-hair aprons'.*

25 *The regalia and throne of the* awenekongo *(kings) of Kongo, inspired by Portuguese models.*

26 *Mwenekongo Afonso I (r. 1509–1542), who opened Kongo up to the Portuguese, ceremoniously receives a Portuguese embassy. Note the Portuguese soldiers on the left, armed with arquebuses.*

27 *São Salvador, or Mbanza Kongo, the capital of the rulers of Kongo. By the end of the sixteenth century it had six Roman Catholic churches and ten thousand inhabitants. It was actually built on top of a hill in rolling savannah country, and not on a towering bluff as shown in this seventeenth-century engraving.*

DE RIEVIERE LELUNDA.

28 *A late seventeenth-century view of the city of São Paulo da Assumpção de Loanda (now known as Luanda) founded by the Portuguese in 1576.*

29 *The ferocious Imbangala of Angola, as imagined by a European artist inspired by contemporary travellers' descriptions.*

30 *The fortress of São Jorge da Mina, or El Mina, erected by the Portuguese on the Gold Coast in 1482 and captured from them by the Dutch in 1637.*

31 *The meeting of Queen Nzinga of Ndongo and João Correira de Sousa, the Portuguese Governor of Luanda, in 1622.*

32 ABOVE *Mwenekongo Garcia II (r. 1641–1660) receives an embassy in 1642 from his newfound Dutch allies. Note the imported brass chandelier and the European boots worn by the* mwenekongo *and his courtiers.*

33 RIGHT *Salvador Correira da Sá e Benavides, who recaptured Luanda from the Dutch in 1648 and was Governor of Angola from 1648 to 1652.*

34 *Seventeenth-century Dutch soldiers manning the cannon at Fort Nassau, Isle of Goeree (Gorée), with Fort Orange in the background.*

might be expected. Like Kongo, Ndongo in the later sixteenth and seventeenth centuries fielded a core of highly skilled soldiers. However, these professional units were different in crucial particulars from the Kongo ones. They developed out of the push by sixteenth-century *ngolas* to concentrate more power into their hands. Traditionally, the command of Mbundu armies had been in the hands of the *sobas*, who also recruited the troops. No *ngola* could be sure, therefore, where the loyalty of his army lay, whether with him, or the *sobas* who had raised it. One solution attempted was to appoint only members of the royal family as commanders. Another was to create a military elite answerable to the *ngola* alone. It was recruited from among free men as well as from slaves trained as warriors, and was kept segregated from the general population in special villages. The social standing of these *imbari* (singular *kimbari*) was ambiguous, being akin to that of slaves. Nevertheless, the *imbari* warriors were the mainstay of the Ndongo monarchy.

Unlike the Kongo heavy infantry, the Ndongo *imbari* carried no shields as a matter of pride. Instead, they relied on their extraordinarily agile twisting, leaping and dodging aside to avoid flying arrows or spear thrusts. To perfect these defensive manoeuvres required arduous and extensive physical training in their military villages. Swords and war-hatchets were their offensive weapons of choice, and in constant preparation for war (like their Kongo counterparts) they regularly exhibited their martial arts in military reviews and dances, exuberantly leaping and parrying to the point of exhaustion.

An Ndongo army on campaign suffered from the same logistical difficulties as one from Kongo and was never very large, at its greatest never being more than about 8,000 strong. It nevertheless usually seemed larger than that to the Portuguese on account of the open order in which the warriors attacked, just as they did in Kongo. When drawn up for battle an Ndongo army was typically deployed in three large formations making two wings and a centre. There might also be a strong rear guard positioned to break flanking attacks attempting to envelop the main line of battle, or to stem a rout or cover a retreat. The typical tactic was to attack with clouds of light troops to the front shooting off their arrows while the elite *imbari* manoeuvred to outflank the enemy. In the sixteenth century a few of the Ndongo scouts and light troops began carrying arquebuses, although most of the light troops that supported the *imbari* were archers. Archers continued to predominate over musketeers well into the eighteenth century.

The Mbundu had no walled towns as such, but as the Portuguese would discover they made considerable use of fortifications around their settlements; these included complex patterns of trenches, wooden palisades, obstacles such as stakes and tree branches, and anti-personnel traps like spiked holes. The thinking was that these defences would be sufficient to repel an assault over a few days. No longer was needed because an attacking force would soon run out of food and have to retire. With that in mind, defenders did their best to commandeer all the supplies in their neighbourhood to deny them to the besiegers as well as to feed themselves. The Mbundu were also adept at throwing up temporary fieldworks to protect the encampment of an army on the march, particularly if it were withdrawing in the face of the enemy. In improvising their fieldworks, the best possible use was made of forested or broken terrain such as the Dembo highlands, the mountainous region between the Ndongo and Kongo kingdoms.

Ndongo territory was one of many rivers, easily navigable to vessels of shallow draught. The Mbundu possessed large fleets of river craft hollowed out of forest tree logs (as was also the practice in Kongo). They probably held up to ninety warriors, who carried missile weapons and, unlike the *imbari*, protected themselves with shields. These fleets raided, ferried troops across rivers and generally tried to retain command of the strategic waterways.

When de Novais went to war with Ndongo in 1579 he knew he was facing a tough enemy with field armies, fortifications and fleets, and that the Portuguese would be hard pressed with their limited military resources to defend their colony. They had no siege artillery, but that did not much matter because it would have been ineffective anyway against Mbundu earthworks and ditches. Fortunately for the Portuguese, the rivers, especially the Kwanza, were deep enough to deploy vessels armed with light cannons. In 1580 their Kwanza fleet was made up of two *galeotas* (single-decked coastal vessels propelled by a lateen sail and oars) with cannon at both bow and stern, a caravel of 100 tons with its multiple sails and cannon, and two smaller boats. Vessels such as these allowed the Portuguese to control the rivers and neutralise the Ndongo fleets. Indeed, they were vital for Portuguese survival because they could support the strategic forts the Portuguese built on the riverbanks and relieve their garrisons if besieged. They also played a crucial role in aggressively taking the war to the enemy, raiding far upstream from the river forts.

What the Portuguese singularly lacked in 1579 was a large field force. One expedient was to arm their own slaves, and these slave soldiers continued to serve in Portuguese armies in Angola up to the end of the eighteenth century. Another was to hire mercenary *mwisikongo* and their armed bands from Kongo, even if they were less reliable than the Portuguese's own slave soldiers. A third was to form alliances with dissident Mbundu *sobas* with their light troops. These were always undependable and likely to desert if the fighting went against them, but the Portuguese had little choice if they wanted the foot soldiers who always made up the mass of their forces in the Ndongo wars. The fourth option was to recruit bands of Imbangala into their service. De Novais encountered the Imbangala as he advanced up the Kwanza river, and because some of their commanders were enamoured of European trade goods they decided to fight for the Portuguese (whether as allies or mercenaries is a mute point) in exchange for them. This was fortunate for the Portuguese because Ndongo was also recruiting Imbangala warriors who, in their unprecedented ferocity and destructiveness, would dominate warfare in the region for the next fifty years.

The origins of the Imbangala are mysterious, although they were comparable to the Zimba with their martial culture, and also to the Jaga, with whom the Portuguese regularly confused them (as have some recent historians). It seems likely, though, that they originated on the vast Benguela plateau south of the Kwanza river – that is, in a part of the country outside the palm-tree region where bananas and cattle predominated. Their huts were made of mud and straw over wooden frames, and settlements were protected by palisades of stout stakes. There were a number of states in this part of the highlands, but the dominant power and regional rival to Ndongo was the Ovimbundu kingdom of Benguela. Drought and the extension of slave raiding were likely disrupting the region during the mid-sixteenth century. In these turbulent conditions renegade soldiers broke away from the Benguela armies and were joined by escaped slaves to form their own marauding bands that answered to no central authority such as a king. Many of these bands were attracted by the rich lands of Ndongo and fell like ravenous hyenas upon the unfortunate peasantry of the Kwanza valley.

Andrew Battell, an English sailor serving unwillingly with the Portuguese in Angola, spent seventeen months with these Imbangala between 1600 and 1601. Drawing on his account and that of other observers we can form a picture of this people's singular social organisation.[5] The Imbangala lived purely and entirely by war. Before they set out on campaign, war doctors ritually strengthened the warriors for combat during a full day of ceremonies. These rituals were accompanied by women singing and shrilling interminably, by pounding drums and by the harsh notes of trumpets made of elephant tusks that could be heard a mile away. At sunset the chief of the Imbangala band, wearing a cap adorned with royal peacock feathers, sacrificed a quaking adolescent boy and four men along with a like number of cattle, goats and dogs. All the carcases were then thrown on to fires and sprinkled with ritual medicines for all the warriors to consume and be 'strengthened' by.

On campaign the Imbangala were highly mobile, suddenly entering populated regions and encamping in round, closely hutted camps protected by entrenchments, wooden stockades and thorn entanglements. In camp they never relaxed their vigilance and worked on the nerves of the terrified surrounding local population by playing all night on their drums and other percussion instruments. From these strong-points they sallied out with daunting alacrity to brush aside any attack by the local people and to ravage the vicinity. The major purpose of an Imbangala raid was to take prisoners. The circumcised, adult men and mature women they captured were sold to slavers or executed. Some of the younger women prisoners would be kept as concubines – never wives – and any children they bore were killed. That was because, to the horror of Mbundu and Ovimbundu societies where ancestors and lineage were the cement of society, the Imbangala deliberately renounced all kin and family relationships. Without offspring of their own they kept up their numbers through capturing adolescent, uncircumcised boys who had not yet been initiated into manhood in their own societies, and incorporating them into their ranks.

The process of assimilation was alarmingly similar to that endured by child soldiers in Africa today, who are forcibly inducted into merciless, freebooting bands of predatory bush fighters. Captured youths were sternly trained in the military skills of the Imbangala warriors and became adept with bow and arrow, hardened wooden lance and war-hatchet. Like the Ndongo *imbari* they learned to despise the use of shields. They also underwent traumatic initiation into Imbangala rituals that included cannibalism – the appalled Battell called the Imbangala 'the greatest cannibals and man-eaters that be in the world'.[6] Cannibalism was absolutely abhorred by Mbundu and Ovimbundu peasants, who believed that only witches and evildoers symbolically ate their victims. Therefore, to force the captured youths to eat human flesh was to rupture their moral training, break any connection with their own kin and forever place them outside their old society.

Made harshly aware that cowards were killed and eaten, these now kinless youths made every effort to master the required military arts and prove they were brave, ruthless and totally loyal to the band. When they had done so to the satisfaction of their commanders (Battell stated that this was achieved when they brought an enemy's head to their general)[7] they were finally integrated into the Imbangala as men. That was the moment they threw off the collar that had been placed around their neck as a symbol of their disgrace when first they were captured. Promotion thereafter, even to senior commander, was based solely on loyalty and service. It was awarded through democratic election, because, since there were no lines of descent or hereditary authority within the band and all were by origin slaves, there was equality of status. In other words, from highest to lowest the Imbangala were technically all slaves, and this too horrified the traditional societies they preyed upon.

We have Battell's vivid description of Gaga Calandola, the general of the particular Imbangala band he lived with. Gaga Calandola wore his hair very long, knotted with valuable seashells; his nose and ears were pierced with long, copper ornaments. Around his neck was a collar of shells, and a bead girdle enclosed his waist, holding up a palm-cloth kilt. Distinctive scarifications covered his body and Battell claimed they were 'every day anointed with the fat of men'.[8] To complete his terrifying appearance his body was always painted red and white. His many concubines wore strings of beads around their necks, arms and legs, and worked their hair high with shells. They perfumed themselves with civet,* and all followed the custom of extracting their two top and two bottom front teeth.

---

* Civet cats were abundant in the Angolan highlands.

The Imbangala bands lived entirely by plunder and left only devastation in their wake. Characteristically, when they came upon the precious, carefully tended palm trees that were (as we have seen) so essential to the peasants' existence, they would chop them down, draw out the sap for making wine, and then pass on. The Portuguese would find their Imbangala mercenaries' love of palm wine very convenient, for they discovered that when laced with cheap, imported European alcohol the Imbangala would accept it in lieu of pay.

It was with this hotchpotch of European and African troops – free men, retainers, slaves and Imbangala mercenaries – that the Portuguese faced the armies of Ndongo. They had gained much experience in local warfare from their campaigns in Kongo, and in combat adopted a formation that replicated the typical Mbundu battle order. The Portuguese themselves mimicked the heavy infantry of Kongo and fought in an impregnably tight formation, or 'battle', bristling with their matchlocks and long swords. They wore their heavy armour that easily deflected arrows and spears, but it was impossibly hot and restrictive and they began gradually to replace it with padded cotton armour as the wars went on.

This formidable Portuguese 'battle' was the anchor of their battle line, but it was not large and seldom numbered more than several hundred men. The 'battle' was always supported on its flanks by the light African troops in Portuguese service, who typically outnumbered it thirty to one. It was these African troops who did most of the actual fighting. The 'battle's' role was to defend the *kikumba*, and to act as a reserve, moving out to break up the enemy's flank attacks or to deliver the final, crushing blow to his core of *imbari*. It was also effective in assaulting fortified positions. If the fortunes of the day turned against the Portuguese army, the secure 'battle' could stabilise the faltering line and lead a counter-attack. However, if the light troops abandoned the field the isolated 'battle' was left in an impossible position. It could fight on alone for quite some time, but without support it was usually broken up in the end and slaughtered.

In 1579, after successfully defending his fort at Nzele, de Novais' forces began inching up the Kwanza river into the Ndongo heartland, establishing fortified bases as they went. From each of these forts a military captain administered the *presidio* (surrounding territory). The prime Portuguese strategic objective was Cambambe, upstream, where the fabled silver mines were supposed to be situated. By 1583 they had pushed just beyond the confluence of the Kwanza and Lukala rivers and were still short of reaching Cambambe when in the mid-winter of that year they fought a significant battle with the forces of Ndongo.

The Portuguese general, André Ferreira Pereira, deployed his 'battle' of 140 Portuguese matchlockmen in the centre with some 8,000 African light troops (most of them archers) on either flank. The Ndongo army was anything between 6,000 and 12,000 strong and included forty or so arquebusiers in its ranks. The Portuguese stood fast on the defensive while the Ndongo attacked in a series of waves. Sangi a Ndala commanded the leading division of the centre, which was composed of the best *imbari* warriors in Ndongo, including members of the royal family and *makota* of the court. Under a blizzard of arrows it flung itself at the Portuguese centre opposite. The Portuguese stood firm, volley-fired and then charged forward with their drawn swords, throwing Sangi's elite warriors reeling back. The Ndongo division drawn up behind them in support then advanced to the attack, but they too wilted under the fire directed from the Portuguese formation, which bristled with steel. The two Ndongo flanking formations then entered the battle. The right wing under Kari kia Luanji, and the left under Kabuku kia Mbilo simultaneously assaulted both flanks of the Portuguese, but were driven back. In desperation, the Ndongo reserves mounted a final charge, but could not break the Portuguese line either.

The Ndongo army would not admit defeat, however, and sullenly bivouacked overnight on the battlefield in sight of the campfires of the Portuguese who would not withdraw either. When the two stubborn armies resumed the battle next morning it was in a snowstorm (which do occur in the highlands in the cold, winter months). Both sides quickly lost their stomachs for fighting in the dreadful weather and gratefully used it as an excuse to break off the engagement and retire.

Pereira's victory was a crucial one, for it allowed the Portuguese to establish a new fortified settlement nearby at Massangano on the left bank of the Kwanza river, which evolved into their main military base upriver. Massangano also became the hub of commercial activity in the interior, because, being sited just above the confluence of the Kwanza and Lukala rivers, it commanded the network of waterways and trails on the surrounding highlands and served as the key staging post for slavers. By the middle of the seventeenth century

Massangano possessed the obligatory fort, four churches, a Jesuit house and a Capuchin convent that all catered to a small community of 600 Portuguese and Afro-Portuguese traders, as well as to the soldiers of the garrison.

Despite such successes, the Portuguese still had failed to reach their objective at Cambambe or to penetrate the Ndongo heartland. In all their military operations they were hampered by severe logistical problems and by difficulties in keeping their African auxiliaries and mercenaries in the field. Nor were they always victorious. Just after Christmas in 1589, on 28 December, the Portuguese flotilla under Luiz Serrão, supported by 100 matchlockmen and large bodies of African troops on the banks, was severely trounced at Ngwalema as it tried to advance up the Lukala river. The Portuguese managed to make an effective fighting withdrawal to Massangano, but they had suffered heavy casualties and had been compelled to abandon everything in their camp. Daunted, they made no more serious efforts for the time being to advance further into the interior. They made no formal peace with Ndongo, however, but were content to observe an uneasy truce while they consolidated their gains downstream the Kwanza.

De Novais died in the same year as the defeat on the Lukala river. Back in Portugal where King Filipe I (who was also Felipe II of Spain) had been ruling since 1581, the Habsburg monarch resolved that in distant Angola the aggressive search for the elusive silver mines should not be left in abeyance, but must be resumed. He also decided that instead of the colony being ruled by another *donatário* like de Novais with all his practically untrammelled powers, Angola should have a royal governor who jumped obediently to Lisbon's command.

The first royal governor arrived in Luanda in 1592, and he and his successor had some trouble in bending the independently minded local settlers and Jesuits to their will. Meanwhile, under them the Portuguese resumed their advance into Ndongo. In 1604 they finally reached Cambambe, thirty miles upstream from Massangano, only to find that the fabulous silver mines were purely the stuff of legend. That was the end of the long-held dream of an Angolan El Dorado to rival the Spanish silver mines of the Americas. Henceforth the hunt for gold and silver in Ndongo was all but abandoned. Both the crown and the governors of Angola acknowledged that the prosperity of Angola must rest almost exclusively on the success of the slave trade. The governors also grasped that there were better ways of taking advantage of slaving than by merely taxing the trade passing through the colony. Rather, they saw that the greatest profits were to be derived from using Angola's armed forces to seize slaves directly from surrounding African kingdoms. That meant becoming involved in constant local warfare, not for strategic objectives, but to procure slaves in ever-mounting numbers to feed the insatiable needs of Brazil's plantation owners.

In these seventeenth-century slave wars against Ndongo the Portuguese began to make somewhat more effective use of their superior weaponry. All of the members of their 'battle' now carried matchlocks, and increasing numbers of their African light troops did too, although even by the early eighteenth century there were still ten bowmen to every musketeer. Only by the very end of the eighteenth century would Portuguese soldiers and their African troops all carry muskets. The Portuguese introduced some light field artillery during the course of the seventeenth century. These guns were not very effective when they fired cannon balls, because of the typically dispersed Ndongo formations, but at close-quarters grapeshot could be very effective. Field artillery came more into its own as the Portuguese encountered Ndongo rocky fastnesses deep in the forests, where their armies withdrew after being worsted in battle. Mortars were the most useful pieces of all in overcoming the redoubts and mutually supporting bulwarks with which their enemies strengthened the natural features of their forts.

Under Governor Luís Mendes de Vasconcelos (1617–1621) the Portuguese began a determined advance into the Ndongo heartland, greatly assisted by their mercenary bands of Imbangala, whom the governor grimly praised as 'hunting dogs to get slaves'.[9] De Vasconcelos' forces inflicted a number of smarting defeats on the Ndongo armies and established a new fortress at Mbaka, far upstream the Lukala river. From this base they sacked the Ndongo capital at Kabasa and garnered a great haul of slaves.

Overcome by this disaster the *ngola*, Mbande, took refuge on Kindonga Island in the Kwanza river and attempted to negotiate with the Portuguese. Nothing came of these initiatives, and in despair he committed suicide (or perhaps was murdered) in 1624. The Portuguese seized the opportunity to install a puppet *ngola*, Hari a Kiluanje, who came from a junior branch of the royal house and was lord of the rocky fortress of Mpungo a Ndongo. He died almost immediately of smallpox and the Portuguese replaced him with Filipe Hari a Ngola. Filipe Hari would remain loyally but uncomfortably in the pocket of the Portuguese until his death in 1664, and would regularly furnish them with large contingents of light infantry for their various campaigns.

Meanwhile, the unfortunate Mbande had a sister, Ana de Sousa Nzinga Mbande, a woman of enormous character and unflagging determination. There was no tradition in Ndongo of women rulers, but she seized power with the support of the *ijiko*, who brought the *imbari* warriors over to her. As a woman she had constantly to struggle to maintain her position against rivals and enemies, and felt she could only do so successfully by assuming the virile attributes of a man and warrior. This was not unprecedented among powerful queens in Africa, where it was recognised that a difference exists between sex as a biological state and gender as a social condition. At some point in the 1640s Nzinga accordingly decided to become fully a 'man'. She took several husbands at a time and made them wear women's clothes and sleep among her women attendants. She personally led her troops into battle, where the Portuguese saw her right behind the battle line. Her personal guard were women of her household whom she trained and armed. She herself possessed all the military skills of a *kimbari*, and at the age of eighty could still leap and dodge with the best of them.

As soon as she was precariously on the throne, Nzinga struck an alliance with Kaza, the leader of a major Imbangala band who had her young nephew and potential rival in his custody. As part of the deal Kaza handed the boy over to Nzinga in 1626. Blood not being thicker than water in royal families, she unsentimentally executed him to secure her position. That done, she set about building up an alliance to confront the invading Portuguese. She had, besides her own followers and Kaza's Imbangala, the *sobas* opposed to Filipe Hari and his Portuguese masters, whom she skilfully drew into her camp.

Unfortunately for Nzinga, any alliance with the predatory Imbangala was fated to be unstable, and she was nearly undone in 1628 when they suddenly changed sides right in the middle of a battle with the Portuguese. Nzinga eluded her pursuers through daring escapades down deep gorges and broken country, but the Portuguese captured her two sisters and had them baptised as Barbara and Engraçia. Despite the Imbangalas' treachery, Nzinga knew they were still undoubtedly the best warriors to be had. So she allied herself with other Imbangala bands. This time, to make sure the arrangement stuck, she began operating like an Imbangala commander herself and her armies adopted Imbangala customs including the election of their officers. The Ndongo elite hated this development. They only put up with it because of the catastrophic military situation that by 1629 saw Nzinga almost driven out of Ndongo altogether, leaving the kingdom to the Portuguese and their puppet, Filipe Hari.

In 1631 Nzinga made a dramatic move that secured her survival. East of Ndongo on the high plateau lay the large Mbundu kingdom of Matamba, which had succeeded in maintaining its independence from both its aggressive neighbours – Kongo and Ndongo. It had a tradition of women rulers and became vulnerable during the uneasy succession of a new *muhongo* (queen), which coincided with the sudden death of the *kambole* (her male consort and war leader). Nzinga struck decisively with her army and Imbangala allies and conquered Matamba, reputedly taking the *muhongo* captive and branding her as a slave (a practice learned from the Portuguese). She became the new *muhongo* herself and used Matamba as a base to rebuild her forces. From there she continued to resist the Portuguese in the rump of Ndongo, where she carried the fight to Filipe Hari, their loyal client ruler.

At the same time as Nzinga was conquering Matamba, those remaining Imbangala who had not been incorporated into her army or into the Portuguese forces began to settle down and give up their entirely destructive ways. Some bands established their own states in the central highlands. The most renowned was Kasanje, founded in the mid 1630s between the Lui and Kwango rivers southeast of Matamba. The Portuguese grasped Kasanje's potential as a military counterweight to Matamba and saw how it would also make an excellent trading partner because it was well positioned to control the trade routes into central Africa. Kasanje consequently soon took over from Ndongo as the principal supplier of slaves for export. The exceedingly unfortunate corollary was that Kasanje was encouraged to continue chronically at war with its neighbours to acquire them. South of the Kwanza river, on the Benguela plateau inhabited by the Ovimbundu, other Imbangala warlords set up their own states or overran and reorganised established kingdoms such as Bembe. There too they engaged in endemic warfare to provide slaves for the Portuguese.

The Dutch Enter the Fray

In Ndongo continuing military successes against Queen Nzinga caused the Portuguese to believe that it required only one more good blow to defeat her once and for all, conquer Matamba and go on to impose their control over the Imbangala state of Kasanje as well. They were just about to launch their campaign in 1641 when a Dutch attack from across the Atlantic almost snuffed out the Captaincy of Angola and threatened to expel the Portuguese from west-central Africa altogether.

It could not be said this was an entirely unexpected development – even if the timing was unanticipated – for the Dutch had long been sniffing and scrabbling around the Portuguese bases on both sides of Africa.* In Atlantic waters they raided Príncipe and São Tomé in 1598 and again in 1599, and from 1606 they began to trade with the kingdom of Loango, north of Kongo, and to challenge the Portuguese trade monopoly in west-central Africa. In West Africa they established Fort Nassau at Mori in 1612 and made severe inroads into the Portuguese control of the gold trade. In 1625 the Portuguese only just managed to beat back a Dutch attack on São Jorge da Mina, their great *feitoria* on the Gold Coast. Dutch privateers cruised the coast and periodically captured Portuguese merchantmen and fought duels with Portuguese men-of-war. After all, the Dutch were engaged in a global struggle against the Habsburg rulers of Spain and Portugal and felt justified in attacking their colonies and *feitorias* wherever they could in the Atlantic as well as in the Indian Ocean.

Then, in a very dangerous development for the Portuguese Atlantic empire, on 2 June 1621 the Dutch Republic granted the *Geoctroyeerde Westindische Compagnie*, or the Chartered West India Company (GWIC), a charter for a trade monopoly in the West Indies and gave it jurisdiction over the African slave trade to Brazil, the Caribbean and North America. As far as Atlantic Africa was concerned, the GWIC was given licence to operate between the Tropic of Cancer and the Cape of Good Hope, where it was encouraged to eliminate the Portuguese competition. The GWIC was thus to be very like the Dutch East India Company (VOC) established in 1602 – with the difference that it was not free to conduct military operations except with the permission of the Dutch government. It immediately set out establishing trading posts

---

* See Chapter 4 for Dutch attacks on the Captaincy of Moçambique.

and colonies in the Americas, attacking Portuguese and Spanish posts and engaging in vastly profitable privateering against their shipping.*

One of the greatest prizes up for grabs was Brazil,† discovered for Portugal in 1500 by Pedro Álvarez Cabral. Colonisation had begun in 1534 and sugar rapidly became the mainstay of its economy with slaves from west-central Africa providing the workforce for the plantations. In 1630 the GWIC captured the port of Recife and the flourishing Captaincy of Pernambuco, the rich, northeasternmost coastal region of Brazil with its heavy concentration of settlers and its 350 sugar mills. The next logical step was to seize the Portuguese slaving stations in West Africa and Angola to secure the essential source of slaves for Pernambuco and to deny them to the remainder of Portuguese Brazil.

In 1637 Count Johan Maurits of Nassau-Siegen, the GWIC's Governor-General of Pernambuco, masterminded the critical capture of São Jorge da Mina and eliminated the Portuguese presence on the Gold Coast. Angola was to be his next objective, and the Portuguese revolt in 1640 against Spanish rule provided the opportunity. Although King João IV of the House of Bragança was crowned on 15 December 1640 and the Habsburg Filipe III deposed, Portugal remained mired in a desperate struggle to fend off a Spanish reconquest and was in no position to divert resources to defend its distant colonies.

Even though the Portuguese were currently trying to negotiate an armistice with the Dutch, Count Maurits assembled a fleet of twenty-one ships in Recife and a task force of 2,000 soldiers. The Dutch ships appeared unheralded off a stunned Luanda on 24 August 1641, where the townspeople were innocently celebrating the accession of King João the Liberator. Taken by surprise, they put up an exceedingly feeble resistance. With Luanda secured, the Dutch then proceeded to take all the smaller Portuguese posts along the coast as far south as Benguela on the Bay of Santo António, a settlement established in 1617 and inadequately protected by its fort. The loss of all the slaving ports in Angola (along with thirty ships and a hundred cannon) was a stunning blow to the

---

* By the end of the eighteenth century the GWIC was losing its ability to defend its possessions against the British in particular. The Dutch government bought in its stock in 1791 and all its territories reverted to the States General.

† Brazil would gain its independence from Portugal in 1822, first as an empire until 1889 under a branch of the House of Bragança, and subsequently as a republic.

sugar economy of Portuguese Brazil, which simply could not operate without a regular supply of fresh slaves.

The defeated Portuguese governor, Pedro Cezar Menezes, his 900 white troops and many settlers hastily retired inland to their strongholds in the Kwanza valley at Massangano, Cambambe and other places. From there they began a grim struggle for survival on two fronts. To the west, the Dutch had secured their flank by clinching an alliance with Mwenekongo Garcia II Nkanga a Lukeni of Kongo. The *mwenekongo* was resentful of constant Portuguese meddling in the affairs of his kingdom, particularly over matters of church patronage. Besides, Dutch trade goods were more desirable. When he learned that the Dutch had seized Luanda, Garcia decided (prematurely, as it would turn out) that the Portuguese were finished. To the east, Queen Nzinga allied herself to the Dutch with alacrity and moved in for what she hoped would be the kill.

It was a campaign in which the outcome trembled in the balance. Nzinga's troops possessed many more matchlocks traded for slaves than in the past, and in battle her musketeers took up position in the vanguard, where their shot mingled with the clouds of arrows fired by the still more numerous bowmen. At the battle of Massangano in 1645 Nzinga's forces broke the African light troops supporting the heavy Portuguese infantry marching to relieve the besieged garrison. They fled, abandoning the Portuguese 'battle' of musketeers to be slaughtered where they stood.

However, at Cavanga in January 1646 the Portuguese under Gaspar Borges de Madureira more than retrieved the situation. He drew up his army with a centre and two wings and with field artillery in support. Instead of detaching troops to defend the *kikumba* left behind the battle line, he positioned it right in the middle of the army. That proved a most fortunate decision. When the Ndongo (who were supported by some 300 Dutch soldiers) broke the Portuguese right wing and started to roll up the centre, they lost momentum when they came upon the *kikumba* and started to loot it and rape the women camp followers. That fired the black Portuguese troops to rally and protect their womenfolk, and allowed space for the Portuguese reserve of heavy infantry (who had been stationed on a hill off the left flank) to mount a ferocious counter-attack.

The Portuguese musketeers drove the Ndongo army from the field in rout, and penned many of the fugitives against the barrier of the Dande river to be cut down. Hundreds more drowned when trying to cross the river on a hastily constructed field bridge that broke under their weight. *Pombos* kept up the pursuit for days and almost managed to capture the flying Nzinga. Her sisters, whom the Portuguese had released after their capture in 1628, fell again into their hands. This time, although they kept Barbara in comfortable captivity until 1657, they promptly strangled Engraçia for treachery. Back on the battlefield, the victorious Portuguese comprehensively looted Nzinga's camp at their leisure, knowing that she would not be able to rally her army for many days to come.

In Brazil there was mounting consternation at the Dutch interruption of the West African slave trade. Accepting that metropolitan Portugal was in no position to intervene, the slave-owning settlers and town council of Rio de Janeiro (who effectively ran the rich and populous Captaincy of Rio de Janeiro) raised the funds necessary to outfit an amphibious expedition to retake Angola. With Lisbon's cautious approval the fleet of nineteen vessels with 900 soldiers on board sailed out from Rio in 1648 under the command of Salvador Correira da Sá e Benavides, a leading citizen, plantation owner and former Governor of Rio de Janeiro.

Da Sá cast anchor in the harbour of Luanda on 12 August and called on the Dutch to surrender. They refused, and the 1,000 men of the Dutch garrison withdrew to Fort São Miguel. Da Sá landed his troops, bombarded the fort with his ships' guns, and once they had opened a breach took it by storm on 15 August, the Feast of the Assumption of the Virgin Mary. Some 163 Portuguese died in the furious assault, but the sacrifice was deemed worth it. Not only did the Dutch in Luanda lay down their arms, but so too did those garrisoning Benguela as well as their troops operating with Nzinga. The Portuguese promptly shipped them off to Europe, and Angola was freed after its seven-year captivity.

The Dutch surrender did not mean they immediately disappeared from the scene. Until a peace treaty between the Portuguese and Dutch was finally signed in 1662 Dutch privateers continued to operate off the Angolan coast. In Angola itself the baleful repercussions of the Dutch occupation were felt for some time. The first Governor of Angola after the Portuguese reconquest was

Salvador da Sá (1648–1652), the victorious commander of the expeditionary force. He hailed from Rio de Janeiro, but the series of assertive, ruthless governors who succeeded him in the latter half of the seventeenth century were all from Pernambuco. Their rich homeland had finally risen up in 1645 against the unwelcome Dutch occupation. After considerable fighting, in which these later governors of Angola all nobly distinguished themselves, the Dutch were finally driven out in 1654. But Pernambuco's economy was left in a shambles after so many years of deliberately destructive warfare.

The Pernambucan governors of Angola saw it as their paramount obligation to assist in their homeland's recovery. They knew they could do this best by restoring and increasing the flow of Angolan slave labour to its sugar plantations. Consequently, they insisted on a policy of more aggressive slaving than Angola had ever experienced before. No longer content to allow private contractors to purchase slaves in the interior from their African captors, these governors encouraged their Portuguese or Afro-Portuguese soldiers to take them captive themselves in raids and other military operations and then to sell them on to the coast. It also became the firm practice to extract slaves as tribute from defeated African rulers.

The defeat and expulsion of the Dutch was, therefore, a double disaster for Queen Nzinga. She had lost a valuable ally in her mortal struggle against the Portuguese, and now the victorious Angolans were prosecuting the war even harder to acquire slaves. To survive, she had to temporise and accommodate. Nzinga had been baptised in 1622, but she had apostatised and not permitted missionaries into her kingdom. Now she ostentatiously embraced Christianity again, thanks (according to missionary report) to the spirits of five of her ancestors she had consulted. They conveniently informed her 'to her no small terror, that they were suffering eternal torments, which she could only escape by once more embracing the Christian faith and seeking the friendship of the Portuguese'.[10] As part of the cleansing process she and her court divested themselves of the vicious, socially transgressive Imbangala style they had affected, and tried with less success to break Imbangala control of her army.

These moves pleased the Portuguese and made negotiating with Nzinga much more acceptable. Even more acceptable to them was Nzinga's decision to cease disrupting the flow of slaves to Luanda from the interior. Agreement could thus be reached in 1657. The Portuguese recognised Nzinga as queen of both Matamba and Ndongo, with the boundary of Ndongo with Angola fixed along the Lukala river. It was agreed that Nzinga would pay no tribute, but a Portuguese resident captain was appointed in Matamba to oversee the revived flow of slaves. On the payment of a ransom of 200 slaves the Portuguese also released Nzinga's sister, Barbara, whom they had captured in 1646.

When the aged Nzinga died on 17 December 1663 the Governor of Angola, André Vidal de Negreiros (1661–1667), decided to accept the *status quo* and recognised her sister Barbara Mukambu Mbande as queen in her stead. Any more conclusive reckoning with Ndongo and Matamba would have to wait because the governor had first to settle with Kongo.

The Portuguese–Kongo Wars

As far as the Portuguese were concerned, Garcia II of Kongo had to pay some penalty for so readily abandoning them and making common cause with the Dutch when the heretics attacked Angola in 1641. They consequently wasted no time in invading his kingdom to make the point. Intimidated, Garcia accepted the terms of a peace treaty. It was confirmed in 1651 in Lisbon, although it took the threat of another Portuguese invasion before Garcia ratified it in 1656. However, the terms were steep. They gave the Portuguese exclusive access to Kongo (thereby cutting out the Dutch) and ceded the Portuguese crown all the kingdom's gold and silver mines. Kongo also surrendered all the country south of the Dande river to Angola, including Luanda Island, which as the source of the *nzimbu*-shell currency had been such a valuable asset to the Kongo kings. As if all that were not enough, by the treaty the humiliated *mwenekongo* acknowledged he was a tributary of Portugal.

Even so, the Portuguese in Angola were not prepared to abide scrupulously by the terms of the treaty. Governor de Negreiros began military operations north of the Dande river into the mountainous region of the Dembo highlands, which was still technically Kongo territory. His intention was to bring more slaves into the Portuguese net and to secure the mines surrendered to Portugal in the treaty. This brought him into increasing dispute with the new *mwenekongo*, António I Nvita a Nkanga (r.1661–1665), who had promised his dying father to avenge the humiliation forced on him by the Portuguese. As tension escalated, de Negreiros (that hard-nosed soldier) flicked off the

Portuguese crown's concerns that he should abide by the requirements for a just war before taking the field. His mission was to further the interests of the slavers of Angola and Pernambuco, and he was not to be constrained by legalistic scruples.

In 1665 the ruler of Mbwila in the Dembo highlands was facing a dynastic challenge from his aunt, Dona Isabel, who was allied to the Portuguese and was banking on their military support. Mwenekongo António decided in July of that year that the moment had come to put an end to Portuguese meddling in the affairs of Kongo. He was encouraged by the royal diviners, who promised him an easy victory. Accompanied by all of Kongo's *mwisikongo* he personally marched one of the largest armies ever assembled in Kongo into Mbwila territory. The hard core of António's army was made up of 800 professional shield-bearers and 190 musketeers under the experienced Afro-Portuguese Captain Pedro Dias de Cabra. Supporting them were well in excess of 10,000 light troops who were, however, little more than a mass of conscripted peasants with scant military experience.

Dona Isabel only had a small force of 400 men to oppose António, but she was supported by a considerable Portuguese army. It was under the command of Luís Lopes de Sequeira, who had at his disposal 466 musketeers (thanks to recent reinforcements from Brazil), a force of professional *imbari* under allied *sobas*, a detachment of fierce Imbangala and 6,000–7,000 bowmen, largely supplied by Filipe Hari, the puppet *ngola* of Ndongo. The latter were hardened light infantry who had taken part in many campaigns since the expulsion of the Dutch. De Sequeira also had two light field pieces, which were destined to play a crucial role in the coming battle. Thus, despite being outnumbered, the Portuguese forces held the definite advantage in terms of firepower and experience. Both sides were inevitably trammelled by a great number of non-combatants – the porters and camp followers in the Portuguese *kikumba* being estimated at well in excess of the number of soldiers who took the field.

On 29 October 1665 the two armies faced off near the lion rocks in the valley of the Ulanga river in Mbwila. Both were drawn up in conventional array and were expecting to fight the sort of set-piece battle they were accustomed to. If we are to believe what soldiers later recounted, they were treated before joining combat to a spectral dual in the sky above them between a Kongo heavy infantryman carrying his great shield, and an Imbangala warrior characteristically without one. Ominously for António's great host, it was the ghostly Imbangala who triumphed.

De Sequeira deployed his somewhat outnumbered army defensively, with the Portuguese musketeers in a lozenge-shaped formation in the vanguard supported by the two artillery pieces. As was customary, he placed his light troops on either flank of the Portuguese 'battle' and held a large force in reserve to the rear with the *kikumba*. The Kongo army seems to have been drawn up in two supporting lines. The Marquis of Mpemba was in command of the front line. In the centre were all the musketeers and half the shield-bearing heavy infantry, while a good 4,000 light troops supported its flanks. The *mwenekongo* himself commanded the second line, which replicated the first in its dispositions. The Duke of Bengo commanded the rearguard and baggage.

Mpemba's vanguard advanced with great determination on the Portuguese line. After fierce hand-to-hand fighting in which the Portuguese made telling sorties from their tight formation, and in which grapeshot from their two field pieces ripped open the Kongo ranks, Mpemba's battered troops finally fell back. António himself then brought up the second line in support, with its reserve of shield-bearers in the centre. Their presence steadied Mpemba's men, who joined in the renewed attack. This time their superior numbers told. The Kongo wings drove off the opposing light African troops supporting the Portuguese centre and then swung in to envelope it completely. The men of Kongo believed they had victory in their grasp, but the Portuguese reserve rushed forward to succour the beleaguered lozenge of Portuguese musketeers. They smashed into the mêlée, and the battle became a dreadful, formless brawl.

The carnage only ended after six hours of fighting, when António (who was said to have left the security of his own ranks to seek out de Sequeira with the intention of engaging him hand-to-hand) was wounded by two musket balls and tried to leave the field. The Portuguese spotted his plight. In a determined sally they caught up with him and his entourage and slew the disabled *mwenekongo*. The exalting Portuguese then hacked off his head and stuck it on a pike, which they elevated above the fray. When they saw the grisly trophy the Kongo army began to fall back in complete disarray, a fiery rain (according to the missionary priests with the Portuguese) falling on the idolaters. Emulating the spectral duellist in the sky earlier that day, the fearsome Imbangala with the Portuguese spearheaded a relentless counter-attack. The Duke of Bengo began to pull back with the Kongo rearguard, but he failed to save the *kikumba* and became caught up in the terrified rout.

Thousands upon thousands of Kongo fell on the field of Mbwila. The elite of the kingdom were almost completely decimated, with no less than ninety-eight titled *mwisikongo* and some 400 lesser chiefs losing their lives. Several clergy were killed too, including António's personal chaplain. The Portuguese captured many important members of the *mwenekongo*'s court alive and maliciously sold them out of Kongo into slavery. As for António, the Portuguese triumphantly carried off his severed head along with his looted crown and sceptre. They brought them back to Luanda, which was *en fête* for several days at the heady news of the victory at Mbwila. Chivalry at length prevailed. While they despatched António's royal regalia to King Afonso VI in Lisbon as trophies, the Portuguese finally buried the *mwenekongo*'s head with royal pomp in the Church of Our Lady of Nazareth in Luanda. Decorative *azulejo* tiles that used to adorn the entrance façade depicted António's severed head on a large salver or shield along with his crown and other items of the royal regalia.

Mbwila was a watershed for Kongo. In its aftermath the central power of the *awenekongo* began to collapse and the kingdom lurched into a protracted, confusing and increasingly destructive era of succession disputes and civil wars. The first step for a pretender to the throne from one of the various branches of the royal house was to gain control of a province – and governors were still nominally appointed by the ever weaker *awenekongo*. Once he had secured his governorship, a contender for the throne was then free to mobilise the male population of his province for war, and in this period governors did so far more comprehensively than had ever been the case in the past. To win, it was essential to control the capital, São Salvador, and be crowned there. Even so, not many of these ephemeral, upstart *awenekongo* were strong enough to conquer and control all the provinces at once, so the debilitating fighting never quite stopped. When a powerful *mwenekongo* did sometimes emerge for a space, civil war inevitably flared up between his heir and other contenders. São Salvador became a frequent victim of these wars, and was even abandoned for a while between 1678 and 1709. Without it as the keystone of the kingdom, central authority collapsed.

Of course, it was a trump card in these civil wars if an alliance with the Portuguese could be secured. The Portuguese knew this perfectly well and set the price of their assistance high. However, it was in items other than slaves because their export from Kongo was in decline. The central state was no longer raiding for slaves, and the fractious, warring *mwisikongo* were more interested in keeping their captives for their own armies or to work their agricultural estates. An alternative to slaves was valuable minerals (the Portuguese would never give up their quest for them), and in 1667 and 1670 they wrung mining concessions from ephemeral *awenekongo* in return for propping them up. The Portuguese were also keen to secure control of the lucrative trade along the Congo river. To do so they knew they had to build a fort to command the key port of Mpinda in northwestern Kongo.

Providentially, in 1670 Rafael I Nzinga a Nkanga managed to seize the throne of Kongo even though he was beset by unreconciled rivals, chief of whom was the Count Estavão de Silva of Nsoyo, in whose province Mpinda lay.* The deal was struck. Governor Dom Francisco de Távora (1668–1676) despatched an army under João Soares de Almeida of 500 Portuguese along with the usual ratio of African light troops (including a detachment of Imbangala) with orders to crush Count Estavão on Rafael's behalf, and then to go on to erect the desired fort at Mpinda.

At first, all seemed to go to plan. De Almeida's men even used *nzimbu* shells to buy provisions as they advanced, so as not to alienate the people of Nsoyo through foraging. Count Estavão gathered his forces to oppose them and made a determined stand with his musketeers intermixed in the centre with his shield-bearing infantry in a very up-to-date formation. Kongo had early seen the potential of artillery, and the count deployed four field pieces in support of his infantry. The intensity of the Portuguese musket and artillery fire shattered the Nsoyo warriors as they advanced, and they broke and fled. Count Estavão was among the many dead.

As the Portuguese should have known, if Kongo armies could be quick to break they were also easy to rally. However, many of the Portuguese officers were newly arrived and nevertheless allowed their own forces to disperse in undisciplined pursuit of slaves and other booty. As a result, on 18 October 1670 the regrouped Nsoyo army under Pedro, the dead count's brother, caught the Portuguese quite unprepared at Kitombo near the coast.

---

* The rich maritime province of Nsoyo had become effectively independent of Kongo in 1636, but its ruling counts maintained the right to participate in the choice of the *awenekongo*.

The Portuguese had no time to deploy their artillery, which had been so crucial in the previous engagement, or to get their musketeers into proper formation. To make things worse, the green Portuguese officers made the mistake of chivvying their light infantry into the sort of tight formation normal on European battlefields, but which made them very vulnerable to the clouds of arrows the Nsoyo archers rained down on them. Caught up in the mêlée and out of their usual close formation, the Portuguese took up the heavy shields they had captured in the previous battle and defended themselves in hand-to-hand fighting with their long swords. It was to no avail. The Imbangala units broke and fled, and the Portuguese joined in the rout. The Mbrize river blocked their flight, and hundreds died while trying to swim it. Thousands more perished on the battlefield and all the artillery was lost. When the Portuguese fleet showed up a few days later, the Nsoyo derisively sent them dismembered bits of Portuguese soldiers.

Kitombo was one of the very worst defeats the Portuguese ever suffered in Africa. Thereafter, they concentrated on coming to terms with the victorious Nsoyo and concluded a treaty in 1690. The Portuguese did maintain tepid trading relations with the rest of Kongo too, but these regions were not as well placed as Nsoyo for commerce, and had ever fewer goods to trade, not even many slaves. The problem was that during the eighteenth century central authority continued to shrink away in the kingdom, and Kongo slowly dissolved into a congeries of squabbling chiefdoms. Provincial armies degenerated into robber bands under lawless warlords. To avoid being taken as slaves the inhabitants of the shrinking towns threw up defences, and the peasantry withdrew to natural fastnesses in forests and on mountain tops.

By the end of the eighteenth century São Salvador itself, repeatedly sacked and looted and its churches in ruins, had reverted to a rustic settlement of huts behind a palisade. Christianity in Kongo did not quite die out, but merged ever more closely with local forms of worship. Literacy only just survived, but correspondence was carried out on dried banana leaves because of the unavailability and high price of paper. Such was the dismal dénouement of Kongo's long and ultimately destructive relationship with Portugal.*

---

* In 1888 Pedro VI of Kongo signed a treaty whereby he became a vassal of Portugal. Manuel III rebelled against Portuguese control in 1914 but was defeated, and the victors finally abolished the Kongo monarchy.

The Portuguese–Matamba Wars

Largely turning their backs on Kongo after their disaster at Kitombo, from the later seventeenth century the Portuguese concentrated on securing their colony of Angola and consolidating their control of the slave trade. They dealt first with Filipe Hari, their long-time Ndongo puppet. He was becoming increasingly disaffected with Portuguese ingratitude for all his unstinting military support in their wars against Nzinga, the Dutch and Kongo. In particular, he was upset by the treaty of 1657, which had recognised Nzinga as Queen of Ndongo and Matamba and had left him as ruler only of Mpungo a Ndongo. In 1670 he finally revolted. After being thoroughly defeated in the field he holed up in his apparently impregnable rocky stronghold of Mpungo a Ndongo. After a long siege, on 18 November 1671 a scaling party of African light troops under an intrepid officer called Manuel Cortes finally surprised the fortress. Filipe Hari was captured alive. Ignoring his decades of invaluable service the Portuguese beheaded him as a traitor. They also took a gratifyingly large haul of slaves from Mpungo a Ndongo.

Filipe Hari's ignominious and cruel fate made the interior states of Matamba and Kasanje doubly determined to maintain their independence. The prosperity of both depended on their incessant, highly organised raiding for slaves and their stranglehold on their transference to Luanda. The Portuguese, still pursuing their aggressive strategy of military slaving, were determined to wrest the trade from them. This could be done through diplomacy and trade agreements, and Kasanje showed itself more willing than Matamba to work with the Portuguese. Otherwise, war was the alternative.

Yet the forces available to the Portuguese in Angola at that time and well into the eighteenth century were but a mixed bag. The best were the regular units of professional musketeers who served under the command of the governor himself and were stationed at the fortress in Luanda and at seven other forts at strategic points about Angola. Almost as dependable were the professional African warriors referred to in this period as *empacaceiros* (antelope-hunters). They were the retainers of *sobas*, who were the sworn vassals of Portugal. Imbangala mercenaries still gave good value for money. Less useful were the poorly trained companies of Portuguese and Afro-Portuguese militia raised in Angola after 1695. Outside the colony itself, a web of treaties permitted the Portuguese to call on the admittedly unreliable light infantry of allied African rulers.

As unsatisfactory as many of the forces at their disposal might have been, the Portuguese did not shy away from war to gain their ends in the interior. In Matamba, Nzinga's successor, her sister Barbara, died in 1666. After a period of civil war, in 1680 Francisco Guterres Ngola Kanini, Nzinga's nephew, seized the throne. Kasanje was currently also embroiled in a succession dispute, and in 1681 Francisco Guterres intervened in support of the anti-Portuguese claimant. In the course of the fighting he was implicated in the killing of the Portuguese *pombeiros* operating in Kasanje. Concerned with safeguarding the interior slave trade routes, and growingly suspicious of Francisco Guterres' ambitions, the Portuguese resolved to intervene decisively with the largest army they could field.

Accordingly, de Sequeira, the famed victor at Mbwila, marched deep into Matamba at the head of a strike force of 530 infantry, all armed with muskets. They were supported by about 10,000 *empacaceiros*, as well as a contingent of Imbangala. Most unusually, the Portuguese even deployed thirty-seven horsemen. Francisco Guterres gathered an army to face the Portuguese and barred their path at Katole, only three days' march from the Matamba capital. The two armies clashed on 4 September 1681.

Francisco Guterres launched an initially successful attack at dawn, but the Imbangala contingent with the Portuguese rallied and retrieved the day. The two sides then settled down to a bitter slogging-match at close quarters. Francisco Guterres perished in the bloody fighting, but so too did de Sequeira. In the end, the Matamba army fell back, but were not routed. The Portuguese remained in command of the field at Katole, but the victory was a hollow one. With their general dead and with many casualties, the severely battered Portuguese withdrew. There was no pursuit from the equally mauled and leaderless Matamba forces.

Verónica I Guterres Kandala Kingwanga succeeded her slain brother as Queen of Matamba. She would rule until 1721 and devoted her reign to consolidating her kingdom. That meant above all coming to terms with the Portuguese. On 7 September 1683 the two parties signed a treaty whereby Verónica accepted nominal vassalage to Portugal. She also agreed to recognise the independence of Kasanje with which she had been at war, and which was now firmly in the Portuguese camp. These terms broke Matamba's monopoly of the slave routes into the interior, and opened them to Portuguese *pombeiros*. Nevertheless, Verónica considered the concession worthwhile and necessary. And so it proved. Even though hostilities broke out between her and the Portuguese in 1689 and again in 1692–1693 they were low keyed and containable, and Matamba entered a period of stability.

The Eighteenth-Century Slave Wars

Slaving ties between Angola and Brazil continued to strengthen during the eighteenth century, with most of the shipping transporting slaves being specifically Brazilian rather than Portuguese. By a peculiar irony these unfortunates were mainly destined to labour on the very sugar plantations that produced *cachaça*, the cane brandy that proved such an extraordinarily successful item of exchange in the Angolan interior for slaves, where it was known as *jeribita*.

As alcohol kept the slave mill relentlessly turning, so too did the muskets the Portuguese traded in ever-growing numbers. By the beginning of the eighteenth century safer flintlocks were increasingly replacing matchlocks as the ignition mechanism on muskets. When the trigger is squeezed a piece of flint, held in the jaws of the lock, springs forward and strikes a metal plate to produce sparks. The plate is simultaneously knocked up by the impact and exposes the priming powder in the pan to the sparks. This was a far more efficient system than the matchlock one, and cheaper and simpler than the wheel-lock alternative. Moreover, only seven distinct drill movements were required to fire a flintlock. Africans of the Angolan interior became increasingly adept with these firearms, and the musketeers of Kasanje in particular were reputed to be every bit as proficient as the picked troops commanded by the Governor of Angola.

During the course of the eighteenth century the catchment area for slaves began to expand in size thanks in large measure to the westward advance of the Lunda empire. The original home of the Lunda was deep in central Africa, east beyond what is now Shaba province in the Democratic Republic of the Congo. By the mid-eighteenth century Lunda armies armed with spears, swords and shields (they regarded firearms as cowards' weapons and refused to use them) were fighting all along the Kwango river against the warriors of Matamba and Kasanje. These wars and the thousands of desperate refugees they displaced produced a wonderful fresh crop of slaves to be sold to the Portuguese. Once the Kwango stabilised as the boundary between the Lunda and Matamba and Kasanje to the west, these states did their best to seal the Lunda empire off from the Portuguese. The reason was that the Lunda slaving network stretched thousands of miles into the interior and Matamba and Kasanje were anxious to assert their role as sole trading intermediaries for this enormous new slave reservoir.

For their part, although the Portuguese were never powerful or numerous enough to place permanent garrisons outside the stabilised late seventeenth-century limits of Angola proper (where Portuguese and Afro-Portuguese soldiers held the string of frontier forts and outposts), they nevertheless remained as determined as ever to force their African neighbours to trade only through them. To that end, they continued to mount inconclusive campaigns, build forts on major trade routes which they later had to abandon for lack of troops, and send in punitive raids against rulers who had defied them. In 1744 there was a renewal of war with Matamba over its ill treatment of *pombeiros* trying to operate in its territory. Some heavy fighting ensued that cost the Portuguese one heavy reverse during its course, but in the end Matamba was forced to reaffirm the treaty of 1683 and acknowledge its vassalage to Portugal.

The most demanding eighteenth-century war was waged between 1773 and 1776 against Viye and Mbailundu, two kingdoms that had recently arisen on the south-central Benguela highlands. Much of the slogging, indecisive fighting concentrated around earthwork fortifications surrounded by ditches and lines of sharpened stakes. The Portuguese had to be content in the end with imposing only nominal authority over the rulers of the two states as their lukewarm vassals.

As for the slave trade, this dreadful traffic continued to be operated by the local Afro-Portuguese and Brazilian networks. Caravans of porters, armed guards and professional guides carrying firearms, gunpowder and fabrics for trade regularly made their way deep into the slave-trading zones of the interior. There the African slave brokers, like flies on carrion, gained steadily in wealth and influence, quite eclipsing the old nobility. Finally, in 1850 the government of Brazil abolished the slave trade and made it an act of piracy to import slaves. It took a little time to enforce the law, and it was only in 1856 that the last recorded shiploads of African slaves landed in Brazil. In Brazil itself the institution of slavery came to end only on 13 May 1888 with the passing of the Golden Law, which liberated 725,000 slaves.

The Final Portuguese Conquest of Angola

After the ending of the slave trade in Angola the actual authority of the Portuguese crown remained confined to little beyond Luanda and the agricultural estates of the surrounding lowlands, Benguela further down the coast and a handful of isolated interior settlements. Portuguese colonisation and administration beyond these points barely existed. Only when the Scramble for Africa frenetically broke out in the 1880s, and Portugal was threatened by the incontinent appetites of other colonial powers, did Portugal bestir itself to lay claim to the vast territories that comprise the modern state of Angola. A series of treaties concluded in 1886, 1887 and 1891 between Portugal and Great Britain, France and Germany defined its boundaries.

The problem for Portugal was that, for its ownership of Angola to be respected by the other colonial powers, it was necessary (as was also the case on the other side of the continent in Portuguese East Africa) to demonstrate effective occupation of the entire colony. However, the military burden of 'pacifying' an Angola that still existed for the main part only on the map was one that a chronically bankrupt Portugal was extremely reluctant to shoulder. It took the secret Anglo-German convention of August 1898 to galvanise Portugal into action. Details of the convention rapidly leaked out, and Portugal learned that Britain and Germany had agreed to partition its African colonies if it could not maintain them. Rather than let that happen, in the first decade of the twentieth century the Portuguese at last set about militarily staking out their claim to Angola. Many years of heavy, cruel fighting were required – in which Portugal employed its modern technological advantages to their fullest extent – before the conquest was finally accomplished, just as the First World War was ending.

In their recorded folklore, the Kimbundu-speaking Pende people of the plains inland from Luanda pithily summed up their reaction to the Portuguese from the moment they landed on their shores: 'From that time until our days the whites brought us nothing but wars and miseries.'[11] These words echoed the very same plaint by an anonymous Arab historian, writing in Malindi on the far side of Africa, who bewailed the Portuguese destruction of the vibrant civilisation of the Swahili coast. These voices speak for all those Africans who suffered from their violent contact with the Portuguese during the age of gunpowder and sail, and particularly for the millions of slaves the Portuguese carried away from their homes to servitude across the oceans.

Notes

CHAPTER ONE

1   Quoted in Mercedes García-Arenal, *Ahmad al-Mansur: The Beginnings of Modern Morocco*, Oxford: Oneworld, 2009, p. 28.

2   Emanuel de Faria y Sousa, *The History of Portugal from the First Ages of the World to the Late Great Revolution, under King John IV, in the Year MDCXL, Translated, and Continued down to this Present year, 1698 by Capt John Stevens*, London: W. Roger and Abel Roper, 1708, p. 346.

3   Mustapha ibn Hassan Husayni Jannabi, quoted in Weston F. Cook, Jr, *The Hundred Years War for Morocco: Gunpowder and the Military Revolution in the Early Modern Muslim World*, Boulder, CO: Westview Press, 1994, p. 241.

4   Quoted in García-Arenal, p. 17.

5   Jewish doctor's (Joseph Valencia's) letter, quoted in Cook, p. 253.

CHAPTER TWO

1   João de Barros, 'Da Asia: Of the deed which the explorers performed in the conquest and exploration of the lands and seas of the east', in George McCall Theal (ed.), *Records of South-Eastern Africa Collected in Various Libraries and Archive Departments in Europe*, London: William Clowes and Sons for the Government of the Cape Colony, Vol. 6, 1900, p. 167.

2   De Barros, in Theal, Vol. 6, p. 170.

3   Duarte Barbosa, *The Book of Duarte Barbosa*, quoted in Basil Davidson (ed.), *The African Past: Chronicles from Antiquity to Modern Times*, Boston, MA and Toronto: Little, Brown, 1964, p. 132.

4   De Barros, in Theal, Vol. 6, p. 173.

5   Vasco da Gama's logbook, quoted in Davidson, p.124.

6   *The Book of Duarte Barbosa*, quoted in G. S. P. Freeman-Grenville (ed.), *The East African Coast: Select Documents from the First to the Earlier Nineteenth Century*, Oxford: Clarendon Press, 1962, p. 130.

7   Anon., *An Arabic History of Kilwa Kisiwani c.1520*, quoted in Michael M. Pearson, *Port Cities and Intruders: The Swahili Coast, India, and Portugal in the Early Modern Era*, Baltimore, MD and London: The Johns Hopkins University Press, 1998, p. 48.

8   Vasco da Gama's journal, quoted in Zoe Marsh (ed.), *East Africa through Contemporary Records*, Cambridge: Cambridge University Press, 1961, p. 17.

9   Quoted in Pearson, p. 143.

10   Quoted in Freeman-Grenville, p. 81.
11   *The Book of Duarte Barbosa*, quoted in Freeman-Grenville, p. 131.
12   Quoted in Freeman-Grenville, p. 108.
13   Quoted in Marsh, p. 12.
14   Quoted in Freeman-Grenville, p. 103.
15   Quoted in Freeman-Grenville, p. 103.
16   Friar João dos Santos, *Ethiopia Oriental (1609)*, in George McCall Theal (ed.), *Records of South-Eastern Africa Collected in Various Libraries and Archive Departments in Europe*, London: William Clowes and Sons for the Government of the Cape Colony, Vol. 7, 1901, p. 187.

CHAPTER THREE

1   Miguel de Castanhoso, 'A discourse of the deeds of the very valorous Captain Dom Christovão da Gama in the kingdom of the Preste John, with the four hundred Portuguese, his companions', in R. S. Whiteway (ed.), *The Portuguese Expedition to Abyssinia in 1541–1543, as Narrated by Castanhoso, with Some Contemporary Letters, the Short Account of Bermudez, and Certain Extract from Correa*, Millwood, NY: Hakluyt Society, 2nd series, No. X (1902; Kraus reprint, 1967), p. 17.
2   Castanhoso, in Whiteway, p. 20.
3   Francisco Alvares, 'A true relation of the lands of Prester John as seen and described by Father Francisco Alvares', in C. F. Beckingham and G. W. B. Huntingford (eds), *The Prester John of the Indies: A True Relation of the Lands of the Prester John Being the Narrative of the Portuguese Embassy to Ethiopia in 1520 Written by Father Francisco Alvares*, Millwood, NY: Hakluyt Society, 2nd series, No. CXIV (1958; Kraus reprint, 1975), Vol. I, p. 312.
4   Manoel de Almeida, 'The history of High Ethiopia or Abassia', in C. F. Beckingham and G. W. B. Huntingford (eds), *Some Records of Ethiopia, 1593–1646: Being Extracts from The History of High Ethiopia of Abassia by Manoel de Almeida, Together with Bahrey's History of the Galla*, Millwood, NY: Hakluyt Society, 2nd series, No. CVII (1954; Kraus reprint, 1990), p. 82.
5   Alvares, in Beckingham and Huntingford, Vol. I, p. 304.
6   Alvares, in Beckingham and Huntingford, Vol. II, pp. 445–6.
7   Richard K. P. Pankhurst (ed.), *The Ethiopian Royal Chronicles*, Addis Ababa: Oxford University Press, 1967, p. 71.
8   Remedius Prutky, 'Travels', in J. H. Arrowsmith-Brown and Richard Pankhurst (eds), *Prutky's Travels in Ethiopia and Other Countries*, London: Hakluyt Society, 2nd series, No. 174 (1991), p. 184.
9   Pankhurst, p. 52.
10   Pankhurst, p. 54.
11   Pankhurst, p. 50.
12   Pankhurst, p. 50.
13   Castanhoso, in Whiteway, p. 32.
14   Castanhoso, in Whiteway, p. 44.
15   Castanhoso, in Whiteway, p. 46.
16   João Bermudez, 'A short account of the embassy which the Patriarch D. João Bermudez brought from the Emperor of Ethiopia . . . to the most Christian . . . King of Portugal', in Whiteway, p. 156.
17   Prutky, in Arrowsmith-Brown and Pankhurst, pp. 151–2.

18   Castanhoso, in Whiteway, p. 67.

19   Isabel Boavida, Hervé Pennec and Manueal João Ramos (eds); Christopher J. Tribe
      (trans.), *Pedro Páez's History of Ethiopia, 1622*, Farnham, Surrey: Ashgate for Hakluyt
      Society, 3rd series, No. 23 (2011), Vol. 1, p. 291.

20   Jerónimo Lobo, 'The itinerário', in Donald Lockhart, M. G. A. da Costa and C. F.
      Beckingham (eds), *The Itinerário of Jerónimo Lobo*, London: Hakluyt Society, 2nd series,
      No. 162 (1984), p. 217.

21   Letter from the King of Abyssinia to the Governor of India, which was despatched in
      1551, quoted in Whitelaw, p. 120.

22   Castanhoso, in Whiteway, p. 76.

CHAPTER FOUR

1   Quoted in C. R. Boxer and Carlos de Azevedo, *Fort Jesus and the Portuguese in Mombasa
      1593–1729*, London: Hollis and Carter, 1960, p. 86.

2   Quoted in John Middleton, *The World of the Swahili: An African Mercantile Civilization*, New
      Haven, CT: Yale University Press, 1992, p. 47.

3   Manoel Barretto, 'Report upon the state and conquest of the rivers of Cuama,
      commonly and truly called the rivers of gold' (1667), in George McCall Theal (ed.),
      Records of South-Eastern Africa Collected in Various Libraries and Archive Departments in Europe,
      London: William Clowes and Sons for the Government of the Cape Colony, Vol. 3,
      1899, p. 480.

4   Dos Santos, in Theal, Vol. 7, p. 296.

5   Dos Santos, in Theal, Vol. 7, p. 300.

6   De Barros, in Theal, Vol. 6, p. 400.

7   Dos Santos, in Theal, Vol. 7, p. 301.

8   Dos Santos, in Theal, Vol 7, p. 302.

9   Pedro Barretto de Rezende, *Livro de Estado*, quoted in Freeman-Grenville, p. 177.

10   Dos Santos, in Theal, Vol. 7, pp. 316–18.

11   Dos Santos, in Theal, Vol. 7, p. 335.

12   Quoted in Eric Axelson, *Portuguese in South-East Africa 1600–1700*, Johannesburg:
      Witwatersrand University Press, 1964, p. 84.

13   Manuel de Faría y Sousa, 'Asia Portuguesa (1666–75)', in Marsh, p. 22.

14   Anonymous account in Italian, quote in Freeman-Grenville, p. 173.

15   George Percy Badger (trans. and ed.), *History of the Imâms and Seyyids of 'Omân by Sálîl-
      ibn-Razník from AD 661–1856*, London: Hakluyt Society, 1st series, No. 44 (1871),
      p. 92.

16   Anon., 'A history of Mombasa, c.1824', in Freeman-Grenville, p. 214.

CHAPTER FIVE

1   Dos Santos, in Theal, Vol. 7, pp. 275–6, 278.

2   De Barros, in Theal, Vol. 6, p. 266. Although written in the mid-sixteenth century, this
      account was first published in 1778.

3   Dos Santos, in Theal, Vol. 7, p. 273.

4   Dos Santos, in Theal, Vol. 7, pp. 267–8.

5   Antonio de Bocarro, 'Extracts from the decade written by Antonio de Bocarro, His
      Majesty chronicler for the state of India, of the performance of the Portuguese in the

east', in Theal, Vol. 3, p. 356. Although written in the mid-seventeenth century, this account was first published in 1876.

6   Dos Santos, in Theal, Vol. 7, p. 288.

7   Dos Santos, in Theal, Vol. 7, pp. 206, 289.

8   Barbosa, c.1518, quoted in D. N. Beach, *The Shona and Zimbabwe 900–1850: An Outline of Shona History*, New York: Africana, 1980, p. 98.

9   Damião de Goes, 'Chronicle of the Most Fortunate King Dom Emanuel of glorious memory', in Theal, Vol. 3, p. 130. This is a work based on official documents and first published in 1566.

10   Dos Santos, in Theal, Vol. 7, p. 207.

11   Dos Santos, in Theal, Vol. 7, p. 287.

12   Dos Santos, in Theal, Vol. 7, pp. 201, 290.

13   de Bocarro, in Theal, Vol. 3, p. 358.

14   Dos Santos, in Theal, Vol. 7, p. 218.

15   Dos Santos, in Theal, Vol. 7, p. 281.

16   'Decision of the lawyers: With the conditions on which war may be made upon kings of the conquest of Portugal, especially upon the Monomotapa, 23 January 1569', in Theal, Vol. 3, pp. 153–6.

17   Diogo de Couto, 'Of the deeds which the Portuguese performed in the conquest and discovery of the lands and seas of the east', in Theal, Vol. 6, p. 387. De Couto died in 1616 and his manuscript was published in 1778.

18   De Couto, in Theal, Vol. 6, p. 372.

19   De Couto, in Theal, Vol. 6, p. 375.

20   De Couto, in Theal, Vol. 6, p. 376.

21   De Couto, in Theal, Vol. 6, p. 378.

22   De Couto, in Theal, Vol. 6, p. 389.

23   De Couto, in Theal, Vol. 6, p. 405.

24   de Bocarro, in Theal, Vol. 3, p. 358.

25   de Bocarro, in Theal, Vol. 3, p. 363.

26   de Bocarro, in Theal, Vol. 3, p. 390.

27   The Dominican Father Luís Espírito Santo quoted in Eric Axelson, *Portuguese in South-East Africa 1600–1700*, p. 70. He refers to 15,000 *chikunda* and 100,000 Kalanga in the final battle – obviously a grossly inflated figure.

28   Faria y Sousa and Sousa de Meneses, cited in Axelson, *Portuguese in South-East Africa 1600–1700*, p. 77.

29   João Julião de Silva's description of 1844, cited in H. H. K. Bhila, 'Southern Zambezia', in B. A. Ogot (ed.), *UNESCO General History of Africa*, Vol. V, *Africa from the Sixteenth to the Eighteenth Century*, Berkeley, CA: University of California Press, 1992, p. 659.

30   Father Antonio da Conceição, quoted in Richard Gray, 'Portuguese musketeers on the Zambezi', *Journal of African History*, Vol. XII, No. 4 (1971), p. 533.

CHAPTER SIX

1   Father José Antonio de Souza, who lived in São Salvador from 1881 to 1887, quoted in E. G. Ravenstein (ed.), *The Strange Adventures of Andrew Battell of Leigh, in Angola and the Adjoining Regions*, Nendeln, Liechtenstein: Hakluyt Society, 2nd series, No. VI (1901; Kraus reprint, 1967), pp. 134–5.

2   Quoted in Alan Scholefield, *The Dark Kingdoms: the Impact of White Civilization on Three Great African Monarchies,* New York, NY: William Morrow, 1975, p. 20.

3   The king, Dom Afonso, to Dom João III, 6 July 1526, quoted in Davidson, pp. 191–2.

4   Quoted in John K. Thornton, 'The art of war in Angola, 1575–1680', *Comparative Studies in Society and History*, Vol. 30, No. 2 (April 1988), p. 375. Unfortunately for him, the young man died in 1659 of an arrow wound to his unprotected eye.

5   Andrew Battell, 'The strange adventures of Andrew Battell of Leigh in Essex, sent by the Portguals prisoner to Angola, who lived there, and in the adjoining regions, near eighteen years (1625)', in Ravenstein, pp. 19–35; and Samuel Purchas, 'On the religion and customs of the peoples of Angola, Congo and Loango (1617)', in Ravenstein, pp. 83–7.

6   Battell, in Ravenstein, p. 21.

7   Battell, in Ravenstein, pp. 32–3.

8   Battell, in Ravenstein, p. 31.

9   Luís Mendes de Vasconcelos in a letter of 28 August 1617, quoted in John K. Thornton, *Warfare in Atlantic Africa 1500–1800*, London: University College London Press, 1999, p. 137.

10   Antonio Cavazzi de Montecuccolo, a Capuchin monk whose account of his visits to Angola was published in 1687. Cited in Ravenstein, p.176.

11   Quoted in David Birmingham, *Trade and Conquest in Angola: The Mbundu and Their Neighbours under the Influence of the Portuguese 1483–1790*, Oxford: Oxford University Press, 1966, p. 27.

Bibliography

General

AFRICA

Dapper, Olfert, *Description de l'Afrique*, Amsterdam: Wolfgang, Waesberge, Boom & Van Someren, 1686

Davidson, Basil (ed.), *The African Past: Chronicles from Antiquity to Modern Times*, Boston, MA and Toronto: Little, Brown, 1964

De Villiers, Marq, and Sheila Hirtle, *Into Africa: A Journey through the Ancient Empires*, Toronto: Key Porter Books, 1999

Ehret, Christopher, *The Civilisations of Africa: A History to 1800*, Charlottesville. VA: University of Virginia Press, 2002

Eltis, David, and David Richardson, *Atlas of the Transatlantic Slave Trade*, New Haven, CT: Yale University Press, 2010

Fage, J. D., with William Tordorf, *A History of Africa*, London and New York, NY: Routledge, 2002, 4th edn

Heueisen, Elizabeth, Anna Meissner and Glenn Riedel (eds), *The New Atlas of the Arab World*, Cairo and New York, NY: The American University in Cairo Press, 2010

Hilliard, Constance B, *Intellectual Traditions of Pre-Colonial Africa*, Boston, MA: McGraw-Hill, 1998

Iliffe, John, *Africans: The History of a Continent*, Cambridge: Cambridge University Press, 1995

Isichei, Elizabeth, *A History of African Societies to 1870*, Cambridge: Cambridge University Press, 2000

Levtzion, Nehemia, and Randall L. Pouwels (eds), *The History of Islam in Africa*, Athens, OH: Ohio University Press, 2000

Lovejoy, Paul E., *Transformations in Slavery: A History of Slavery in Africa*, Cambridge: Cambridge University Press, 2000, 2nd edn

Mair, Lucy, *African Kingdoms*, Oxford: Clarendon Press, 1977

Northrup, David, *Africa's Discovery of Europe 1450–1850*, New York, NY and Oxford: Oxford University Press, 2009, 2nd edn

Oliver, Roland, and Anthony Atmore, *Medieval Africa, 1250–1800*, Cambridge: Cambridge University Press, 2001

Reader, John, *Africa: A Biography of the Continent*, London: Hamish Hamilton, 1997

Robinson, David, *Muslim Societies in African History*, Cambridge: Cambridge University Press, 2004

PORTUGUESE EMPIRE

Abshire, David M., and Michael S. Samuels (eds), *Portuguese Africa: A Handbook*, New York: Praeger Publishers, 1969

Anderson, James M., *The History of Portugal*, Westport, CT: Greenwood Press, 2000

Boxer, C. R., *The Portuguese Seaborne Empire 1415–1825*, New York: Alfred A. Knopf, 1969

Darwin, John, *After Tamerlane: The Rise and Fall of Global Empires, 1400–2000*, London: Allen Lane, 2007

De Oliveira Marques, A. H., *History of Portugal*, Vol. 1, *From Lusitania to Empire*, New York, NY: Columbia University Press, 1972

Diffie, Bailey W., and George D. Winius, *Foundations of the Portuguese Empire, 1415–1580*, Minneapolis, MN: University of Minnesota Press, 1977

Disney, A. R., *A History of Portugal and the Portuguese Empire*, Vol. 2, *The Portuguese Empire*, Cambridge: Cambridge University Press, 2009

Livermore, H. V., *A New History of Portugal*, Cambridge: Cambridge University Press, 1976, 2nd edn

Newitt, Malyn (ed.), *The First Portuguese Colonial Empire*, Exeter Studies in History No. 11, Exeter: University of Exeter, 1986

Parry, H., *The Age of Reconnaissance: Discovery, Exploration and Settlement 1450–1650*, London: Cardinal, 1973

WARFARE

Black, Jeremy, *Tools of War: The Weapons that Changed the World*, London: Quercus, 2007

Black, Jeremy, *War and the World: Military Power and the Fate of Continents 1450–2000*, New Haven, CT and London: Yale University Press, 1998

Chandler, David, *The Art of Warfare on Land*, London: Hamlyn, 1974

Chase, Kenneth, *Firearms: A Global History to 1700*, Cambridge: Cambridge University Press, 2003

Dobson, Mary, *Disease: The Extraordinary Stories Behind History's Deadliest Killers*, London: Quercus, 2007

Duffy, Christopher, *Siege Warfare: The Fortress in the Early Modern World 1494–1660*, London: Routledge & Kegan Paul, 1979

Gat, Azar, *War in Human Civilisation*, Oxford: Oxford University Press, 2006

Headrick, Daniel R., *Technology: A World History*, Oxford: Oxford University Press, 2009

Howard, Michael, *War in European History*, Oxford: Oxford University Press, 1976

Iliffe, John, *Honour in African History*, Cambridge: Cambridge University Press, 2005

McNeill, William H., *The Pursuit of Power: Technology, Armed Force, and Society since AD 1000*, Chicago: University of Chicago Press, 1982

Parker, Geoffrey (ed.), *Cambridge Illustrated History of Warfare*, Cambridge: Cambridge University Press, 1995

Parker, Geoffrey, and Angela Parker, *European Soldiers 1550–1650*, Cambridge: Cambridge University Press, 1977

Tallett, Frank, *War and Society in Early-Modern Europe, 1495–1715*, London and New York, NY: Routledge, 1997

Thornton, John, 'Armed slaves and political authority in Africa in the era of the slave trade, 1450–1800', in Christopher Leslie Brown and Philip D. Morgan (eds), *Arming Slaves from Classical Times to the Modern Age*, New Haven, CT and London: Yale University Press, 2006

Townshend, Charles (ed.), *The Oxford History of Modern War*, Oxford: Oxford University Press, 2000

Uzoigwe, G. N., 'The warrior and the state in pre-colonial Africa', in Ali A. Mazrui (ed.), *The Warrior Tradition in Modern Africa*, Leiden: Brill, 1977

White, Gavin, 'Firearms in Africa: An introduction', *Journal of African History*, Vol. 12, No. 2 (1971), pp. 173–84

Angola

Balandier, Georges, *Daily Life in the Kingdom of Congo*, New York, NY: Pantheon, 1968

Birmingham, David, 'The African response to early Portuguese activities in Angola', in Ronald H. Chilcote (ed.), *Protest and Resistance in Angola and Brazil*, Berkeley, CA: University of California Press, 1972

Birmingham, David, *The Portuguese Conquest of Angola*, London and New York, NY: Oxford University Press, 1965

Birmingham, David, *Trade and Conquest in Angola: The Mbundu and Their Neighbours under the Influence of the Portuguese 1483–1790*, Oxford: Clarendon Press, 1966

Boxer, C. R., *Salvador da Sá and the Struggle for Brazil and Angola 1602–1686*, London: University of London, Athlone Press, 1952

Henderson, Lawrence W., *Angola: Five Centuries of Conflict*, Ithaca, MI and London: Cornell University Press, 1979

Heywood, Linda M., 'Slavery and its transformation in the kingdom of Kongo: 1491–1800', *Journal of African History*, Vol. 50, No. 1 (2009), pp. 1–22

Hilton, Anne, *The Kingdom of Kongo*, Oxford: Clarendon Press, 1985

Hilton, Anne, 'The Jaga reconsidered', *Journal of African History*, Vol. 22, No. 2 (1981), pp. 191–202

Miller, Joseph C., *Kings and Kinsmen, Early Mbundu States in Angola*, Oxford: Clarendon Press, 1976

Miller, Joseph C., 'Nzinga of Matamba in a new perspective,' *Journal of African History*, Vol. 16, No. 2 (1975), pp. 201–16

Newitt, Malyn, 'Angola in historical context', in Patrick Chabal and Nuno Vidal (eds), *Angola: The Weight of History*, New York, NY: Columbia University Press, 2008

Ravenstein, E. G. (ed.), *The Strange Adventures of Andrew Battell of Leigh, in Angola and the Adjoining Regions*, Nendeln, Liechtenstein: Hakluyt Society, 2nd series, No. VI (1901; Krause reprint, 1967)

Scholefield, Alan, *The Dark Kingdoms: The Impact of White Civilization on Three Great African Monarchies*, New York, NY: William Morrow, 1975

Thornton, John K., 'The art of war in Angola, 1575–1680', *Comparative Studies in Society and History*, Vol. 30, No. 2 (April 1988), pp. 360–78

Thornton, John K., *The Kingdom of Kongo: Civil War and Transition 1641–1718*, Madison, WI: University of Wisconsin Press, 1983

Thornton, John K., 'Legitimacy and political power: Queen Njinga, 1624–1663', *Journal of African History*, Vol. 32, No. 1 (1991), pp. 25–40

Thornton, John K., *Warfare in Atlantic Africa 1500–1800*, London: University College London Press, 1999

Vansina, Jan, *Kingdoms of the Savanna*, Madison, WI: University of Wisconsin Press, 1966

Vansina, Jan, based on a contribution by T. Obenga, 'The Kongo kingdom and its neighbours', in B. A. Ogot (ed.), *UNESCO General History of Africa*, Vol. V, *Africa from the Sixteenth to the Eighteenth Century*, Berkeley, CA: University of California Press, 1992

Wheeler, Douglas L., and Rene Pélissier, *Angola*, Westport, CT: Greenwood Press, 1971

Ethiopia

Abir, Mordechai, *Ethiopia and the Red Sea: The Rise and Decline of the Solomonic Dynasty and Muslim–European Rivalry in the Region*, London: Frank Cass, 1980

Adejumobi, Saheed A, *The History of Ethiopia*, Westport, CT: Greenwood Press, 2007

Arrowsmith-Brown, J. H., and Richard Pankhurst (eds), *Prutky's Travels in Ethiopia and Other Countries*, London: Hakluyt Society, 2nd series, No. 174 (1991)

Beckingham, C. F., and G. W. B. Huntingford (eds), *The Prester John of the Indies: A True Relation of the Lands of the Prester John Being the Narrative of the Portuguese Embassy to Ethiopia in 1520 Written by Father Francisco Alvares*, Millwood, NY: Hakluyt Society, 2 Vols, 2nd series, No. CXIV (1958; Kraus reprint, 1975)

Beckingham, C. F., and G. W. B. Huntingford (eds), *Some Records of Ethiopia, 1593–1646: Being Extracts from The History of High Ethiopia of Abassia by Manoel de Almeida, Together with Bahrey's History of the Galla*, Millwood, NY: Hakluyt Society, 2nd series, No. CVII (1954; Kraus reprint, 1990)

Boavida, Isabel, Hervé Pennec, and Manueal João Ramos (eds); Christopher J. Tribe (trans.), *Pedro Páez's History of Ethiopia, 1622*, 2 vols, Farnham, Surrey: Ashgate for Hakluyt Society, 3rd series, No. 23 (2011)

Crawford, O. G. S. (ed.), *Ethiopian Itineraries circa 1400–1524 Including Those Collected by Alessandro Zorzi at Venice in the Years 1519–24*, Cambridge: Cambridge University Press for Hakluyt Society, 1958

Crummey, Donald, *Land and Society in the Christian Kingdom of Ethiopia from the Thirteenth to the Twentieth Century*, Urbana, IL: University of Illinois Press, 2000

Haberland, E., 'The Horn of Africa', in B. A. Ogot (ed.), *UNESCO General History of Africa*, Vol. V, *Africa from the Sixteenth to the Eighteenth Century*, Berkeley, CA: University of California Press, 1992

Lockhart, Donald, M. G. A. da Costa and C. F. Beckingham (eds), *The Itinerário of Jerónimo Lobo*, London: Hakluyt Society, 2nd series, No. 162 (1984)

Marcus, H. G., *A History of Ethiopia*, Berkeley, CA: University of California Press, 1994

Markham, C. R., 'The Portuguese expeditions to Abyssinia in the fifteenth, sixteenth and seventeenth centuries', *Journal of the Royal Geographical Society of London*, Vol. 38 (1868), pp. 1–12

Pankhurst, Richard K. P. (ed.), *The Ethiopian Royal Chronicles*, Addis Ababa: Oxford University Press, 1967

Pankhurst, Richard K. P. (ed.), *The Ethiopians: A History*, Oxford: Blackwell, 2001

Parkyns, Mansfield, *Life in Abyssinia: Being Notes Collected during Three Years' Residence and Travels in That Country*, London: John Murray, 1868

Salt, Henry, *A Voyage to Abyssinia and Travels into the Interior of that Country Executed under the Orders of the British Government, in the Years 1809 and 1810*, London: F. C. and J. Rivington, 1814

Sanceau, Elaine, *The Land of Prester John: A Chronicle of Portuguese Exploration*, New York, NY: Alfred A. Knopf, 1944

Whiteway, R. S. (ed.), *The Portuguese Expedition to Abyssinia in 1541–1543, as Narrated by Castanhoso, with Some Contemporary Letters, the Short Account of Bermudez, and Certain Extract from Correa*, Millwood, NY: Hakluyt Society, 2nd series, No. X (1902; Kraus reprint, 1967)

Morocco

Bovill, E. W., *The Battle of Alcazar: An Account of the Defeat of Don Sebastian at El-Ksar El-Kebir*, London: Batchworth Press, 1952

Cook, Weston F. Jr, *The Hundred Years War for Morocco: Gunpowder and the Military Revolution in the Early Modern Muslim World*, Boulder, CO: Westview Press, 1994

Davis, Robert C., *Christian Slaves, Muslim Masters: White Slavery in the Mediterranean, the Barbary Coast and Italy, 1500–1800*, New York, NY: Palgrave Macmillan, 2004

De Faria y Sousa, Emanuel, *The History of Portugal from the First Ages of the World to the Late Great Revolution, under King John IV, in the Year MDCXL, Translated, and Continued Down to this Present Year, 1698 by Capt John Stevens*, London: W. Roger and Abel Roper, 1708

El Fasi, M., 'Morocco', in B. A. Ogot (ed.), *UNESCO General History of Africa*, Vol. V, *Africa from the Sixteenth to the Eighteenth Century*, Berkeley, CA: University of California Press, 1992

Hoffmann, Eleanor, *Realm of the Evening Star: A History of Morocco and the Land of the Moors*, Toronto: Ambassador Books, 1965

García-Arenal, Mercedes, *Ahmad al-Mansur: The Beginnings of Modern Morocco*, Oxford: Oneworld, 2009

Rogerson, Barnaby, *The Last Crusaders: The Hundred-Year Battle for the Centre of the World*, London: Little, Brown, 2009

Mutapa and Zambezia

Beach, D. N., *The Shona and Zimbabwe 900–1850: An Outline of Shona History*, New York, NY: Africana, 1980

Bhila, H. H. K., 'Southern Zambezia', in B. A. Ogot (ed.), *UNESCO General History of Africa*, Vol. V, *Africa from the Sixteenth to the Eighteenth Century*, Berkeley, CA: University of California Press, 1992

Gray, Richard, 'Portuguese musketeers on the Zambezi', *Journal of African History*, Vol. XII, No. 4 (1971), pp. 531–3

Isaacman, Allen F., and Barbara S. Isaacman, *Slavery and Beyond: The Making of Men and Chikunda Ethnic Identities in the Unstable World of South–Central Africa, 1750–1920*, Portsmouth, NH: Heinemann, 2004

Isaacman, Allen F., and Derek Peterson, 'Making the Chikunda: Military slavery and ethnicity in southern Africa, 1750–1900', in Christopher Leslie Brown and Philip D. Morgan (eds), *Arming Slaves from Classical Times to the Modern Age*, New Haven, CT and London: Yale University Press, 2006

Newitt, M. D. D., 'The Portuguese on the Zambezi: An historical interpretation of the Prazo system', *Journal of African History*, Vol. 10, No. 1 (1969), pp. 67–85

Newitt, M. D. D., *Portuguese Settlement on the Zambesi [sic]: Exploration, Land Tenure and Colonial Rule in East Africa*, New York, NY: Africana, 1973

Theal, George McCall (ed.), *History and Ethnology of Africa South of the Zambesi 1505–1795*, Vol. 1, *The Portuguese in South Africa from 1505 to 1700*, Cambridge: Cambridge University Press, 2010

Theal, George McCall (ed.), *Records of South-Eastern Africa Collected in Various Libraries and Archive Departments in Europe*, London: William Clowes and Sons for the Government of the Cape Colony, Vols 3, 6 and 7, 1899, 1900, 1901

Swahili Coast

Axelson, Eric, *Portuguese in South-East Africa 1488–1600*, Johannesburg: Struik, 1973

Axelson, Eric, *Portuguese in South-East Africa 1600–1700*, Johannesburg: Witwatersrand University Press, 1964

Axelson, Eric, *South-East Africa 1488–1530*, London: Longmans, Green, 1940

Badger, George Percy (trans. and ed.), *History of the Imâms and Seyyids of 'Omân by Sálîl-ibn-Razník from AD 661–1856*, London: Hakluyt Society, 1st series, No. 44 (1871)

Boxer, C. R., and Carlos de Azevedo, *Fort Jesus and the Portuguese in Mombasa 1593–1729*, London: Hollis and Carter, 1960

Cliff, Nigel, *Holy War: How Vasco da Gama's Epic Voyages Turned the Tide in a Centuries-Old Clash of Civilisations*, New York: HarperCollins, 2011

Elphick, Richard, *Kraal and Castle: Khoikhoi and the Founding of White South Africa*, New Haven, CT and London: Yale University Press, 1977

Freeman-Grenville, G. S. P. (ed.), 'The coast 1498–1840', in Roland Oliver and Gervase Mathew (eds), *History of East Africa*, Vol. 1, Oxford: Clarendon Press, 1963

Freeman-Grenville, G. S. P. (ed.), *The East African Coast: Select Documents from the First to the Earlier Nineteenth Century*, Oxford: Clarendon Press, 1962

Furber, Holden, *Empires of Trade in the Orient, 1600–1800*, Minneapolis, MN: University of Minnesota Press, 1976

Hall, Richard, *Empires of the Monsoon: A History of the Indian Ocean and its Invaders*, London: HarperCollins, 1998

Horton, Mark, and John Middleton, *The Swahili: The Social Landscape of a Mercantile Society*, Oxford: Blackwell, 2000

Kirkman, James, *Fort Jesus: A Portuguese Fortress on the East African Coast*, Oxford: Clarendon Press, 1974

Marsh, Zoe (ed.), *East Africa Through Contemporary Records*, Cambridge: Cambridge University Press, 1961

Middleton, John, *The World of the Swahili: An African Mercantile Civilization*, New Haven, CT: Yale University Press, 1992

Pearson, Michael M., *Port Cities and Intruders: The Swahili Coast, India, and Portugal in the Early Modern Era*, Baltimore, MD and London: The Johns Hopkins University Press, 1998

Salim, A. I., 'East Africa: The coast', in B. A. Ogot (ed.), *UNESCO General History of Africa*, Vol. V, *Africa from the Sixteenth to the Eighteenth Century*, Berkeley, CA: University of California Press, 1992

Theal, George McCall (ed.), *History and Ethnology of Africa South of the Zambesi 1505–1795*, Vol. 1, *The Portuguese in South Africa from 1505 to 1700*, Cambridge: Cambridge University Press, 2010

Theal, George McCall (ed.), *Records of South-Eastern Africa Collected in Various Libraries and Archive Departments in Europe*, London: William Clowes and Sons for the Government of the Cape Colony, Vols 3, 6 and 7, 1899, 1900, 1901

Index